Gladiator
Ace

Gladiator Ace

Bill 'Cherry' Vale, the RAF's forgotten fighter ace

Squadron Leader William 'Cherry' Vale
DFC and Bar, AFC, MiD, Greek DFC

BRIAN CULL

With
Ludovico Slongo
and
Håkan Gustavsson

Haynes Publishing

First published in 2010 by Haynes Publishing

A catalogue record for this book is available from the British Library

ISBN 978 1 84425 657 0

Library of Congress control no. 2009936975

Published by Haynes Publishing, Sparkford, Yeovil, Somerset BA22 7JJ, UK
Tel: 01963 442030 Fax: 01963 440001
Int. tel: +44 1963 442030 Int. fax: +44 1963 440001
E-mail: sales@haynes.co.uk
Website: www.haynes.co.uk

Haynes North America Inc.
861 Lawrence Drive, Newbury Park,
California 91320, USA

Printed in the USA

CONTENTS

GRANDDAD BILL

It is through a strange set of circumstances that I came to meet Brian Cull – the author of this book. About 18 months ago I was on a business trip to the UK (I live in the US now) and was at a loose end at the weekend. For some reason I decided to take a trip down memory lane and visit Framlingham – the small Suffolk town where Granddad Bill grew up and where he and I both went to school at Framlingham College.

While visiting the school I suddenly remembered that when I left I paid for a lifetime subscription to the Society of Old Framlinghamians. They had long since lost track of me and I had not had any contact with the school for years. I decided to see what had become of some of the rogues that I went to school with so I got in touch with the society through its website and reacquainted myself. I am very glad that I did – it has been great to find out what some of my old mates are up to.

Out of the blue I was approached by Chris Essex who runs the overseas bag of Old Framlinghamians. Chris told me that Brian Cull, an author, had got in touch with the school looking for any known living relatives of Bill Vale as he was writing a book about him. This was way too intriguing not to follow up! Why would anyone want to write a book about my grandfather? I contacted Brian and in no time at all we were sitting at my mother's house drinking tea and swapping stories about Granddad Bill. It came as something of a surprise to find that Brian, in some respects, knew more about him than we did.

When I read the draft of this book, aside from a sense of awe, I conjured up a mental picture of a bunch of rag-tag pilots, hopelessly outnumbered, often in inferior and/or damaged equipment, lacking in munitions and supplies, with almost certain defeat staring them in the face, going up there time and time again and fighting until someone died. I also noted that as new names and characters get introduced into the story they slowly but surely, one by one, disappear. All, it seems, except my grandfather.

When Winston Churchill said, 'Never in the field of human conflict was so much owed by so many to so few', he was of course referring to the Battle of Britain pilots. However, these guys were cast in the same mould and reading this book really puts a saying like that into its true context.

I have many childhood memories of my grandfather. He was of course my idol. I remember his famous Christmas visits – which seemed to go on for weeks and weeks. I remember him claiming his favourite chair from my father and arranging his stuff all around it – his pipe and tobacco on one side, his Tom Thumb cigars on the other and his unfiltered Woodbines in the middle. Nobody ever dared touch a thing until he left and the house reeked of him for weeks. I remember his obnoxious little poodle, Carla, that he would feed chocolates until all of its teeth fell out and we had to feed it liquidised chicken.

I remember that he would hold court and was the world's greatest expert on everything, especially the technical flaws in war films and anything to do with aviation or sport. I remember his trips to the seaside planned for days to minute detail despite the fact that we always went to the same place at breakneck speed – the whole family screaming for him to slow down while the kids were car sick in the back!

I remember his fantastic stories of scoring a century at Lords, of scoring goals in hockey while trying out for England, his athletics, his rugby, his shooting – he was an expert at all of them. It was hard to believe and a part of me never did, but as a young boy looking up at him I certainly wanted to.

I remember his devotion to the RAF. As with all kids, all my memories are that it snowed every winter and was scorching hot every summer, so I don't know if there ever was a time that I didn't see him wearing his RAF tie, cravat or blazer, but if there was one I don't remember it.

I remember his crazy cars. I don't know if they really were the fastest cars in the world, but he certainly said that they were and did his best to prove it. The first time I ever went 100mph was in his Riley 1.6 – no seat belts, nose pressed against the windshield. It's a wonder I survived the experience, but have to admit I have been doing it ever since. I too inherited that gene and have a collection of things that go fast. He always drove everywhere at breakneck speed right on the edge of losing it completely. It is sadly ironic that he was killed in a car that he wasn't even driving. I was of course shocked at the news and especially at the way he died – I had always imagined something much more romantic. I can't say that I was devastated as, since he had met Kay, the family had much less contact from him and we had drifted apart somewhat. I don't recall that there was a family feud, he just had other things to do.

I also probably have more to thank him for than I have ever acknowledged. He was a big influence in my life as a child. He had a massive ego and nothing that I ever achieved in sports or at school was good enough. It is kind of sad in a way, but it sure made me try harder and push myself to achieve things I didn't know I could. There are many examples, but one such relates to the shooting team. It was my grandfather's dream that, like him, I would attend Framlingham College even though there was no way we could afford it. Due to a combination of my mother's determination and hard-earned cash, and a scholarship from Cambridge County Council, I did go and it changed my life. It would never have happened had it not been for him.

My grandfather took me to one side and told me that my first day at Framlingham I was to go to the Drill Master and tell him that I was Bill Vale's grandson and that he should put me into the shooting team. I took him at his word and followed his instructions to the letter. The Drill Master – Bill Pritchard – had quite a glint in his eye when he informed me that being Bill Vale's grandson did not exempt me from having to earn a place on the shooting team like everyone else. He then introduced me to the shooting team who were all sixth-formers and grown men in my eyes (I was 12 and about 90lb soaking wet). However, since I was the great Bill Vale's grandson and had presented myself to the range he said he would let me have a go.

It was the only sport that I have ever been able to do without even trying. Two weeks later I was in the cadet pairs, the following term I was in the Second VIII, the following term I was in the First VIII and two years later I was Captain of Shooting – a position I occupied until I left the school. I remember vividly that when I told my grandfather that I had come in 2nd place in the Captains' competition at the All England boys meeting at Bisley his exact words were 'Well you only have one place to go to beat the old man!' Things were a bit frosty between us for a while after that. Nevertheless, had it not been for his guidance, I would never have even tried something that I later came to excel at. I could give many more similar examples.

Now here is what I don't remember, and it might take a psychologist to figure this one out. I remember him talking about the RAF, talking with passion about flying, talking about life in the war, Libya, Greece, Crete, I remember him talking about planes and how they worked and how marvellous the Hurricanes were and how old the Gladiators were. I remember him talking about his fellow pilots and their war rations and I remember him talking about some of the pranks they used to get up to. However, I don't remember one single story about one single battle. As a young boy who was riveted to every war movie and spent most of my time simulating mock battles in the backyard one would think that I would remember every word about every battle parrot fashion, but he never said a word about them as far as I recall. We all knew that he was a hero and had been decorated, but we (myself and the family) learned more about his actual exploits from Brian Cull than we ever did from him!

Of course I am hardly impartial, but I found this book absolutely fascinating. I hope that you do too.

Andy Roberts

[Bill would have been equally extremely proud of his grandson Andrew, who holds the position of Global Division Director, Metals and Minerals Division, Inspectorate International. He would also have been very proud of Andrew's lovely family and his great-grandsons Harry, George and Vaughn, and great-granddaughter Pascalle Vale.]

ACKNOWLEDGEMENTS

Ludovico Slongo and Håkan Gustavsson, authors in their own right, are thanked for contributing material from their research archives. Ludovico has recently co-authored *Desert Prelude: Air War in North Africa 1940–41*, while Håkan's website – surfcity.kund.dalnet.se – is highly recommended.

My continued thanks go to my wife Val, who accompanied me on all of the research trips, while Bill's daughter Gaynor and grandson Andrew Roberts were instrumental in filling in much of Bill's background. Andrew also kindly wrote the Foreword.

Old Framlinghamians Jim Blythe, Leigh Cunningham, Chris Essex, Norman Porter (*Framlingham College Old Boys* editor), James Ruddock-Broyd and Trevor Trevethick provided much help and several anecdotes, as did Bill's friends Sqn Ldr John Hopper and Reg Kingman.

Television presenter and author Jonathan Dimbleby kindly responded to my enquiry regarding his father. Peter Elliott and staff at RAF Hendon Museum were most courteous and helpful, as were the staff at The National Archives. Derek Larkin at www.oldhaltonians.co.uk kindly provided information regarding Bill's time at Halton. Author James Aldridge is acknowledged in regard to his novel *Signed With Their Honour*.

TOCH members Dennis Burke, Kiran Toor, and author Alex Crawford, provided information during the course of my research. Ruy Horta and Snautzer are thanked for providing translations of German-language material. Both Andy Thomas and Tom Willis are thanked for the loan of photographs.

Also remembered fondly are the late Wg Cdr Edward Howell OBE, DFC, who gave permission to use extracts from his book *Escape to Live*, and the late Bill Winsland DFC for anecdotal material. Eminent author Dr Jochen Prien generously provided extracts from *Jagdgeschwader 77*, while author Chris Shores is thanked for permission to use the 1940 Desert Overview Appendix, and also for the loan of photographs.

Finally, my gratitude is extended to Jonathan Falconer of Haynes Publishing for making it possible to publish this tribute to a fine fighter pilot, a hero almost forgotten in the mists of time.

Author's note

Due to the lack of personal written material, I have made a number of assumptions and educated guesses regarding Bill's career and the many stories that surround him. It is not my intention to either sensationalise or fabricate, nor perpetuate myths, but without information to the contrary I have relied on various sources in an endeavour to pay tribute to a somewhat larger-than-life character whose fighting career has been mostly overlooked and forgotten. Passages from contemporary accounts have been widely used, since the experiences of others would have been similar to those of Bill.

With claims for 30 enemy aircraft destroyed plus 4 shared, Bill occupies No. 3 position in the RAF's unofficial list of 'Top-Scoring Pilots of World War II'. Only his one-time contemporary and friend Sqn Ldr Pat Pattle (50+2 shared), and Wg Cdr Johnny Johnson (34+7 shared) are listed above him. Other notables such as Flt Lt Screwball Beurling had 30+1 shared, Grp Capt 'Sailor' Malan gained 27+7 shared, and Wg Cdr Paddy Finucane 26+6 shared.

Presented differently, Pattle had 52 including 2 shared, Johnson 41 including 7 shared, Bill 34 including 4 shared, Malan 34 including 7 shared, so Bill retains No. 3 status – truly the 'forgotten ace'. It should be emphasised that all pilots' scores were credited *claims* for enemy aircraft destroyed, and not *actual* enemy aircraft destroyed.

INTRODUCTION

When Sqn Ldr Bill Vale DFC AFC RAF (Rtd) was tragically killed in a car accident in 1981, he did not leave a written account of his life in the RAF during the Second World War; only his logbook survived to tell the story of his exploits. This has been used extensively to re-create his operational career with 33 and 80 Squadrons in 1940 and 1941, initially flying Gladiators before progressing to Hurricanes, during which he claimed more than 30 aerial victories and was awarded the DFC and Bar.

This account, therefore, relies heavily on the records of the two squadrons and, in effect, records these squadrons' respective operational histories in the relevant periods when Bill was a member – 33 Squadron, 1937–40, and 80 Squadron 1940–1. The successes and losses of the squadrons would have affected Bill – their story is Bill's story, and Bill's story is their story.

Reference is also made by the author from time to time of James Aldridge's novel *Signed With Their Honour* published in 1943. Aldridge was an Australian-born journalist, novelist and war reporter who was in Greece when Bill and his colleagues of 80 Squadron were defending Greece's north-western border against the Italian incursion. He was one of a group of journalists that included Richard Dimbleby and Leland Stowe, who attempted to cover the warfront. In late 1943, *Signed With Their Honour* was published in England by Michael Joseph and was dedicated to Sqn Ldrs Pat Pattle and Bill Hickey. Its introduction reads:

> Greece 1941 . . . This is the story of a handful of British fliers, with
> their out-of-date and battered Gladiators, fighting a desperate battle
> to stem the advance of the Nazi hordes. 'Signed With Their Honour'
> is also the story of John Quayle, a fighter pilot who fell in love with
> a Greek girl. Against a background of war-torn Greece, this dramatic
> novel sweeps on to a tremendous and unforgettable climax.

A number of Bill's contemporaries, as well as his family, believe that the hero of the novel, 'John Quayle', is based upon some of the adventures and experiences of Bill (note the similarity of names); other characters in the book bear nicknames of 80 Squadron pilots, Tap (Gordon 'Tap' Jones[1]) and Pat (Pat Pattle), while Sqn Ldr Hickey (80 Squadron's CO) is also mentioned.

However, James Aldridge has recently advised the author that this was not the case, and that he never knowingly met Bill, only Pattle and Hickey.

Bill's daughter Gaynor, and his grandson Andrew (Gaynor's son) have provided many anecdotes of their early life with Bill and his first wife Bette, although following divorce in 1969, the family saw less of him.

PREAMBLE

William Vale – known as Bill to his family and friends and as Cherry to his RAF contemporaries – was born on 3 June 1914 at 254 Castle Road, Chatham in Kent, the third son of Royal Marine Sgt George Robert Vale (born in Framlingham in Suffolk in 1883) and his wife Catherine (neé Webb, also Suffolk-born). Their first son Arthur was born in 1909, followed by George at the end of 1912 and, after Bill, came Jack (1916).

At the time of Bill's birth, his father was stationed at the Royal Naval Barracks, Chatham, where he was a physical training instructor (PTI) with the Royal Marine Light Infantry. It is not known if Sgt Vale was on duty during the night of 3–4 September 1917, when German Gotha bombers targeted Chatham Barracks, a raid in which 120 naval personnel were killed or died from their injuries. One assumes that the whole family was in danger although none was directly involved.

With the First World War over and following his retirement from the Royal Marines, Sgt-Maj Vale (as he then was) returned to his Suffolk roots and settled in Framlingham with his young sons. Their final child Vera – a girl at last – arrived early in 1921 to complete the family. George had applied for and was successful in gaining a position at the prestigious Framlingham College as PTI. The position fortuitously entitled his sons to be granted free admission to the fee-paying college.

> The Albert Memorial College was founded in 1864 in memory of Queen Victoria's husband, Albert, Prince Consort, whose statue takes pride of place at the front of the College. It was later named after the town of Framlingham. The original school building is an example of Victorian era mock-Gothic architecture and faces the twelfth-century Framlingham Castle across a large, shallow lake called The Mere. The building is Grade II listed. Brandeston Hall, or Framlingham College Junior School, is located in the nearby village of Brandeston, and is named after the Tudorbethan manor house that forms its main building. Brandeston Hall is a war memorial. The College enjoys a magnificent situation, looking out across the Mere to the twelfth-century castle. The College grounds are extensive and the original

mock-Gothic buildings have been developed over the years, as a result of significant building initiatives.[1]

Although he retained the soubriquet 'Sergeant-Major' he was in fact appointed to the rank of Lieutenant in the Special Reserve of Officers, later being promoted to Captain. Known to friends and family as 'Nips' due to his fondness of a drop of Navy rum, he was nonetheless an accomplished marksman, and he was appointed to command the College Cadet Force. A story is told of a chamber pot perched on top of the chapel spire by some high-spirited miscreant, and of marksman Nips shooting it to smithereens with one shot from an ancient Lee-Enfield .303 rifle at an estimated 500yd.

Bill gained entry to the college in September 1923, when he was just 9 years old, where he became a member of Stradbroke House. Although he was a high achiever in academic studies, particularly maths and science, he had developed an interest in mechanics and was also a very keen sportsman, who excelled at most sports including shooting and hockey, in particular. He gained a Cambridge Certificate, but chose to pursue an engineering course in the Royal Air Force.

Chapter 1

BILL JOINS THE RAF

On leaving Framlingham College in December 1930 – shortly after the death of his mother – 16-year-old Bill immediately applied to join the RAF and was accepted as an apprentice (Service No. 565293) at Halton, the RAF's prestigious technical training college near Wendover in Buckinghamshire. He was a member of the 23rd Entry comprising some 300 apprentices, of whom 48 were to be lost during the coming war.

> Following the end of the Great War, the Air Council purchased the former Rothschild Estate to house its new No. 1 School of Technical Training as the home for the Aircraft Apprentice Scheme when this was introduced in 1920. The three-year course was initiated to train 155 Apprentice Entries between 1920 and 1923 and the training they received was thorough and broad-based. Apart from the basic syllabus, which combined the academic and practical disciplines, sporting and spare-time activities were closely supervised and enthusiastically encouraged. For the less athletic there was gliding and shooting. All could indulge their interests and talents in the Halton Society, which supported acting, debating, aero-modelling, wireless building, expeditions to the battlefields of Belgium and many other activities. Their most ambitious project was the design and construction of a light aircraft, which became a successful competitor in air races in 1927 and 1928.[1]

The idea for the technical training school was Lord Trenchard's, the founding father of the RAF, and graduates became known as 'Trenchard Brats'. As one of such an elite band, Bill must surely have loved his time at Halton.

> Entry to Halton was a considerable achievement attained by passing a stiff examination and character assessment. The Halton system was designed to mould an intelligent youth into a tough, practical and self-reliant man skilled in his profession. For three years life for the apprentice consisted of drill and physical training, of long days spent on engineering and academic studies, with reveille at 6.30am

17

and cease work at 5.30pm; of one half day a week for recreation on the playing fields and in the swimming bath; of church parade every Sunday; of winning distinction at rugby football, boxing, golf [and shooting]. Pay was three shillings a week, of which one shilling was retained to pay one's fare home on holiday at the end of the term. Any breach of rules incurred at least seven days' confinement to quarters, with other sundry restrictions on the defaulter's freedom and an hour on the parade ground in the evening.[2]

While at Halton Bill represented the RAF Rifle Association at the 11th Annual Meeting at Bisley in 1931, competed for Suffolk in the Queen Alexander's Cup event in 1932, and the Apprentices' Challenge Cup at Bisley in 1933. He had certainly inherited his father's expert eye and marksmanship. On completion of his training in 1933, he was fortunate to be posted to RAF Martlesham Heath, just north-east of Ipswich and only a few miles from Framlingham, so leave was presumably spent at home.

RAF Martlesham Heath, a grass airfield, was officially opened in January 1917, when the Experimental Aircraft Flight transferred from Upavon, Wiltshire. Original airfield structures comprised two large hangars for the aircraft and wooden huts for the mess, quarters and flight offices. The Flight's tasks included cloud flying (blind flying), quite hazardous in those days. The aeroplane was still evolving and many types of experimental aircraft were sent to Martlesham for testing. The role of the Station was changed in 1924 to Aeroplane and Armament Experimental Establishment (A&AEE), and two squadrons were established, albeit without operational aircraft although in an emergency the Air Ministry would have provided a number of DH9As. Meantime, the squadrons continued in their specialist roles, one dealing with armaments and the other with aerodynamic testing. Such flights were fraught with danger and a number of Martlesham Heath test pilots lost their lives during this period.[3]

By 1934, when Bill arrived at Martlesham Heath on his first posting, a scheme had been devised in order to provide air experience for ground staff airmen. Two Vickers Virginias of the Armament Test Flight were made available and there was never a shortage of volunteers since the six ground staff airmen with the most flying time at the end of each month were paid 1s a day for the month concerned. It is likely that Bill would have been one of the keenest of volunteers, since he qualified as an air gunner while at Martlesham Heath.

The station's various sporting teams participated in the local rugby, hockey and football leagues with some success. Wednesday afternoons were devoted to sporting and recreational activities and Bill was soon able to hone his sporting skills. He represented Suffolk in 1934 and 1935, and was invited for a hockey trial with England. He was also a member of the RAF Shooting Team for 1934.

In 1935 Bill, having qualified as a Fitter/Aero Engines and Aerial Gunner, applied for and was accepted for pilot training, being posted to Hamble airfield near Southampton, arriving on 29 September. Hamble was the home of Air Services Training and 3 Elementary and Reserve Flying Training School (E&RFTS), formed to provide aviation training for both civil and military pilots. Bill's first flights were made in an Avro Cadet. Having proved his suitability for further pilot training, the end of the year found him posted to 4 FTS (Flying Training School) at Abu Sueir, Egypt, and he set sail from England aboard one of the many troop transports plying the route. Trooping by sea was carried out mainly twice a year, often in the most uncomfortable circumstances. It is not known aboard which vessel Bill travelled, but the conditions as described by another pilot were probably par for the course:

> Conditions for the 2,000 troops aboard were reminiscent of a mid-eighteenth century prison-ship. Six levels of wooden planks had been fitted in the holds to make decks. These had beams roughly six feet apart. From these beams the soldiers and airmen slung navy-type hammocks each night and took them down again each morning. They were so close together that you could not walk between them – you had to crawl underneath . . . The officers were luckier and shared a normally two-berth cabin among four.
>
> Also, being amongst pilots, my colleagues were not seasick. During the two days and three nights of storms in the Bay of Biscay, the OC Troops had delegated all Orderly Officer's duties to the Air Force. Only they had stomachs so toughened by aerobatics that they could get round the troops' decks without being sick. Even then it was touch and go as troops' vomit with its nauseous stench dribbled through the gaps between the boards on to the hammocks of the decks below. For the men themselves, confined there by the storm and with no effective ventilation, it was horrendous. In good weather, when all troops came on deck, none could sit down for lack of room; all had to stand. For the rest of the day, fresh air was taken in shifts. Officers were allowed enough deck space to get fresh air at any time.[4]

Pupils arrived at Abu Sueir from the RAF Depot at Uxbridge (Middlesex) at an average rate of 80 a year and, during their course, received instruction in a wide range of subjects which included Theory of Flight, Rigging, Engines, Elementary Wireless, Meteorology and Navigation. For instructional purposes, the school was divided into the Initial and the Advanced Training Squadrons. These squadrons were again split into flights to offer the pupil specialised training.

> Centrally situated between Cairo and Port Said, 4 FTS was at the time the only RAF training unit located overseas and provided pilots for squadrons in the Middle East. Between 1935 and 1936, as part of the RAF expansion scheme, 4 FTS underwent major changes in its organisation and equipment. Under the new two-stage system of RAF training, civil schools were utilised to provide the *ab initio* stage of flying training, and the FTSs were reorganised so as to concentrate purely on the more advanced Service flying training. As a result, the 4 FTS course length was reduced to six months, with an intake of pupils every three months, and the School was re-equipped with newly available military aircraft. From April 1935, the Avro 504s of B Flight were replaced with Avro Tutors and three months later E Flight was formed, also with Tutors. C and D Flights of the Advanced Training Squadron were re-equipped with Hawker Audax and Hart aircraft to replace the AW Atlas in the Army co-operation role.[5]

Bill was initially attached to 33 Squadron, a light-bomber unit flying two-seater Hawker Hinds, waiting his turn to join a flying course. He was not idle during this period, helping 4 FTS to win the Shell Hockey Cup (1936), and also represented the RAF ME Shooting VIII and RAF ME Boxing Team in the same year. Bill had certainly proved his credentials on the field of sport and in the ring!

But he still had not learned to fly, although his training was to begin on 5 January 1937, going up in a FTS Hart (K4903) under the tuition of Flt Lt John Oliver.[6] Next day he was airborne in K4909 and from then onwards his training continued unabated. His first solo followed on 14 January (Hart K5050) and by the end of the month he had clocked up 28 flights totalling 31.15 hours dual, and 32.45 hours solo. Another of his instructors was Flt Lt Paddy Coote. By 7 July, when he was awarded his 'wings', Bill had amassed 77.45 hours solo, including a night flight, and was assessed as 'Average' as a pilot, 'Above Average' as pilot/navigator, 'Average' in bombing, and 'Above Average' in air-gunnery.

Finally came the big day for Bill – 20 July 1937 – when he joined 33 Squadron as a fully fledged Sergeant Pilot. He was also welcomed to the squadron due to his sporting prowess and another big day in Bill's life came on 7 January 1938, when he represented RAF Middle East in the annual Inter-Services Hockey Match, which ended in a 2–4 defeat by the Army.

In March 1938, 33 Squadron converted to Gladiators on becoming a fighter squadron. Bill made his first Gladiator flight, in K8053, on 4 March. Based at

Ismailia and commanded by Sqn Ldr Hector McGregor, a New Zealander in the RAF, training soon got under way with flying and gunnery practice.

> Ismailia was a pleasant little town, with open-air cafés and many little bars. The European part of the town and the main shopping centre was well laid out with attractive trees planted at intervals along the pavements, and there were scores of good shops in the many small side streets. The native quarter, however, was a complete contrast, filthy, stinking to high heaven, with dirty, straggling mud huts bundled together and domestic animals wandering inside, outside and all over them. Around the town for as far as the eye could see stretched the wilderness of the desert. There were no sand dunes and palms. It was dead flat, an immense waste ground consisting of yellow grit, hard smallish stones, sand and, here and there, a patch of spiky camel thorn. At the edge of the town was the Royal Air Force station, which was in the process of being reconstructed when 80 Squadron arrived, so for the first fortnight they had to manage with temporary accommodation. Until the building operations were complete all the pilots spent most of their time at the United Services Club, a large bungalow surrounded by trees and overlooking Lake Timsah. It had everything: a bar, showers, changing rooms, and an enormous lawn, which stretched right down to the edge of the lake. But the best thing about it was that everything was free, or at least one did not need any money; at the time one just signed for a book of tickets – the cost of the book was then added to the mess bill at the end of the month.[7]

Bill made good progress as an embryonic fighter pilot and excelled in aerobatics and air-to-ground shooting. On 1 August 1938, he received his first assessment as a fully fledged fighter pilot:

As a fighter pilot	Above Average
As a pilot/navigator	Above Average
In air-gunnery	Above Average

His skills were soon to be fully tested.

Chapter 2

BILL'S FIRST WAR – PALESTINE

During the first half of 1929, conflict erupted between Arabs and Jews in Jerusalem. Jews were accused of having seized Muslim holy places in Jerusalem – Al Aqsa and Al-Haram – atop the Jewish holy place called the Temple Mount. In response, enraged Arab mobs attacked Jews in Jerusalem and looted their homes, and the attacks and looting spread to other cities. The Jews in Hebron suffered the most. There, 67 Jews were killed and others injured. The attackers did not spare women, children or the aged. Hebron was a holy city for the Jews, but its settlement of 700 people came to an end. Survivors fled to Jerusalem. At Tel Aviv, armed Jews counter-attacked and killed six Arabs. A British force rushed from bases elsewhere in the Mediterranean and ended the violence, the British having killed 87 Arabs and wounded many more. The total Jewish dead from the disturbances was 133.

In the 1930s, Palestine became enormously important as a destination for Jewish migrants. Anti-Semitism was worse than ever because of the rise of Nazism, and the United States had slowed acceptance of immigrants drastically. The opposition on the part of the native Palestinian Arabs to displacement by the Jews meant that they had to be prepared to defend their interests by force.

Although the RAF had first been called upon to assist ground forces to disperse Arab anti-Jewish demonstrations in and around Jerusalem and Jaffa in late 1933 – on 28 October of that year, for example, nine Gordons from 14 Squadron had scattered crowds by carrying out low-level mock strafing attacks – it was not until 1935 that serious dissent in Palestine erupted when the followers of Sheikh Izz ad-Din al-Qassam, who was killed in a shoot-out with the British, initiated a general strike in Jaffa and Nablus, and then launched attacks on Jewish and British installations.

About one month after the general strike had started, the leadership group declared a general non-payment of taxes in explicit opposition to Jewish immigration. In the countryside, armed insurrection started sporadically, becoming more organised with time. One particular target

22

of the rebels was the major Trans-Arabian Pipeline (TAP) constructed only a few years earlier from Kirkuk (Iraq) to Haifa (Jewish Palestine). This was repeatedly bombed at various points along its length. Other attacks were on railways (including trains), Jewish settlements, secluded Jewish neighbourhoods in the mixed cities, and Jews, both individually and in groups. 14 Squadron was joined in policing actions by 6 Squadron and a flight of 33 Squadron Hinds. Such was the tempo that 6 Squadron lost two crews shot down by ground fire during the latter part of the year.

* * *

Violence continued throughout Palestine in 1938, which saw a section of two Gladiators of 80 Squadron being sent to Ramleh in August for 'policing' duties. Two of these were flown by Plt Offs Pat Pattle and Peter Wykeham-Barnes, who were soon in action strafing rebel bands early the following month.

> They went to Palestine and were stationed first at Samakh, a small landing-ground on the southern shores of Lake Galilee. The Arabs had started a rebellion and the Gladiators were there to co-operate with the ground forces of the army against the rebels. The work consisted mainly of message dropping and reconnaissance, although Pat and Pete were occasionally called upon to machine-gun rebel positions or drive off the Arabs when they attacked convoys on the roads. For the first time Pat realised what a lethal weapon a Gladiator could be. The four Browning guns poured a shower of lead in the direction of the enemy and there was not much chance for the poor Arab if he was selected as a target, especially when the guns were under the expert control of such excellent marksmen as Pattle and Wykeham-Barnes.
>
> On the other hand, the Arabs themselves were extremely good shots. In four engagements during one week three RAF aircraft were brought down by their accurate fire. On another occasion, when an assortment of twelve bombers, fighters and reconnaissance aircraft were sent off on a mission, nine of them had to force-land, having received bullets in the engine or fuel tanks. Pat and Pete were lucky, for although their Gladiators received their fair share of bullets during these engagements, they were never seriously damaged and were always able to fly safely back to their own landing-ground.[1]

It was into this hot spot that detachments from 33 Squadron found themselves thrown in September 1938, their task to assist ground forces to round up armed bands of tribesmen who were terrorising certain areas. Bill was one of four pilots chosen to fly to Ramleh for co-operation with the Army in maintaining order, and was allocated Gladiator L7614 as his 'personal' aircraft. The move resulted in three months of intense operations against rebels in the area. This mainly involved ground troops going in and searching villages that were suspected of supporting these armed rebels, while aircraft preceded the troops to drop leaflets informing the inhabitants to remain indoors. Any infringement was met with force.

On 1 October, the detachment flew its first operation, being called upon to attack dissidents. A dozen casualties were reported in return for one Gladiator receiving a bullet through the tail plane strut. Two days later, the Gladiators were off in pairs on local reconnaissance patrols, during the course of which five casualties were inflicted. On 5 October, Bill flew a solo patrol and returned claiming one casualty. Three more pilots arrived for duty at Ramleh on 13 October, allowing Bill and one other to be detached to Haifa four days later. During a patrol on 18 October, he again had cause to open fire on dissidents and reported two casualties.

During this time there were a number of accidents involving 33 Squadron Gladiators, although not all occurred in Palestine. On 17 October, Plt Off Lionel Reed, who was undertaking unauthorised aerobatics near or over a ship transiting through the Suez Canal, was killed. On board the ship was his wife/girlfriend. He came in too close and caught the ship's aerial, which must have jammed his controls as the Gladiator dived into the ground about 1 mile south of Qantara.

November proved to be a particularly intensive period for the Palestine detachment, although Bill, much to his chagrin, experienced a quieter time at Haifa. Meanwhile, heavy rains on 7 November made Ramleh aerodrome unserviceable and the detachment moved to Lydda, from where three days later the squadron suffered its first operational casualty. Sqn Ldr McGregor and four others conducted strafing attacks during an air cordon operation at Beit Fulk. As a result of enemy sniping, Sgt Arthur Tebbs crashed and was critically injured. Although rescued, he died nine days later.

The detachment moved back to Ramleh on 12 November, daily recces and patrols continuing unabated. Several casualties were inflicted on the rebels during this period. On 25 November, troops carried out searches of villages near Jerusalem and the western suburbs of El Kastel on the Jaffa Road in conjunction with the Army's 7th Division in the area west of Jerusalem.

From first light the unit air-pinned the following villages, aircraft being relieved every two hours: Husan, Wadi Fukin, El Maliha, Suba Ein Karim, El Jura, Sataf, Khirat, El Laus, El Waliya, Deir Yasin, El Qastal, Aqqur, and Khan Sueida. Considerable pinning action was taken, but few casualties recorded. One of Bill's colleagues, Plt Off Hudson, carried out a forced landing near El Maliha after being hit by rifle fire. He did not survive. Bill was back in the air on 28 November, he and his flight commander answering a call to investigate an incident at Um Ay Zind, but found no sign of dissidents. Another pilot carried out a recce of the same area and came under fire. He returned the fire and 'obtained' two casualties. Bill's detachment was recalled and returned to Lydda, he and his section leader strafing dissidents at Bu'eina on 20 December (one casualty), and being called out again two days later but to no avail.

The Christmas break was spent at Lydda. Circumstances precluded any elaborate decorations or celebrations, but the airmen's dining room was livened up by festoons purchased in Tel Aviv. During the morning carols were sung and in the afternoon the sergeants and airmen engaged in a donkey polo match. Later the squadron beat the Buff's (West Kents) detachment at six-a-side soccer. Bill's involvement in these festivities is not recorded, although it seems likely that he participated.

The local war continued on 27 December though no action was required. Such was the intensity of operations that 33 Squadron had flown 1,850 hours between September and December alone, losing 2 pilots killed, 2 wounded and 3 aircraft, while a further 14 suffered damage from ground fire but were able to return to base. On 2 February 1939, Plt Off John Poynton, who had only been with the squadron for nine days after being posted in from 80 Squadron, was killed when his aircraft crashed during operations near Deir Ballut. It was believed he had also been hit by rifle fire from the ground.

The tactics adopted by the RAF proved successful and by June order was eventually restored. It transpired that the decision of the French to crack down on Arab leaders in Damascus might have been a significant factor in stopping the conflict. By the time the violence ended in June 1939, more than 5,000 Arabs, 400 Jews, and 200 Britons had been killed and at least 15,000 Arabs wounded. For his leadership in the operations 33 Squadron's CO, Sqn Ldr Hector McGregor, was awarded the DSO, while Flt Lt Hale Bolingbroke (Bill's detachment commander) received a DFC. For his participation Bill received the Palestine Medal and was Mentioned in Dispatches:

> For specially distinguished or meritorious service of a high standard. The faithful or zealous performance of ordinary duty is not sufficient in itself. There must be either special services of a high degree of merit superior to ordinary work, or highly meritorious performance of ordinary duties when these have entailed work of a dangerous or specially trying character.[2]

War had by now broken out in Europe but training continued in the Middle East, which was largely unaffected by events. A few of the more experienced aircrew were posted home, including Sqn Ldr McGregor. The New Year of 1940 saw 33 Squadron and its sister unit 80 Squadron, also equipped with Gladiators, move to Helwan. At the end of January, air-to-ground firing exercises were held at Mersa Matruh, Bill and another pilot sharing top spot

25

with 185 hits out of 200 rounds fired. Various air defence exercises were held over the ensuing few months.[3] Further exercises revealed alarming inadequacies in the Gladiator's performance. During practice interceptions against Blenheims, the Gladiator pilots found that they could only make one pass before the Blenheim's superior speed enabled it to escape.

33 Squadron was now commanded by Sqn Ldr D.V. Johnson and equipped with 21 Gladiators (mainly Mk.IIs). It had 22 pilots in three flights. Bill was in C Flight commanded by Flt Lt Hale Bolingbroke DFC. Serving with A Flight was Flt Sgt Len Cottingham from Grimsby, who had been at RAF Halton as an apprentice the same time as Bill, as had Sgt Ron Slater. Presumably they had known each other before joining 33 Squadron. On 11 May, Bill was advised that he had been selected for appointment to commissioned rank.

Chapter 3

TOTAL WAR!

A t the outbreak of the Second World War, Italy had two armies in Libya: Fifth Army and the Tenth Army. Both armies were commanded by the Commander-in-Chief of Italian North Africa and Governor-General of Italian Libya, the charismatic Marshal of the Air Force (*Maresciallo dell'Aria*) Italo Balbo. The Fifth Army in Tripolitania was commanded directly by Gen Italo Gariboldi and had six infantry divisions and two blackshirts divisions. The Tenth Army in Cyrenaica was commanded directly by Gen Mario Berti and had three infantry divisions, one blackshirts division and two Libyan infantry divisions. In late June 1940, the principal force on the border with Egypt was the Tenth Army. The Italian air forces (Aeronautica della Libia of the Regia Aeronautica) available in Libya greatly outnumbered the British forces in Egypt. The British, however, had an advantage in quality.

On 11 June 1940, the day after Italy declared war on the Allies, the Italian forces stationed in Libya and the British and Commonwealth forces stationed in Egypt began a series of raids on each other. Among the more notable achievements of these raids was the capture of Fort Capuzzo by the British Army's 11th Hussars.

* * *

When Italy entered the war, 33 Squadron was ordered to move B Flight's six Gladiators to Sidi Barrani to carry out bomber escort duties. C Flight and Bill remained at Helwan. The **14th June** saw the first combats between opposing RAF and Regia Aeronautica fighters over North Africa. This occurred when the 11th Hussars, joined by elements of 4th Armoured Brigade and 1/Royal Rifle Corps, assaulted Fort Capuzzo and Fort Maddalena (the two most important Italian frontier posts). The offensive was supported by attacks by Blenheims from 45, 55, 113 and 211 Squadrons. To protect both bombers and ground forces, 33 Squadron flew offensive sweeps as far as Bardia, meeting the Regia Aeronautica twice in the morning.

At 0735, Flg Off Dixie Dean,[1] with Flg Off Bob Couchman, Plt Offs Vern Woodward and Alf Costello, took off from Sidi Barrani to provide indirect escort to Blenheims from 45 Squadron. Two Blenheims were tasked to attack the nearby airstrip of Sidi Azeiz while three others headed for Fort Maddalena. One of the bombers that attacked Sidi Azeiz was shot down by light AA fire, killing the crew. The four Gladiators returned at 0925 and reported a successful low-flying attack carried out on a Ca309 Ghibli reconnaissance-bomber after forcing it down at Sidi Aziez.

The Ghibli was flown by Tenente Adriano Visconti, who had been tasked to carry out a reconnaissance over Sidi Azeiz. During the attack by the Gladiators, the gunner (1°Av. Luigi Moroso) was wounded and one engine was put out of action, obliging Visconti to carry out the forced-landing at Sidi Azeiz, where fierce fighting was taking place. Visconti dismounted the front gun of the Caproni and with it defended the aircraft for more than one hour before another Ca309 from his unit landed and rescued him and his crew. The abandoned aircraft was later captured intact by British troops. For this mission Visconti was awarded the *Medaglia di bronzo al Valor Militare* for bravery. The official citation stated that:

> During a mission he was attacked by three enemy aircraft that seriously damaged his plane. With skilful manoeuvre he landed it and immediately organised the defence of his crew displaying courage and great determination.

Thirty-five minutes later, at 1000, after refuelling the Gladiators, Dean and Woodward were off again, followed a few minutes later by Sgt John Craig. Near Fort Capuzzo they intercepted three Ca310B light-bombers of 159ªSquadriglia escorted by CR32s. Dean shot down one of the fighters while Woodward and Craig jointly attacked one Caproni, setting its engine on fire, before engaging a second. The former crashed among British tanks near Fort Capuzzo. The pilot, Sergente-Maggiore Stefano Garrisi, managed to bale out, as did 1°Av. Montatore Ubaldi, but the gunner, Av.Sc.Arm. Giuseppe Pascali, jumped too low and was killed. The second bomber, flown by Tenente Mario Virgilio Corda, was hit by 130 rounds and Sergente-Maggiore Giovanbattista Trevisan wounded. Woodward also became engaged with the escort and claimed a CR32 before returning to base with a single bullet hole in one of his wings. Of the action Dean recalled:

> An inoffensive-looking light-bomber was seen, and I detached Woodward and Sgt Craig to attack, whilst I stayed aloft to cover. Within a short spell I saw six aircraft in line astern heading from the west. I recognised them as CR32s. I remember being quite calm, and wondering what the heck to do. I flew towards them, keeping them well to my right – with the thought of getting behind them (and shooting them down one by one – silly boy!). Before I got close enough to them, they split in all directions and formed a ring around me – the

sitting duck! I remembered somewhere about flying extraordinarily badly to present a very bad target. I throttled back, yawed and waffled up and down and around, and could hear the thump of their half-inch cannon at each pass, and as each came into my sights having a rapid squirt at them. This seemed to go on for ages, and eventually one of them dropped away and suddenly the remainder disappeared, and I was thankfully alone in the sky and flew back. I heard upon my return to base that one CR32 had been destroyed, apparently by me, whilst Woodward and Craig had shared the bomber. I did hear later that the pilot of the CR32 had been struck by a single bullet through the heart.[2]

The CR32s were from the 8°Gruppo led by Capitano Martino Zannier, CO of 92ªSquadriglia. The Italian pilots reported that they had chased seven Gladiators and one of them was claimed by Tenente Ranieri Piccolomini and a second jointly by Sergente Ernesto Pavan and Sergente Edoardo Azzarone, before the latter was shot down and killed over the British lines.

While on an early morning patrol from Helwan on **16 June**, a section of three Gladiators from C Flight, including Bill in N5763, entered a heavy mist and the pilots became disorientated resulting in Flt Lt Hale Bolingbroke's aircraft crashing into the sea; the 29-year-old pilot was killed. The other two Gladiators had better luck and force-landed in the desert without much damage or injury, Bill simply noting in his logbook 'force landing No. 2'.

During the month the Italians moved two divisions up to the frontier to retake Fort Capuzzo, and also increased their air activity. To assist 33 Squadron's Gladiators in combating this, two Blenheim 1Fs of 30 Squadron and a Hurricane (which had recently arrived in theatre) from 80 Squadron, were attached to the squadron at Mersa Matruh, arriving on 17 June. Dean remembered:

> When the first Hurricane arrived in Egypt to 80 Squadron at Amriya, each pilot of the unit was allowed to complete a modest test on it. It flew superbly, balanced and well trimmed, and was a joy to fly. Take-off and landing was no problem.

Bill was one of the unlucky pilots who did not get an opportunity to fly the Hurricane.

Two days later (**19 June**), four Gladiators flown by Sqn Ldr Johnson, Flt Lt Hawkins, Flg Off A.H. Lynch and Sgt Roy Green, accompanied by the Hurricane and the two Blenheim fighters, took off to patrol the Sollum area. A dozen CR42s were encountered and the aircraft at once became involved in a dogfight with nine of them. In fact only five CR42s, of 10°Gruppo, were involved, the other aircraft seen by the British pilots were CR32s of 8°Gruppo. Nine of these Fiats had taken off at 0825 loaded with 2kg bombs with the dual role of escorting the Bredas from 159ªSquadriglia and ground-attack. The formation comprised six CR32s of 92ªSquadriglia and three from 94ªSquadriglia. The former unit returned with nothing to report, but the latter section was back at 1055 claiming the destruction of Sollum's electrical station by the use of 36 2kg bombs, but noting enemy fighters that had attacked them. No losses were suffered by the CR32s.

The Hurricane pilot (Wykeham-Barnes) claimed two, but Green was shot down and killed, most likely by Sergente Giuseppe Scaglioni. Two CR42s were shot down, Sergente-Maggiore Ugo Corsi crashing into the sea, while TenCol Armando Piragino, the commanding officer of 10°Gruppo, was injured when his Fiat crashed at Sollum, being taken prisoner. Sergente Scaglioni described the combat:

> Over Bir el Gib we were surprised by a number of Glosters and a Hurricane that attacked with height advantage giving us a lot of trouble. I saw the commander doing a violent overturning while I was doing a break on the left, this manoeuvre put me behind a Gloster that I shot down with my 12.7 mm guns.
>
> I lost sight of the commander immediately and after landing I knew he was missing. In the same combat we lost Sergente-Maggiore Corsi shot down by a Hurricane that I attacked trying to distract it from its action but in vain. For sure Corsi was taken by surprise because he was considered a pilot of exceptional skill and the very best aerobatic pilot of the Stormo.

On **21 June**, one of those unfortunate incidents known as 'friendly fire' occurred when a Seagull V amphibian seaplane – A2-21 from the Australian cruiser HMAS *Sydney* spotting for the Royal Navy's bombardment of Bardia – was attacked in error by Gladiators from 33 Squadron (pilots unknown). It was badly damaged and the port undercarriage collapsed on landing at Mersa Matruh, although the crew – Flt Lt Tom Price RAAF and Lt Jack Bacon RN (also Australian) – were unhurt. Although Bill was flying that day he was not involved. Three days later he was advised of his commission as Pilot Officer (44065).

The next successful engagement for 33 Squadron occurred on **29 June**, when three Gladiators flown by Dean, Craig and Plt Off Peter Wickham (a 112 Squadron pilot on attachment) took off to patrol the front lines. These were followed by two more flown by Woodward and Plt Off Jerry Harrison (also from 112 Squadron). At 1230, a Ro37 was sighted and forced to land three miles west of Sidi Aziez after being attacked by Wickham. The rear gunner was apparently hit and the aircraft landed in British lines. Three CR32s were then encountered in the Ricotta Capuzzo area. A dogfight ensued and Woodward forced down one two to three miles north of Fort Capuzzo, near the road between Capuzzo and Bardia. He then pursued another, which he shot down after a long dogfight. Both Fiats fell behind British lines. Harrison claimed a third damaged. One of Woodward's victims was Sottoten Antonio Weiss, adjutant of 12°Gruppo, who was killed.

These successes were followed by two more the next day (**30 June**). At 0800, three CR32s of 160ªSquadriglia took off from Ponticelli to escort another reconnaissance Ro37. Over Bir Sceferzen they were attacked by two Gladiators flown by Dean and Wickham. The former recalled:

> Peter Wickham and I were patrolling near Bardia, and spotted two CR42s [*sic*]. We each took one, and within minutes there were two black plumes on the ground. I got involved with another CR42, a quite aggressive 'Eyetie' (most rare), and I unfortunately got into head-on attacks with him, which are not recommended. We had three passes at one another but with no apparent damage, except that when we reached base together I didn't perform any victory rolls, although Peter was performing perfect flick rolls in formation. Lucky for me, because my riggers reported to me that my centre section was badly damaged, and it was well I had overcome my exuberance.

Tenente Ivano Vanni baled out from his burning aircraft while Sergente Aldo Santucci force-landed his CR32 close to T5 airstrip, west of Tobruk. While doing this he hit an Army truck, seriously injuring the driver and writing off the aircraft.

At 0400 on the morning of **1 July**, C Flight was ordered to fly to Sidi Barrani, Bill flying N5769. The transfer flight from Gerawla took 50 minutes. At 0940, Bill was airborne with his section to carry out a patrol over the Capuzzo–Bardia area, returning at 1130 having not made contact with the enemy. But his luck and opportunity changed on the next patrol, when he engaged a CR32 while patrolling with his section between Sidi Barrani and Capuzzo, claiming this shot-down for his first victory. It seems unlikely that the Italian fighter crashed; it may have temporarily force-landed but was able to return to its base. Bill carried out two more patrols before nightfall, and by the time he turned in for a well-earned rest he had been in the air for over seven-and-a-half hours during the day.[3]

Bill was given a short break and missed the action on **4 July** when no fewer than 11 CR42s were claimed in two actions by A Flight together with the attached 112 Squadron pilots. At 0900, five CR42s of 8°Gruppo took off to escort a Ro37 reconnoitring the Sollum area. The Italian formation reported being intercepted by several Gladiators, which attacked the Ro37. The Italian fighters intervened and managed to save the observation aircraft, but almost all of the Fiats suffered gun-jamming during the combat and two CR42s were shot down, Tenente Giovanni Tadini and Sergente-Maggiore Arturo Cardano both of 94ªSquadriglia were taken prisoner, Tadini having baled out while Cardano crash-landed. Their opponents were in fact a section of three Gladiators from A Flight, Plt Off Chico Woods and Len Cottingham being the victors.

During the evening, six Gladiators – two from A Flight and four flown by attached 112 Squadron pilots – took off to escort a Lysander on a reconnaissance sortie over the front lines. Nine CR42s were reportedly seen taking off from Monastir LG, west of Bardia, and the Gladiators dived to attack. In fact, there were only five Fiats involved in this action. The section led by Flg Off Tony Gray-Worcester, including Cottingham and Woods, attacked just as the Fiats left the ground and Gray-Worcester[4] claimed four of them while Cottingham claimed two and Woods one. The other three Gladiators led by Flg Off Waldo Price-Owen with Flg Offs Bob Smith and Flg Off Dick Bennett, all from 112 Squadron, apparently attacked the same hapless flight. Taking the barely airborne Fiats by surprise Smith and Bennett each claimed one shot down. All five Fiats were shot down against nine claims made by the Gladiator pilots.

In quick succession Sergente-Maggiore Trento Cecchi was shot down and killed and Sottoten Nunzio De Fraia was obliged to bale out, wounded, from his burning aircraft. Capitano Franco Lavelli was the next to fall and then Tenente Alberto Bevilacqua, who, although seriously wounded, disengaged and landed a heavily damaged aircraft. Only Sergente-Maggiore Agostino Fausti remained in flight, fighting against the whole RAF formation. From the ground it was seen that his fire hit two Gladiators that were obliged to leave the combat area (no victories were claimed), but the other four Gladiators pounced on the hapless and gallant pilot, hitting his aircraft while he (probably already wounded) was trying a last evasive manoeuvre diving in westward direction towards the fading sun. Fausti died in his burning plane and was awarded a posthumous *Medaglia d'Oro* for bravery.[5]

For the Gladiator patrol, the only casualty was Price-Owen, whose aircraft it would seem had been damaged by Fausti before his demise, as later recalled by Flt Lt Joe Fraser of 112 Squadron:

> During July, pilots from 112 Squadron, on detachment at Sidi Barrani, were gaining operational experience rapidly and many dogfights resulted around the bay of Sollum between Gladiators with CR42s, for the CR42 pilot had not yet learnt to respect the Gladiator – his senior, with its greater manoeuvrability. It was during one of these flights that F/O Price-Owen was badly shot up, though uninjured himself, and then decided to bale out. However, unfortunately, he was wearing

a parachute belonging to a friend of far greater stature and on pulling the rip cord, the loose harness gave him a very severe jerk between his legs which almost cost him his manhood – a very serious matter. He was incapacitated for some time and posted from the Squadron.

Bill was back flying routine patrols that continued unabated, carrying out two on the 5th, four on the 6th, three on the 7th and two on the 8th. A further five followed on the 10th, 11th and 12th – all uneventful. But then he scored again, on **15 July** while flying N5766, when he engaged an SM79 with his leader, Flg Off Harry Starrett, near Mersa Matruh at about 1630, this being claimed shot down jointly. Records show that a mission by a reconnaissance SM79 was flown over Alexandria in daylight, the aircraft also bombing the harbour. It seems unlikely that this was the machine intercepted by Bill. Another Savoia was reported by 5ªSquadra Aerea as lost during the day due to non-operational causes, but no more details have come to light.

Before the month was out, more victories came the way of B Flight's Plt Off Woodward, who claimed two and a third shared with one of the 112 Squadron pilots in two separate engagements, but Plt Off Preston was obliged to bale out, victim of the Italian ace Tenente Guglielmo Chiarini of 13°Gruppo. On **24 July**, a patrol by five Gladiators of B Flight flown by Dean, Woodward and Plt Off Costello, with Sgts Ron Slater and Dickie Shaw, encountered an estimated 18 CR42s over the front lines. In the ensuing skirmish, Woodward claimed one and a probable, Slater one and Costello one damaged. It seems that Shaw's aircraft was hit in return, force-landing east of Buq-Buq on his way back to the airstrip. He rejoined the squadron following a long trek across the desert.

Their opponents were 11 CR42s from 10°Gruppo led by Maggiore Carlo Romagnoli, plus a further six from 13°Gruppo. They reported meeting 15 Gladiators escorting 9 Blenheims, which were attacking Bardia. Three of the bombers were claimed damaged by Tenente Franco Lucchini before the Gladiators engaged, one of which was claimed shot down by Tenente Giovanni Giuducci. Another was damaged by Tenente Giuseppe Aurili, but Capitano Aldo Lanfranco became separated, was shot down and obliged to bale out in the Sidi Azeiz area. A British patrol took him prisoner a little later. Lanfranco was one of the oldest pilots of 10°Gruppo and a few days later a message was dropped near Tobruk by a British aircraft, advising that he was wounded and in Alexandria hospital. Meanwhile, Tenente Enzo Martissa of 91ªSquadriglia reported that he had forced down a Gladiator, and then, on returning to base, had seen his wingman in difficulties against the determined attack of another Gladiator. Although his guns had jammed, he had attacked and forced the Gladiator to break away. The next day Martissa was out again searching for the fighter he had obliged to land and having found it, he strafed it to destruction, most likely the machine of Shaw. Sergente Luigi Ferrario returned to base with a damaged fighter and Tenente Giulio Torresi from 13°Gruppo claimed another, raising the total claims to three for loss of one and one damaged. It seems that Capitano Lanfranco was taken to Ma'atan Bagush, where a Blenheim observer noted:

> Our latest Italian prisoner is a snooty major [*sic*]. He had the cheek to down one of our Gladdies, but one of ours pranged him. He has a broken ankle and two broken ribs, says Doc Turner, who had him in his truck for running repairs. The damage was caused by a bad harness design, and hitting his own tail-plane. The parachute, though, is gorgeous white silk and has been spirited away by the CO. 30 [*sic* – 33 Squadron] rang and claimed it. Fat chance!
>
> Two of the Lysander pilots [from 208 Squadron] looked in on us this evening and entertained us with some good yarns. One of their lot, taken prisoner, marched into the Iti Mess and shouted: 'Who in here speaks English?' A small Italian shot to his feet. 'I speak-a d'English,' he said. 'Then f--- you for a start,' said the 208 pilot. This yarn was told by an Italian pilot who is now our prisoner. I feel there should be more, but that's it.[6]

At 0915 on **25 July**, Derna/North airstrip suffered a heavy air attack by six Blenheims of 211 Squadron, which destroyed two SM79s on the ground and seriously damaged two more. Five personnel were killed and thirteen more wounded. B Flight of 33 Squadron was detailed to sweep the border area to cover eventual stragglers. Five of the Gladiators were flown by the same pilots as the previous day – Dean, Costello, Woodward, Slater and Shaw – and they were joined by Flg Off Peter Strahan of 112 Squadron. Seven CR42s were encountered over Bardia. Woodward and Slater each claimed one, of which Woodward's went down in flames, before they shared a third. Slater was then seen spinning down, out of the fight (although he returned safely), and Woodward became separated from the remaining Gladiators. He was attacked for seven or eight minutes at low level by several CR42s before escaping. He later revealed that this was probably his hardest combat against Italian fighters, and was very impressed by his opponents. Costello claimed one shared, probably with Strahan, whose aircraft was hit during the skirmish and he was forced to make an emergency landing on the return flight. He was returned to base aboard an infantry vehicle.

The Gladiators had clashed with CR42s from 13°Gruppo, but without the success they believed they had achieved. At 0910, Sergente-Maggiore Leone Basso of 77ªSquadriglia had scrambled from El Adem following an air raid alarm. Tenente Giovanni Beduz of 78ªSquadriglia joined him ten minutes later. With them were also Sergente Rovero Abbarchi, Sottoten Natale Cima and

Sergente Ernesto Taddia (all of 78ªSquadriglia). The fighters were directed to an interception course along the probable return route of the Blenheims that had attacked Derna. While cruising over Bardia waiting for the bombers, the Gladiators carried out a surprise diving attack on the Fiats. At least three of the Italian fighters turned the tables against their opponents. Basso attacked a Gladiator, which was left smoking, while Abbarchi followed a Gladiator deep (30 miles) inside British territory and finally claimed it shot down. All the Fiats returned to base between 0940 and 1025.

33 Squadron was now sent back to Helwan, where it was to be re-equipped with Hurricanes that were arriving in the Middle East in small numbers. Its Gladiators were handed over to newly arrived 3 (RAAF) Squadron. During its two-and-a-half months of operations, 33 Squadron's pilots had claimed an estimated total of 38 Italian aircraft shot down (including those claimed by the attached 112 Squadron pilots) and numerous others damaged.

Chapter 4

POSTED TO 80 SQUADRON

Bill was not destined to remain with 33 Squadron and re-train on the Hurricane. Instead, he found himself posted on **27 July** to sister unit 80 Squadron, joining B Flight at Amirya commanded by Flt Lt Pat Pattle. Serving with the squadron were two more of Bill's old acquaintances from his Halton days, Sgts Cas Casbolt and Don Gregory.

* * *

80 Squadron had been sharing battle duties with 33 Squadron and was commanded by Sqn Ldr Paddy Dunn, but Bill now spent what must have been a frustrating four weeks engaged in mainly training flights, while his colleagues continued the fight. His log records 11 flights in Gladiators during August, mainly formation practice, with two harbour patrols, plus five trips in the station's Magister.

Meanwhile, on **4 August**, B Flight – without Bill – was ordered to provide an escort for a 208 Squadron Lysander, which was to carry out a reconnaissance of troop movements at Bir Taieb el Esem. Flt Lt Pattle led Wykeham-Barnes, Plt Off John Lancaster and Sgt Ken Rew. Pattle and Lancaster took up position 4,000ft above the Lysander and slightly to its starboard side. The other two Gladiators flew 1,000ft below the top cover and positioned themselves behind the Lysander. This formation crossed the border and after going about 30 miles a Very light was observed coming from the Lysander. The top cover dived down to investigate, but failed to spot anything unusual. Pattle then saw several Breda Ba65 single-engine light bombers in two formations, one of three and the other of four. These aircraft had earlier taken off with an escort of CR32s to attack a British supply depot 25 miles south-west of Sollum. The Italians had completed their second pass over the target when they spotted the lone Lysander. Wykeham-Barnes and Rew attacked the formation of four Ba65s, which were heading for the Lysander. Wykeham-Barnes claimed one of the Bredas in flames but he was then attacked by a CR32, believed to be that flown by M.llo Romolo Cantelli. He claimed to have shot down one of the fighters before baling out of his badly damaged aircraft. Rew was last seen attacking one of the Bredas, but he failed to return. He was later reported dead. He was probably shot down by Capitano Duilio Fanali, who claimed a Gladiator during the initial combat.

Pattle went after two Bredas that were flying in close formation. Dropping down to about 200ft the Bredas released their bombs and gradually began to outpace the slower Gladiator. The Italians made the fatal mistake of turning to the north, which allowed Pattle to cut the corner and close the range to 150yd. He came in for a quarter attack, which slowed the Italian down. Two of his guns then jammed but, undeterred, he continued to attack and the Breda finally went down to crash in a cloud of dust. By this time the second Breda had escaped.

In the middle of a mêlée Lancaster had the discomfort of having all four guns jam. He was then hit and wounded in the left arm and shoulder – possibly also by M.llo Cantelli. Fearing he might pass out due to loss of blood he managed to evade his attackers and with his right hand stemming the blood flow he was able to fly his badly damaged aircraft back to Sidi Barrani, where he landed and was rushed off to hospital. His Gladiator was later declared a write-off. Pattle, meanwhile, had come under attack from the escorting Fiats. More fighters had joined the fray, these being identified as CR42s. Turning into five attacking aircraft he hit one from close range whereupon it rolled on to its back and crashed into the ground. Breaking free from the others he headed for friendly territory only to find his way barred by at least a dozen enemy aircraft. At this point his remaining guns jammed and for 15 minutes he was able to avoid any major damage before his controls were then hit and he was forced to bale out. After landing on the ground Pattle set out on foot towards the front lines. He was later rescued by elements of the 11th Hussars and taken back to Sidi Barrani. It was thought that all three pilots had been lost, but then Pattle returned, as did Wykeham-Barnes, who was also picked up by the 11th Hussars.

On **8 August**, it was decided to operate 14 Gladiators (again without Bill) over the El Gobi area where large formations of Italian fighters had been operating. Sqn Ldr Dunn planned to lure the Italians into thinking there was only a small formation of Gladiators. To do this three aircraft were to act as bait. Accordingly three Gladiators were to fly at 8,000ft, with three more at 10,000ft. Four flew at 12,000ft and the final four at 14,000ft. All formations flew in a broad vic, which was the standard formation at this stage of the desert war. The leader of the highest formation controlled the formation. A mixed formation of 16 CR42s escorting a single Ro37 observation aircraft were soon spotted at 6,000ft. Leading the Gladiators into the sun, Flt Lt Pattle ordered the lower sub-formation to attack. As this formation reached the Italian fighters the other sections were ordered down. Sqn Ldr Paddy Dunn reported:

> I followed my first target down, who rolled over slowly on to his back
> with smoke coming out: Observed P/O Stuckey (No. 3 on my left)

37

quarry in much the same condition and gave him a burst of my own, then pulled up and across the rear of the formation of 18 that was beginning to peel-off. A CR42 did a steep diving turn away from his formation and I was easily able to give him a full deflection shot for about eight seconds, he continued in a dive with smoke issuing from him but as the formation of 18 was approaching around about me with advantage of number and height, it was impossible to pursue him. I claimed it definitely shot down and consider it to be one of the five observed on the ground by Sub 4 [sub-flight 4] before entering. Then followed a long period of loose play in which numerous targets offered themselves.

At the same time large numbers of enemy aircraft attacked me, chiefly from straight ahead and beam but not driving home determinedly. In one of them I throttled back and stall turned on the attacker's tail before he was quite past me, he then rolled on to his back and dived down in the second half of a loop. I followed and gave this aircraft what I thought was an effective burst with the result that he did not recover and continued down with bluish smoke issuing from him.

The other flights had by now entered and attacked their opponents, and the number of enemy aircraft thinned down. Two or three enemy aircraft were still about. I pulled up steeply to avoid one in particular who was dangerously near to my tail, having chased me down in the dive from the port quarter. In the ensuing black-out I have little knowledge of what he did but at the top of what was the first half of something like a rocket loop, I found myself going in the opposite direction with the aircraft climbing rapidly past me on my left and below, he then appeared ahead of me and did a slow roll, unfortunately, I was too surprised and failed to get him in my sight, whereupon he half rolled and dived out; another stall turn brought me on his tail, but he did a rapid dive, turned to the left and streamed off like a homing rabbit – next stop El Adem.

I engaged one more enemy aircraft but my guns failed to fire (after 300 rounds approx.). I tried to clear them but was only able to get one more short burst. I left the fight, gained height at 12,000 feet and returned to witness a dogfight between three aircraft two of which were Gladiators. I then set off home and picked up two other Gladiators.

The CO was credited with two confirmed and one probable and reported that his sub-flight gained five and two probables, with Stuckey also getting two and a probable and Wykeham-Barnes one. By now the second and third sub-flights had joined the fight. Flt Lt Evers-Swindell claimed one, while probables were awarded to Plt Off Keg Dowding, Flg Off Hugh Wanklyn Flower, Flg Off Bill Sykes and Flt Sgt Mick Richens. Finally, Flt Lt Pattle, having masterfully conducted the action, now joined the fray:

> I saw Nos 2 and 3 sections engage and before I brought my section into the fight, I saw five crashed aircraft on the ground, three of which were in flames. My own section then engaged those e/a who were attempting to reach their own base and immediately became engaged in separate combats. I engaged a CR42 and, after a short skirmish, got into position immediately behind him. On firing two short bursts at about 50 yards range the e/a. fell into a spin and burst into flames on striking the ground. The pilot did not abandon his aircraft. I then attacked three e/a immediately below me. This action was indecisive as after a few minutes they broke away by diving vertically for the ground and pulling out at very low altitude. Whilst searching for other e/a I saw two more aircraft crash and burst into flames. Owing to the widespread area and the number of aircraft engaged it was impossible to confirm what types of aircraft were involved in these crashes or who shot them down.
>
> The sky seemed clear of 42s although several Gladiators were still in the vicinity. I was about to turn for our base when a 42 attacked me from below. With the advantage of height I dived astern of him and after a short burst he spun into the ground into flames. As before, the pilot didn't abandon his aircraft. F/O Graham confirms both my combats which ended decisively. Seeing no further sign of e/a over the area, I turned towards our base. On my way home F/O Graham and F/O Linnard joined me in formation and my section landed at 1910 hrs.

Flg Off Sid Linnard also claimed two, while Flg Off Shorty Graham was credited with a probable. Two Gladiators were lost, Flt Sgt Trevor Vaughan (killed), and Evers-Swindell, although the 11th Hussars picked him up, as he later reported:

> I set the aircraft on fire. First removing the water bottle and Very pistol. I walked for three hours away from the sun and then lay down to sleep. I slept till about 0100 hours finding dense fog and myself wet through. I then dug a hole in some soft sand and buried myself. There I stayed till daylight. At about 0630 next morning when the fog started to lift I started to walk into the sun until 1500hrs, when I saw three armoured cars on the horizon. I fired three Very light cartridges. The next thing I remember I was lying in the shade of the armoured car, the crew told me I was about five miles from the wire.

One of the Gladiators was claimed by Sergente Lido Poli. Although his Fiat was badly shot up and he suffered severe wounds to his arm, he nevertheless stayed in the fight and brought down the Gladiator before he had to land himself due to his injuries. He was picked up by British troops and had to have his arm amputated. When the Italian Command heard of this he was awarded the *Medaglio d'Oro*. The Italians admitted the loss of eight aircraft, those flown by Sergente Aldo Rosa, Sergente Enrico Dallari and Sergente Antonio Valle, who all baled out; Sottoten Alvaro Querci and Sergente Santo Gino, who force-landed in addition to Sergente Poli and M.llo Norino Renzi, who was killed.

An eighth Fiat also failed to return although Tenente Enzo Martissa was recovered a few days later. He had force-landed his CR42 with 100 bullet holes in it, some 10 miles from El Adem. Severely wounded, he survived his ordeal by drinking dewdrops at dawn but, after two days, he was beginning to expect the worst. One of the bullets that had hit his aircraft, had pierced the griffin's head of squadriglia's badge on the port wheel cover and he poignantly scratched with a knife, on the white background disc of the badge, the following epitaph:

> You, little griffin, have been struck in the head. I would have suffered less if I had been likewise! I'm not mortally wounded, but I shall pass away, since I can't walk for 10–20 km to reach a track. And it will be by hunger and thirst.

He was found two days later by a motorcycle patrol led by Tenente Domenico Raspini, who recalled:

> We saw an aircraft in the desert. We approached and found Tenente Martissa under a wing, with a leg almost torn off by an explosive bullet from a British fighter. We rescued him. He told us that if we didn't come to save him, he'd shoot himself in the head with his gun, because he was dying of thirst.

Martissa's CR42 was later recovered, repaired and returned to operational service. In this action, the surviving Italian pilots claimed five Gladiators, all shared, and two probables.

No more enemy aircraft were encountered by 80 Squadron until **17 August**, when B and C Flights provided air support for naval vessels bombarding Bardia and Capuzzo, including Bill flying K7913. Wykeham-Barnes led Dowding and Plt Off Peter Stubbs DFM (won in Palestine) down through the clouds and attacked a Cant Z501. The seaplane, from 143ªSquadriglia, eventually fell in flames and crashed into the sea after several passes. Sottoten Cesare Como and Sottoten di Vascello Renzo Monselesan, the observer, both perished. Flt Lt John Lapsley, flying one of the Hurricanes, met four SM79s over ships near

Bardia and claimed three shot down, one of which crash-landed in the desert (two dead, one wounded, two unhurt), but next day, the Hurricane Flight was removed from the squadron and used to form 274 Squadron. Sqn Ldr Dunn and half a dozen pilots were posted with their aircraft to this new squadron, which was brought up to strength by posting in pilots from 33 Squadron. Flt Lt Tap Jones assumed temporary command of 80 Squadron until Sqn Ldr Bill Hickey, an Australian, arrived on 27 August.

The second week in September found Bill flying five standing patrols over Mersa Matruh (in K8036, K8022, K7912, L8009 and K7892), all of which proved uneventful, before moving with his Flight to Sidi Barrani on 12 September (flying K8013). Sqn Ldr Hickey took off that night in an attempt to intercept a lone bomber attacking Mersa Matruh. As it was illuminated by searchlights, he was able to fire a couple of bursts at it but failed to observe any results. From Sidi Barrani, Bill continued flying routine patrols over Bardia and Fort Capuzzo, before he undertook a Lysander escort sortie on the evening of **13 September** in K8013. Although his aircraft suffered minor damage from AA shrapnel he was able to return and land safely. With the Italians advancing into Egypt, the Gladiators were frequently called upon to provide escort for the Lysanders over the area on reconnaissance missions, but when it became apparent that the Italians were heading for Sidi Barrani, the squadron was ordered back to Mersa Matruh.

On **15 September**, the squadron moved to a new location simply known as 'Y' landing ground. From here ten Gladiators took off to patrol the seaward side of Sidi Barrani. Nothing was seen and the squadron split up into sections. The section led by Plt Off Tony Cholmeley came across five SM79s approaching from the north-east. The Gladiators attacked, forcing the bombers to turn back, but return fire hit Cholmeley's aircraft and it fell into the sea. The 22-year-old was killed.

Following a five-day break, Bill flew a patrol over the fleet on **18 September** (in K7978) and an escort to bombers two days later in the same aircraft. Meanwhile, on **19 September**, one of the squadron's newly qualified pilots, Plt Off Roald Dahl,[1] was ordered to fly his Gladiator from Abu Sueir to the squadron's airstrip 30 miles south of Mersa Matruh, via Amiriya and Fuka. On the final leg Dahl could not find the airstrip and, running low on fuel and with night approaching, he was forced to attempt a landing in the desert. Unfortunately, the undercarriage hit a boulder and the plane crashed, fracturing his skull, smashing his nose in, and blinding him. He managed to drag himself away from the blazing wreckage and passed out. The location he had been given to fly to was in error, and he had mistakenly been sent instead to the no man's land between the Allied and Italian forces. Dahl was rescued and taken to a first-aid post in Mersa Matruh, where he regained consciousness, but not his sight, and was then taken by train to the Royal

Navy hospital in Alexandria. Doctors said he had no chance of flying again, but in February 1941, five months after he was admitted to hospital he was discharged and passed fully fit for flying duties (see Chapter 8).

On the ground the Italian offensive soon ground to a halt and a stalemate ensued. Although numerous patrols were flown no enemy aircraft were encountered. Routine patrols over Mersa Matruh continued for the remainder of the month, Bill alone logging five between the 20th and 30th. In early October, B Flight moved to Bir Kenayis, some 40 miles south-west of Mersa Matruh. By this time the Gladiator Mk.Is were being replaced with Mk.IIs. On 9 October, new arrival Flg Off Nigel Cullen, an Australian known as 'Ape', surprised a flight of five Ba65s. He dived in among them and saw one make off trailing black smoke, but was unable to confirm its crash.

B Flight returned from Bir Kenayis on 17 October, its place being taken by A Flight.

On **31 October**, the Italians planned to launch co-ordinated raids against Mersa Matruh and other targets in the area. A total of 50 SM79s were available, as were 40 CR42s from 2°Stormo. But, before the operation commenced, two formations of Blenheims respectively attacked the airfields at Monastir and Gambut. 80 Squadron Hurricanes and Gladiators provided cover for the Monastir raid, while 33 Squadron similarly flew escort for the Gambut operation, with Bill flying Gladiator N5825.

At about 1000 hours, seven Blenheims attacked the landing grounds at Gambut, destroying three bombers of 9°Stormo and damaging many others. Three CR42s from 82ªSquadriglia and a further three from 78ªSquadriglia scrambled after the bombers but failed to catch them. Two other CR42 pilots, Sottoten Carlo Alberti of 366ªSquadriglia and Sergente Mario Veronesi of 92ªSquadriglia, reported meeting Hurricanes both of which were claimed damaged. The returning Blenheim crews did not record any encounter with Italian aircraft except one crew who mentioned that a CR42 tried to follow them but after firing two bursts from 500yd was set upon by a Gladiator and a Hurricane and last seen diving towards the ground with smoke trailing from it. Bill did not report any contact. The Italian mission against Mersa Matruh was not cancelled and at 1050, 10 SM79s of 9°Stormo took off together with 11 SM79s of 14°Stormo and five from 33°Gruppo. The bombers were escorted by 18 CR42s from 13°Gruppo, which flew as close escort, and 18 more from 151°Gruppo, which was to fly an indirect support sweep. For 151°Gruppo this was the first long-range escort mission since arriving in Libya. They took off from Amseat to arrive over Mersa Matruh at the same time as the bombers.

The bombers gathered over Tmimi and then headed east in groups of five in arrow formations. The fighters from 13°Gruppo flew in flights of three in echelon right formation at 15,000ft, directed to a rendezvous point 15 miles south-west of Mersa Matruh along the road that connected this base with

Bir Kenayis, which they reached at 1256. After the bombers arrived over Mersa Matruh, each formation went for different targets but was attacked by Hurricanes and Gladiators while aiming for their targets. The first formation of five SM79s from 33°Gruppo, led by TenCol Ferri Forte, was able to repel the attack of reportedly three Gladiators. At 1303 they hit with precision the new railway station of Mersa Matruh, built after the old one was definitely put out of action by earlier bombing attacks. At 1246, 14°Stormo, led by TenCol Lidonici, attacked the airfield of Bir Kenayis, but finding it empty they headed for an alternative target of troops south-west of Mersa Matruh. 80 Squadron pilots on the ground noticed the bombers attacking the aerodrome of Bir Kenayis and reported that bombs fell to the south-west and some distance away, obviously thinking that the Savoias had missed their intended target of some miles. Gunners of the 14°Stormo claimed two Hurricanes and a Gladiator destroyed, and another Gladiator probable. One SM79 crash-landed near Sidi Barrani and was written-off while a second crash-landed in the desert near Tobruk and was also written-off. Three more SM79s returned at 1400 so badly damaged that they were classified irreparable and another was sent away for major repairs. Of its original 11 SM79s, only 5 were still fit for further operations.

At 1255, 9°Stormo, led by TenCol Italo Napoleoni, released its bombs on the railway near El Qasaba airfield. The diarist of 208 Squadron reported that around 40 bombs of the 100kg type were dropped by 15 SM79s and that 4 of them fell in the camp damaging 3 lorries and 3 tents while the remainder fell around the railway siding. Two SM79s from 11ªSquadriglia were shot down. The squadriglia flew in a V formation led by Tenente Giovanni Ruggiero and it was the two outer SM79s that were shot down in flames by a Hurricane. A gunner in Ruggiero's SM79, Av.Sc.Arm. Cherubino Mariotti recalled, of this his first combat mission:

> I was on a S79, first left wingman of a five planes formation that was attacked by British fighters after bombing enemy troops near Mersa Matruh. We, gunners, were returning fire when I noticed that the two end wingmen of our formation were hit and were losing height in flames. Suddenly I centred in my gun sight a Hurricane that was closing to the last three planes shooting continuously at us. I was able to aim at its belly and saw my tracers entering it. Obviously hit, the plane directed towards the ground leaving a thick cloud of black smoke. In this way I avenged the Tenente and dear friends lost in the two planes that fell in flames.

Sergente Pilota Armando Zambelli, who was the only survivor of the SM79 flown by Tenente Di Frassineto, recalled:

I was hospitalised in Derna infirmary when I heard that we were going to start for an important bombing mission. Today it can seem a bit excessive all the enthusiasm with which we wanted to take part in war missions, but twenty years old and with the high spirit of those days all seemed normal for us. I left the infirmary and reached the squadriglia. When my Commander Capitano [sic] Giovanni Ruggiero asked me how I felt I told him: 'Perfectly and I'm ready to start.'

The action was one of the most important of the war so far and our forces were fifty S79s with the escort of forty fighters started from an airstrip near Derna and after around an hour of flight we arrived over the airbase of Matruh. Our section was composed by five planes disposed in arrow formation under command of Capitano [sic] Ruggiero. We were almost on the target when a hand on my shoulder made me turning the head. It was the Motorista that told me that we were attacked by enemy fighters of which we had already shot down one. Sadly the Hurricanes and Gloster Gladiators from a superior height continued to fire without respite and after a short while I saw the end wingman opposite to my position falling in flames; pilots were Tenente Fabiani from Rome and Sergente Bigliardi from Bologna. We succeeded in bombing the target but following another enemy's burst of fire our plane started to burn and being made of wood and fabric it burned like a wax match.

I told the members of the crew to bale out but without avail because they tried to fight the fire. Enemy bullets continued to enter the plane and I saw the poor crewmembers hit by the bullets and reached by the flames. We decided to leave the plane, I opened the exit door on the top of the cockpit and immediately air suction threw me against the tail of the plane that was burning; I lost consciousness and I woke up when the parachute opened. I was descending under the area where our CR42s and the Hurricanes were fighting. Moving my legs I tried to move towards the land to avoid falling into the sea but in that moment I lost consciousness again.

When I woke up for the second time I was on a British vehicle between a bearded Sikh driver and an English officer that pointed his gun on me. I was taken to the infirmary because I was burned in the face and in the hands and had a dislocated ankle; there I was left resting for a while. Subsequently I was examined by a General that told me that he was Canadian and that he had fought as our ally during the First World War. He asked me, in an approximate Italian, if in Italy we thought that they killed the aviators that jumped with the parachute.

Chapter 5

ONWARDS TO GREECE

Benito Mussolini had grown jealous of Hitler's conquests and wanted to show his Axis partner that he too could lead Italy to similar military conquests. Italy, in 1939, had already occupied Albania (Greece's north-western neighbour) and several British Commonwealth strongholds in Africa, but could not boast victories such as those of Nazi Germany. Mussolini, who regarded south-eastern Europe as lying within the Italian sphere of influence, decided to invade Greece as it seemed to be an easy opponent. Mussolini told Count Ciano:[1] 'Hitler always faces me with a fait accompli. This time I am going to pay him back in his own coin. He will find out from the papers that I have occupied Greece.'

In the early morning hours of 28 October 1940, the Italian Ambassador awoke Greek Premier Metaxas and presented him an ultimatum. Mussolini demanded free passage for his troops to occupy unspecified 'strategic sites' inside Greek territory. Greece had been friendly towards National Socialist Germany, especially profiting from mutual trade relations, but now Germany's ally Italy was to invade Greece partly to prove that Italians could match the military successes of the German Army in Poland and France. Metaxas rejected the ultimatum. Even before the ultimatum had expired Italian troops invaded Greece from Albania. The invaders crossed the Kalamas river and approached Ioannina (Yannina), but were soon driven back and pursued beyond Greek territory and into Albania. Further north the Greeks checked Italian attempts to advance, and then passed on the offensive.

Within three weeks Greek territory was clear of the invader and a full-scale counter-attack was in place. The counter-attack was met with great success, a change in Italian commanders and the arrival of considerable reinforcements having little effect. Korce, the largest town in Albania fell to Greek forces on 13 November, to be followed by Pogradec and Argyrokastron on 4 December, Himare on 24 December and Kelcyre on 10 January.

In 1939 the United Kingdom had extended a guarantee of military aid if Greek territorial integrity was threatened. The British were committed to fighting in North Africa and could not spare many military units or war material to assist Greece. British public opinion was inspired by the way the Greeks had repulsed the Italians, and Prime Minister Winston Churchill thought it would be dishonourable not to aid the Greeks. The first British help to Greece were a few RAF squadrons under Air Vice-Marshal John D'Albiac, sent to aid the small Royal Hellenic Air Force in November 1940, while with the consent of the Greek government, British forces occupied Crete on 3 October, releasing the 5th Cretan Division for the Albanian front.

* * *

On **8 November**, 80 Squadron was informed of its imminent move to Greece. The squadron was reorganised into two flights fully equipped with Gladiator IIs, and it was arranged for the flights to proceed independently to Greece. B Flight's Gladiators were led by Sqn Ldr Hickey, and included Bill flying N5784 (a former 33 Squadron machine, NW-L), this aircraft having been assigned to him. To ensure that everyone knew it was 'his' machine, Bill had its spinner boss painted cherry red (thereby gaining his subsequent nickname). He also had Framlingham College's coat-of-arms, including its Latin inscription *Studio sapientia crescit* (Wisdom grows with study) painted behind the cockpit access hatch.

The Gladiators departed just after lunch on **17 November**, and flew to Sidi Haneish (a flight of 2 hours, 10 minutes according to Bill's logbook) where the pilots were bedded down for the night; the aircraft were refuelled by the ground crews of 112 Squadron. Early the next morning the Gladiators, navigated by a Bombay transport, headed north-east for Crete. A Sunderland flying boat joined the formation at the coastline, its purpose being to pick up anyone who might have the misfortune to land in the sea. Fortunately it was not needed and all the Gladiators and the Bombay landed safely at Heraklion (2 hours, 15 minutes), where they were refuelled. After a light lunch they took off on the last part of their journey and 90 minutes later were circling over Eleusis aerodrome.

As soon as they landed Sqn Ldr Hickey went off to HQ to get his orders, while the rest of the pilots went into Athens to see the sights of this centre of ancient history. The warmth of their welcome by the Greeks in their capital city was overwhelming. The streets were decorated with flags, the locals cheered and slapped them on the back, the children whistled and waved as the pilots gave them the thumbs-up sign. Everywhere they went the airmen were greeted with open arms and offers of hospitality. That night the local pubs, the tavernas, were crowded, and all the drinks were free to the Royal Air Force. The party was interrupted when Hickey returned from the Grand Bretagne Hotel, with the news that B Flight was to take off next morning and fly to Trikkala, located in the fertile plain of Thessaly in central Greece, where they would refuel and then make their first patrol in Greek skies.

Also gathered at the hotel were a number of British, Australian and American war correspondents, among whom were Richard Dimbleby, James Aldridge and the RAF's official reporter in Greece, Sqn Ldr Tommy Wisdom. On the arrival of 80 Squadron at Eleusis, the latter wrote:

> Other more than welcome arrivals were the men and aircraft of 80 Squadron, our first fighter squadron in Greece. 80, led by a most gallant Australian, Bill Hickey, with 'Tap' Jones and 'Pat' Pattle as Flight Commanders and including men like Cullen and Bill Vale, was to add gloriously to the record which the squadron had set up in the desert. It was equipped with Gladiators, but these, despite their slowness, had tackled the Italians over the desert, and there was no reason – especially with the added advantage of ample and excessive cloud cover – why they should not do the same in Greece.
>
> We now had five squadrons in Greece. While we numbered no modern aircraft in these squadrons, most of the aircrews had considerable fighting experience, and hopes were high. But there were tremendous difficulties. Far worse than the enemy was the weather that came with the winter. The Greeks, who were anxious not to provoke Germany, could not accede to our plan of utilising the Greek aerodromes in the north. The result of carrying out our raids on Albania from Menidi and Eleusis was that the Blenheims, given luck, could just about manage to reach the distant targets and return before their fuel was exhausted.

High mountains rose into the clouds, but the aircraft, heavily loaded, could not go very high, and in any case icing conditions would be encountered if they did; and there were very few strips of beach or fields on which an aircraft could be landed in an emergency. Experienced airline pilots said that the weather of Greece, because it was unpredictable, together with these great mountain ranges, made flying conditions the worst in Europe.

B Flight arrived at Trikkala about midday on **19 November** to find the pilots of a Greek PZL unit (23 Mira) already operating from there sitting on wooden benches in the open, less than 50yd from their ancient aircraft. They were enjoying a meal of bread and cheese and olives, washed down with a very strong-smelling but sweet-tasting wine. After a snack it was decided that the Greek pilots would take B Flight to have its first look at Albania.

As the formation neared the Italian airfield at Koritza, the PZLs were obliged to turn back due to their short range. The Gladiators flew over Koritza from where Italian anti-aircraft opened up. Flt Lt Pattle, who was leading the second section, sighted four CR42s climbing towards them from the starboard beam. It had been arranged beforehand that the Gladiators would not use their radio/telephones unless it was absolutely essential.

Pattle warned Sqn Ldr Hickey of the presence of the CR42s simply by diving past the CO's section and pointing his Gladiator towards the Italian aircraft. Hickey acknowledged that he understood by waggling his wings and Pattle withdrew to his position at the head of his section. As Hickey's section dived towards the four CR42s, Pattle noticed another pair and took his section, consisting of Stuckey and Casbolt, to engage these. Pattle went for the leading aircraft, which attempted to evade the attack by diving steeply and slipping from side to side. Pattle followed, closing in rapidly, but did not fire until his target straightened out. From 100yd astern he opened fire. The Fiat steepened its dive; the pilot had apparently been hit, because he was seen to fall forward over the control column. Pattle pulled away as his victim went straight down to crash about two miles west of Koritza, bursting into flames on striking the ground. Stuckey, following close behind Pattle's Gladiator, gave a thumbs-up signal to Pattle signifying confirmation of the victory.

Pattle then brought down a second Fiat. Stuckey claimed a G.50 and a CR42, while Casbolt also claimed a G.50, probably the same aircraft. Following his second kill, Stuckey was then wounded in the shoulder and leg but was able to regain base safely, from where he was transferred to the Greek Red Cross hospital in Athens. In addition to the five victories claimed by Pattle's section, Graham claimed a G.50 and a CR42, while Bill (N5784) claimed two CR42s, one of which he shared with Plt Off Sammy Cooper. Linnard claimed two more CR42s as probables. Bill described the fight in his official report:

> Nine Gladiators and three PZLs took off from Trikkala in four flights of three aircraft to carry out an offensive patrol over Koritza. I was flying in the second flight as No. 2 to F/Lt Pattle. We arrived over the area at approximately 1440 hours and after patrolling for about five minutes two CR42s were seen approaching our formation at 14,000 feet from starboard ahead. The signal for line astern was given by the flight leader, who immediately attacked the enemy aircraft, which broke formation. F/Lt Pattle engaged one CR42 and after a short dogfight shot it down out of control, with smoke coming from the engine.
>
> The other CR42 was engaged by No. 1 Flight. I tried to regain my flight but finally attached myself to two Gladiators in formation, which I found out to be No. 1 Flight led by S/Ldr Hickey. We carried on the

patrol at about 10,000 feet over Koritza, where we met fairly accurate AA fire. 'Tally-ho!' was then given when three CR42s in formation were seen at about 6,000 feet. The formation split up and I dived on a CR42 which was attempting to escape to the north. I carried out a quarter attack and then slid in to an astern position, which I held while the enemy pilot did evasive tactics. He then carried out a manoeuvre which appeared to be a downward roll and I noticed that smoke was coming from his engine. I carried on firing in short bursts until he went between two hills through a small cloud. I followed over the cloud but no enemy aircraft appeared and so I went below into the valley and saw wreckage in a copse – at the same time getting fired at by enemy troops.

I climbed up immediately and at 6,000 feet saw a shiny monoplane with radial engine diving down. I gave chase but was out-distanced and so gave up after firing a short burst at about 400 yards. I gained altitude and observed a Gladiator and a CR42 in a dogfight very low down over the hill, and also noticed that the enemy pilot was attempting to lead the Gladiator over a group of enemy ground forces. I waited until the Gladiator pilot had manoeuvred into an astern attack and then carried out a quarter attack. I noticed that first white smoke and then black was coming from the engine of the e/a before I opened fire. I carried out quarter attacks until the other Gladiator pilot pulled away and then slid into an astern attack.

I remained in that position until very low over the main road and then the CR42 turned over and slid into the side of a hill. The aircraft did not burst into flames. While pulling up I fired at the enemy ground troops. I gained altitude and waggled my wings for the other Gladiator pilot to join me and then found the other pilot was P/O Cooper, who had apparently run out of ammunition. I then set course for home and finally landed at Eleusis, where I refuelled, before proceeding to the base aerodrome. I inspected my aeroplane and found that I had one bullet hole in my tail plane, which had done no damage. In each encounter with CR42s I found that both pilots used the downward roll manoeuvre at high speed for evasive action.

Actual losses suffered by the Italians were three CR42s and one G.50. Sergente-Maggiore Natale Viola (363ªSquadriglia), M.llo Giuseppe Salvadori (363ªSquadriglia) and Sergente-Maggiore Arturo Bonato (393ªSquadriglia) all failed to return, as did Tenente Attilio Meneghel of 361ªSquadriglia in the G.50. A fourth CR42, flown by Sergente-Maggiore Walter Ratticchieri, was hit and the pilot was wounded in both legs. Another Fiat pilot, Sergente-Maggiore Luciano Tarantini, claimed a Gladiator shot down, two more being claimed as probables, one by Capitano Paolo Arcangeletti, the other by a G.50 pilot. It had proved a resounding success for 80 Squadron.

The pilots of B Flight, now fêted by the locals, who soon learned of the victory, found comfortable quarters in the best hotel in Trikkala, while ground personnel were billeted at the local school. It started raining during the night, and continued unabated for 48 hours, ruling out any operational flying for almost a week when low cloud replaced the rain. It was not until **25 November** that nine Gladiators were able to carry out an offensive patrol. Bill, flying N5784, participated in the patrol led by Sqn Ldr Hickey, who reported:

> Nine Gladiators left Trikkala at 1150. Maintained offensive patrol between Koritza and El Basan via Arai from 1255 to 1335. No enemy fighters encountered. Three separate convoys heading east attacked by No. 1 Flight. Nos 2 and 3 Flights maintained protective umbrella.
>
> (a) First convoy 18 miles west-north-west from datum point. Composition 100 pack-mules plus 20 heavy MT. Small camp and about 2–300 troops. One lorry set on fire, others damaged. Several personnel and pack-mules killed or wounded. One MG nest put out of action. General panic and confusion. MG and rifle fire experienced. One officer [own pilot] very slight flesh wound. Damage to aircraft slight.
>
> (b) Second convoy six miles west of datum point. Composed 12 heavy MT, headed east. Number of horses or mules resting in pens. MT personnel in vicinity. Leading lorry set on fire, others damaged. Several casualties caused.
>
> (c) Third convoy composed four or five MT headed west, but stationary. Leading lorry set on fire, others damaged. Wooden sheds on hilltop also attacked, in which personnel had entered. General panic.

Bill simply entered 'ground strafing' in his logbook.

The next clash with the Italians occurred when nine Gladiators, led by Sqn Ldr Hickey, took off from Trikkala on **27 November** and patrolled to the north of Yannina. Three SM79s were seen, escorted by CR42s from 150°Gruppo. The RAF pilots promptly attacked these and two of the Fiats went down. Flt Lt Tap Jones and Sgt Gregory were the two successful pilots. Capitano Nicola Magaldi was killed and Sergente Negri had his aircraft very badly shot up, but he was able to crash-land back at his base. The Italian pilots made no claims. Bill participated in this patrol but was not involved in the action.

More action followed the next day, when a force of 20 CR42s was encountered over Delvinakion by six Gladiators (not including Bill), which were initially able to gain the upper hand but were then overwhelmed. Gregory claimed three of the fighters, and Jones shot down two off the tails of Gladiators before being wounded in the neck. Although his Gladiator was badly damaged, he was able to land without further mishap. Flg Off Bill

Sykes collided with the Fiat flown by Sergente Corrado Mignani, and both pilots were killed.[2] Meanwhile, Wanklyn Flower had his aircraft badly shot up, but he believed he had shot down one of the biplanes. Price-Owen and Plt Off Hosken also had their Gladiators damaged. Honours to the Fiats on this occasion.

B Flight now moved to the old city of Yannina (Ioannina), which juts into a large green lake surrounded by even greener trees. Needle-sharp minarets and slate-domed mosques dominated the town, which had been in Turkish hands for some 500 years. Snow-capped mountains embraced the lake. The Gladiators took off for the first escort mission from this picturesque location on **29 November**, when Blenheims from 84 Squadron were sent to bomb the Italian supply dumps near Tepelene close to the Albanian coast. The Gladiators then carried out a search for the wreckage of Sykes's aircraft lost the previous day (see Appendix X).

The Gladiators, in pairs, rolled over and dived towards the autumn-tinted hillsides to begin the search for the crashed Gladiator. Pat and Cherry Vale, however, did not dive with the others. Pat had already spotted two formations of aircraft coming towards them. He pointed them out to Vale, and then began to climb into the sun directly in the path of the approaching machines. He could already make out that there were half-a-dozen, two- or possibly three-engined bombers, but as yet could not distinguish their type, or even if they were friendly or hostile. They were flying in two groups of three, the first group slightly in front and just below the second three. Pat brought his Gladiator round into a position where he could nose straight down out of the sun. Cherry Vale was just behind him and a few yards to the right. Pat stared intently at the rapidly approaching formation, taking in every little detail . . . three engines . . . tall single fin and rudder . . . the long nose . . . he was sure now. They were Savoias.

The nose of his Gladiator dipped and he sped like an arrow towards the leading bomber. The Savoia, unaware of the danger hidden in the blinding rays of the midday sun, flew blissfully along its steady course. Pat had the engine at the front of the bomber right in the middle of his sights now, but he held his fire until he could clearly see the faces of the pilot and the co-pilot. He squeezed the trigger button on the control column and felt the whole plane shudder with the recoil of the four machine guns. The Savoia was blurred now, but he held his finger on the gun button until it seemed that he must crash head-on into the bomber. He pulled hard on the stick, and as the black monster passed beneath him he could hear Cherry's guns still firing into it. The leader of the second flight was now almost directly on top of him, and the gunners were sending a hailstorm of white tracer towards him. He fired again, and just had time to see his own tracers burying themselves inside the belly of the Savoia before his Gladiator stalled and fell away. By the time he had regained control of his machine the Savoias were half-a-mile away and he knew he could never hope to catch up with them again. He looked behind and saw Cherry's Gladiator just coming up to join him. Cherry had seen Pat's Gladiator spin down after attacking the second Savoia, and he thought that Pat had been hit by the gunners. He had broken away and followed Pat down.

Pat glanced again at the now rapidly disappearing enemy bombers and wondered how many of them would get back to their base. He could see plumes of smoke billowing out behind the leaders of each trio. If only the whole of his flight had been behind him when he had attacked they would not have got off so lightly. Or better still if he and Cherry had been flying Hurricanes, with their greater firepower and superior speed, they might have downed the lot on their own. When were they going to get those Hurricanes? Surely Headquarters did not expect them to go on flying their veteran biplanes forever. The sight of the snow-capped mountains, now frighteningly close to his starboard wing tips, brought him back to reality. He climbed quickly and headed towards Yannina. The other Gladiators landed soon after Pat and Cherry had got back, but they had not encountered any enemy aircraft. Neither had they been able to find any trace of Bill Sykes or his Gladiator.[3]

Bill (flying N5784) and Pattle could only claim damage to their targets, which were in fact part of a formation of 28 Z.1007bis of the 47°Stormo BT from Grottaglie on a raid. The defending air gunners reported that nine Gladiators attacked them, claiming one probably shot down – presumably Pattle's aircraft, which had spun down after his attack.

War correspondent Richard Dimbleby and some of his companions endured hardships to reach the battlefront, making their way up into the mountains in treacherous conditions and over unmade roads. He later found himself caught up in an Italian air raid:

> One morning during the advance north of Koritza we were returning from an inspection of part of the front when we ran into a collection of mules in the street of a hamlet. We were edging our way through when we heard the increasing noise of bombers. Having been attacked earlier in the day, we were on our guard and ready to jump out of the car, but we were in a most unpleasant position. The mules were wedged tightly round us; their drivers had thrown themselves flat on

their faces in every available doorway. The throbbing of the Savoias grew louder and we could see six of them approaching through our rear window. It was impossible to jump out of the car. Already the animals were beginning to kick and plunge. Then: with a shrill whistle and a clang like the slamming of a great iron door, the first bomb burst on the edge of the village. The terrified mules lifted in unison as though they were puppets on wires. They stayed erect for a second, then broke into mad confusion, kicking and sprawling in the road. In the car we ducked down in our seats and I confess I put my hands over my ears.

The second bomb was nearer and the third rushed down so violently that we thought it must burst on us. It fell behind the nearest houses; one of them trembled and shivered down in a cloud of dust. The car rocked on its wheels and with a jingle the rear window splintered on to the back seat, covering Arthur with fragments and cutting his head. The noise was deafening and in the dust and smoke I could see through my fingers the straining backs and flanks of the mules as they stampeded by.

Then the bombers turned over us and wheeled away to the north. We waited for a few seconds to make sure they were not coming back and climbed out. The hamlet was a shambles. One man had been hit by shrapnel, but only in the foot. He was sitting up in a doorway, shouting for help. The rest were picking themselves up and brushing dirt and mule manure off their faces and clothes. The house at the corner had lost its front. It looked like a cake from which the icing had fallen away. Two old women were standing, gaping at it and one of them had a piece of brick caught in her hair.

But the shambles was round the corner, where the press of mules had been greatest. Fragments of the third bomb had mown down nearly a dozen animals. Two were lying on their sides, kicking convulsively as the blood poured from them. As we were approaching a driver took out his rifle and shot them both through the head. The rest lay in a hideous tangle, heads blown from bodies, legs bent and snapped with bloody bones sticking through the skin. The entrails of one had been blown round its neck in a slippery red garland. Another had been laid open from muzzle to tail, as though by the slaughterer's axe. It was a bloody and terrible sight. Since that day I have seen many corners of battlefields where human beings had been torn apart by the weapons of modern war, but never since have I seen such a surfeit of carnage. These were only the remnants of animals, but we felt sick.[4]

The weather again closed in and no operations were flown until **2 December**. Just before 1100 on that date, Flt Lt Pattle took off from Yannina on a morning weather reconnaissance. In the Argyrokastron area he spotted a lone biplane, which he saw to be a Ro37bis reconnaissance aircraft. He attacked the unsuspecting machine and shot it down in flames near the road about five miles to the south of Argyrokastron. This was an aircraft from 42ªSquadriglia and Sergente Luigi Del Manno and his observer, Capitano Michele Milano, were both killed. At 1430, Pattle was off again, this time at the head of a dozen Gladiators to undertake an offensive patrol over the front lines in support of the Greek Army. Near Premet two more Ro37bis from 72°Gruppo OA were seen 1,000ft below. Pattle led his flight down. He levelled out just behind and beneath the left-hand aircraft and waited for Cooper to get into position astern the second unsuspecting reconnaissance aircraft. They opened fire simultaneously and both Italian aircraft fell in flames. One man was seen to bale out of Cooper's victim, but all four crewmen – Capitano Gardellea/Capitano Fuchs and Sergente Leoni/Sergente Vescia were reported killed.

The 80 Squadron detachment at Yannina left for Larissa on 3 December, the ground crew being transported in Greek Junkers G.24s. Here they would be joined the next day by the rest of the squadron as well as four 112 Squadron Gladiators, which had arrived from Egypt and were on detachment to 80 Squadron. Eleven of 80 Squadron and the four 112 Squadron Gladiators promptly returned to Yannina on detachment.

In the late evening of **4 December**, the Gladiators were out escorting Blenheims bombing Italian communication centres and Wellingtons dropping supplies to Greek units. Over Tepelene the Gladiators engaged an estimated 27 Italian fighters. These were actually a dozen CR42s from 150°Gruppo led by TenCol Rolando Pratelli, and ten G.50s from 154°Gruppo. Flt Lt Pattle claimed one shot down into a hillside near Delvinakion, one in flames from which the pilot baled out, and a third from which the pilot also baled out. He also claimed two probables. During these combats his aircraft was hit in the fuel tank and in one wing strut. Other claims were submitted by Sgt Hewett for two CR42s and a G.50, while Bill (N5784), Sgts George Barker and Gregory each claimed a CR42. Italian claims were for two Gladiators shot down, against actual losses of two CR42s in which Tenente Alberto Triolo and Sottoten Paolo Penna were killed. Quite obviously, there occurred some wild over-claiming over the mountains of Tepelene. Bill's combat report did not survive, but of his own claims Ted Hewett reported:

> The first CR42 I destroyed by a short burst from almost dead astern after a short chase, and a few polished aerobatics on the part of the enemy. The second was a little more difficult but I finally got a long burst into the machine at the top of a loop. The enemy aircraft fell sideways and then burst into flames. It was gutted before it hit the ground. The first CR42 went into a hillside in a vertical dive and I saw the impact.

Gazing below I saw a monoplane flying very low across a snow-clad mountain. I dived upon it and as my range closed I saw it to be a G.50. I opened fire and had a long burst at the aircraft and then pulled away. On sighting the aircraft again I saw it skidding violently sideways about 30 feet up and heading for a hilltop over which there was no possibility of climbing. I was not able to witness the crash because I was distracted at that moment by machine-gun fire from behind. A CR42 was then on my tail. I rolled off the top of a loop and saw him no more. I then returned to base.

After returning to Larissa on **5 December**, 80 Squadron was taken out of the front line for much needed rest and overhaul. New aircraft were ferried over from Egypt, while five of the war-weary Gladiators were handed over to the Greeks. For the next two weeks all was relatively quiet as the weather made flying virtually impossible. This enabled the ground crews to give the aircraft a complete service. The Squadron Diary records:

7 December Owing to the unserviceable state of the squadron, due to operations, extensive major and minor repairs were commenced to rectify this unserviceability. It must be realised that the unit had to undertake repairs, which would normally have been sent back to a maintenance unit. A salvage unit is available to undertake the salvage of aircraft, but owing to the bad state of the roads in Greece, the salvage party could not proceed to Larissa. No flying was carried out. The weather was poor, with rain and snow.

For the next few days work proceeded at a very satisfactory rate. There was no flying because of the very bad weather – rain and snow.

11 December After nearly five days of hard work the u/s aircraft were more or less ready for immediate use. Credit must be given to the ground crews for the hard work they put in during this period. No ops.

12 December Raining hard in the morning. It turned to drizzle in the afternoon. No ops.

13 December Air raid alarm 1205. Three Gladiators (Pattle, Hewett and Casbolt) took off but no enemy seen. All clear 1300. About 40 NCOs and airmen with equipment proceeded in the Junkers to Yannina.

14 December Very cold. 20mph wind from the north. Cloud 10/10th at 6,000 feet. Visibility 20 miles. During the afternoon the cloud base lifted to 15,000 feet and visibility decreased.

At Larissa the weather was too bad for flying from 15 to 18 December.

Two American war correspondents Leland 'Lee' Stowe and Ed 'Steve' Stevens were making their way to the front during this period and encountered some of the horrors of war at first hand. Stowe later wrote:

> We know most of the road up to Kakavia on the Albanian frontier. It's through valleys most of the way and there are dozens of dead horses along the road. Some of them have been pushed into the ditches. Some still lie where they fell. Trucks, in their mad dash for the front, have flattened out the heads of some of them. Others have had their haunches torn or crushed by collisions from the rear. Still others died from exhaustion. There are always more dead horses. Dumb in life, they speak with a bitter eloquence in death. You look at them and know you are in the war zone once more. You look at them and hasten to look away. But they make you think about war. You ride on and there are more dead horses and you keep thinking about war. We don't like it, but they are always there – and so is the war.

It was during a visit to Athens that Bill met Janina. She was the daughter of a Greek family introduced to Bill by one of the war correspondents who had befriended him. Janina, a student before the war broke out, helped at a first-aid post in Athens, but was soon to be posted to the town with a similar-sounding name – Yannina – near to where Bill and the 80 Squadron detachment were based. He arranged to meet her there in the coming days. Bill was smitten.

British servicemen in Greece, officers and other ranks alike, were warned not to become overfriendly with the pretty Greek girls, since it was known that some were in the pay of 'the enemy', particularly in Athens, where the German Legation was situated. Sqn Ldr Wisdom wrote:

> The Legation, on the road from our billets to HQ, always roused our ire. The Swastika flag floated next to the Stars and Stripes – for the American and German Legations occupied adjoining buildings. Athens was full of Germans. Their favourite meeting-place was *Zonars*, the smart society café on the corner of Bucharest Street and University Street. It was also the favourite meeting-place of RAF officers, since it had the only bar in Athens that dispensed draught beer. This came from the German-owned brewery, and was extremely good.
>
> There were naturally a number of incidents in which the Germans were involved and which they doubtless encouraged. However, they got very little change out of the RAF. There was a pretty girl from the Argentine with a large car, who asked three RAF officers out to tea, and when they got indoors they found to their stupefaction that they were to drink tea in the German Legation. They left hurriedly.

One night some of us were dining together at *Maxim's* when the Deputy Assistant Provost Marshal whispered that the table next to us was occupied by a member of the *Geheime Staats Polizei* [Gestapo], in Athens on vacation – these Germans were always on holiday – with his girlfriend. With one accord we all took violent exception, not only having Germans in the place at all, but also to having them listening to what we were saying, even if that were harmless. One of our party, who spoke German, politely told the Huns to get out. The Gestapo man refused. It looked as if we were going to involve ourselves in the incident, which he doubtless wished to provoke. One of the nightclub girls, Marianne, a friend of ours, who was sitting at the bar, watched us with unsmiling eyes.

Englishmen from other tables joined us, and the word went round that the Hun should be kicked out if he wouldn't go quietly. Mac, who spoke German, moved over to the table and spoke for a few moments to the Gestapo man and his girlfriend quite nicely, saying that it would be far wiser if they left. Mac saved the situation. Word must have gone round through a Greek secret police employee – probably one of the dancing girls – for a few moments later the German couple were escorted outside, and they spent the night in gaol, as neither of them had a night pass.

Wisdom added:

Marianne, the dancing girl from *Maxim's* was very nice. She was certainly no ordinary cabaret girl – we spotted that from the first. She was really pretty, to begin with – masses of blonde hair, blue eyes and a figure that was just perfect. Moreover, she was intelligent, and she spoke, or so it seemed, every known European language. Our chaps in Athens came to know her fairly well. Not that anyone knew her really well. Altogether Marianne was a bit of a mystery. She never asked questions but she did give advice. She seemed to know everybody, and, unlike the other dancing girls, she had police passes that admitted her everywhere. She told us to whom it was inadvisable to talk – who were, in fact, spies.

For Bill there was no problem, Janina did not frequent nightclubs or bars, she was a student. Although some of Bill's colleagues frowned upon the relationship, others openly encouraged him. Janina's parents apparently approved.

80 Squadron resumed operations on **19 December**, when Sqn Ldr Hickey led a patrol over Tepelene, during which five SM79s were encountered, one of which was claimed as a probable. Sammy Cooper was wounded by return

fire and he baled out of his damaged aircraft. Hewett's aircraft was hit by
AA fire and he landed some distance from Yannina, his aircraft later being
salvaged. Sqn Ldr Hickey believed he had shot down one of the escorting
G.50s but no losses were recorded. One of the American war correspondents,
Lee Stowe, who was at the front, related how he and Ed Stevens had
witnessed Cooper's fate:

> High above the snowy, 6,000ft shoulders of the Nemeroka range we
> saw another group of planes plunge out of a mass of clouds. A sudden
> flame winked from one of them like a lighthouse beacon. It was a
> hit. A hit from somewhere, we couldn't tell where. She was punch-
> drunk and wobbling. Yes, she was falling! Steve and I shrieked with
> joy. 'They've got one! They've got one!' We saw sheets of fire girdle
> the airplane as she lapsed into a dizzy plunge. Then we saw her shoot
> downward, twisting, twisting, twisting. 'Get your camera,' I yelled
> at Steve. Now I saw the white, flowing break of a parachute, and
> then another plane. It was circling around and around as plane and
> parachutist plummeted down toward the spot where the snowline
> ended and the green hills began.
>
> The plane fell fastest and a cloud of black smoke rose from the
> hill where it crashed across the river. But the fighter kept circling
> around the swaying figure below the white envelope, and long after
> the envelope had settled to earth. We were puzzled by the plane's
> behaviour. If the pilot was a Fascist, why did he risk being plugged
> by Greek batteries, or were they too far away? We went over to ask
> the Greek anti-aircraft boys. They said the pilot was British and he
> had circled around to show Greek soldiers on the mountain where the
> Italian parachutist had fallen, so they could capture him. That seemed
> to make sense.
>
> All this happened just at noon. Steve and I lunched by the
> riverbank. Afterward as we were walking along the road, an
> ambulance rolled up and an officer in RAF blue stepped out. 'I've
> got to get my pilot, the one the Italians shot down over on that
> mountain – as soon as possible,' he said to the Greek major. 'My
> God, was that plane one of yours!' we gasped. The major explained
> that a Greek doctor and soldiers had been on the way to rescue
> the British aviator for more than an hour now. The squadron
> leader wanted to climb up the mountain and meet them, and so
> did we. But you couldn't tell what ravine they would bring him
> down; whether they'd go first to the village over to the east or
> whether they'd strike straight for the river. So there was nothing
> for us to do but wait. 'Who was it?' we asked, almost fearfully,

hoping it wouldn't be one of our friends. 'Don't know for certain,' said Squadron Leader Hickey. 'Anyhow he's wounded. I could see the blood soaking through from his leg. But he's alive, all right. I flew within thirty feet of him and he signalled me. He knew I was sticking by.'

Hickey was one of the few men in the squadron we hadn't met before. He had a chiselled face and fair hair and spoke with an officer's decisiveness. He was tense in the way a man is tense who has just come out of battle and still has responsibilities to fulfil. He must have circled for fifteen minutes over the spot where his pilot fell. Then he had dashed down the valley and managed a dangerous landing on the boggy valley lands below Argyrokastron. In an incredibly brief time he had located an ambulance and an interpreter, and hurried up the valley to the place directly opposite where his man had been shot down.

We had to wait and keep waiting and that was harder on Hickey than on anyone else. 'We've got to get that man back to a hospital,' he said. The tone left no doubt about his follow-through. But we had to wait, lounging beside the river, and we persuaded Hickey to lunch from our well-filled knapsack. Reluctantly he posed for a picture, and just after that – out of a long silence – two Fascist shells came screaming down right at us. Luckily we were in a tiny gully with an eight-foot bank. We threw ourselves against it just as the explosions roared. A lot of dirt and gravel showered down on us. The shrapnel flew much farther. The bursts were only about forty feet away. Obviously the Italians had changed their range at last. We had to get out, and get out fast, running northward under the riverbank as much as we could. Shells kept breaking behind us and Hickey said he'd rather be up in a dogfight. In twenty minutes we were out of their orbit, but much less nonchalant.

We had to wait for more than three hours and it seemed hellishly long. At last a little procession emerged from the tumbling, darkening hills and slowly marched toward the other bank of the river. Then came another interminable delay, which we couldn't figure out. The squadron leader was going to wade the river, but somebody found him a horse. Half an hour later another horseman dashed back for a stretcher. The rescue party had had nothing but a board and had carried the wounded man on it for five hours down the mountain. Finally the Greek soldiers started carrying their burden through the first narrows, wading waist-deep; then across long rocky stretches of riverbed, then through another channel. Hickey got back first. 'He's in pretty bad shape,' he told us. 'Who is it?' 'Cooper,' he replied.

Sammy Cooper. Steve and I wanted to curse. Probably we did. I was thinking of the dinners we'd had with him far behind the lines a month ago. I remembered Sammy especially because he was the gayest, lustiest man in the squadron. One night he drank a lot of wine to kill his lonesomeness. He had a shock of wavy blond hair, clean-cut features, and a fighting jaw. 'I want a woman,' Sammy had growled. 'I tell you I want a woman tonight. But I only want one woman in the world – and she's in England. I don't mind fighting. But why in hell won't they let us fight in England? Why do we have to fight out here in these bloody mountains?' He showed me her picture. She was all that a man like Sammy deserved. 'I want a woman,' Sammy was saying again. 'Somebody who'll be tender and who'll understand me and make me forget this Goddamned war – for one night anyhow. Damn it, you can't even have that.' The words stayed with me long afterward. In wartime, in this kind of war, you understand how men feel like that. But there was nothing ahead but months and months and months of fighting for Sammy and his squadron mates. Even if they came through, it might still be years before they'd get back to England. She was a lovely-looking girl, too. Would she still be there? . . .

Now we were waiting for them to bring Sammy across the river. They were coming, but slow as the hinges of indistinct shapes in the blackening night, with the ambulance waiting behind us on the road.

'Hello, Sammy. Everything's all right, Sammy. It's Steve.'

'It's Lee. We're going to get you in soon.'

The reply was mumbled, almost a groan. Sammy's voice was very thick, partly from cognac, partly from other things. We packed him into the ambulance as gently as we could. 'I'm cold. I'm freezing with cold.' Hickey and Steve and I tucked five or six blankets over and around him. Then we started. There was a little overhead light in the lorry. I sat on Sammy's left, and first Hickey sat on his right. Then Steve sat there when the CO went up front to keep the inquisitive Greek sentries from holding us up with minutes of useless talk – an inevitable Greek failing. Hickey was marvellous at shutting them up fast and pushing the ambulance ahead. In the dim light Sammy's face was covered with grime or something. Gradually I made it out. His eyebrows and eyelashes were burned off. That was why he rarely opened his eyes. For a long time I was afraid he might be blinded, too.

'Cigarette – cigarette, please,' he begged. I lit one for him and he held his mouth open for it. Then his lips clamped down on it and he sucked long and deeply, three times in rapid succession. He didn't have strength for more, but it seemed to ease him for the moment. His lips were swollen. They were dry to the verge of cracking and his teeth gritted at every jolt in the road. The squadron leader held a soldier's canteen to his lips, while I lifted up Sammy's head. He drank as I've never seen anyone drink before – long, devouring gulps. Then his head fell back limply and the pains came back in a little while.

'We got some of them – didn't we?' Sammy would ask when he came out of it. We lied with great emphasis. We had to lie. Now Steve was on the other side and we each held one of Sammy's hands, trying to get them warm, to get the blood circulating again. When the ambulance hit the holes in the road, his clasp tightened like a vice on my fingers and on Steve's. Then the groans broke through his unwilling teeth, and his head went back and back as if he were trying to push the pain out of his body. Sometimes it seemed more than any man could bear. Sometimes I sat and looked at the long damp locks of tangled hair, the fine forehead, and the grey face and I thought about what freedom costs, and how little most people know what it costs. And sometimes I thought about those statesmen who thought you could compromise for freedom and bargain with truth. They were bitter thoughts.

Sometimes the road was fairly good for a short distance. Then Sammy talked a little.

'Did the others get through all right? Did we get any of them? I got that bloke's undercarriage – I'm sure I did. I couldn't do anything more. My cockpit on fire. Sorry I couldn't save the plane. The fire blinded me. I got it in the leg. Then I couldn't see anything.'

Then the long groans again, and Sammy asking if it was much farther now, and we lying again and saying it was just round the bend below, and Steve and I beginning to understand what the wellsprings of hatred and revenge are like and all the time telling Sammy we'd be at the emergency hospital in a couple of minutes now. Then the ambulance lumbering on for twenty more minutes, and on until it seemed we'd never reach it.

When we got up the hill and into the kitchen that served for an operating room, the Greek surgeon worked fast. Several Greek officials clustered around to do everything they could. It was eight hours since Sammy had been shot down. I didn't see how he could stand much more. He was terribly pale from loss of blood. The surgeon snipped away the emergency bandage between the knee and thigh on his left leg. As the scissors snipped higher and higher Sammy stirred. 'Don't let them cut off the old man,' he said. We laughed, nervously but thankfully. In all this tenseness it would still be Sammy who would break the strain and show us how to laugh. Then all the laughter drained out of us when we saw the wound.

We saw it and looked and looked away again, not wanting to see. It was a great raw gash, about fourteen inches long and many inches wide. The CO's lips tightened into a hard straight line. He pulled me aside: 'Explosive bullet,' he whispered. 'Sssh! Don't let him know.' Sammy's cries turned us back toward the operating table. The surgeon had both his hands far inside his leg, running his fingers along the naked bone. He was probing for a fracture. There was one, but not there. It was higher up in the hip, the worst possible place. Even if Sammy pulled through, he'd probably be lame; maybe he wouldn't be able to fly any more, but you must never tell a wounded flier that. Looking at the great ugly hole in his leg, we wondered how Sammy had survived these hours and hours of torturing descent while the Greeks carried him down, without a stretcher.

'They were awfully good to me,' he had said weakly when we first put him in the lorry. 'They carried me for miles and miles.' Now the doctor's hands were outside again. 'I'm sorry, awfully sorry – really couldn't help it,' Sammy was saying. Then they poured the iodine on the raw flesh, and it was almost unbearable to see his face. We begged the surgeon to put him under with morphine. He said Sammy's heart was too weak; he had lost so much blood, and he might not be able to stand it. 'I'll give him a transfusion,' volunteered Hickey, and we echoed him. It was no good. In this place they couldn't test the blood group and they didn't have the necessary apparatus. They could give an anti-tetanus injection, and they were doing it. The pain was terrible as they forced the fluid in. One and then another of us stood beside Sammy and held his hand and brushed his forehead. Why, why in God's name, couldn't they give him morphine?

But it seemed as if every fate conspired to refuse Sammy ease from pain. The pain seemed more than any man could stand. All this time he was begging for water. 'Steve! Water. Water, please. Oh God, give me water.' Then Sammy's voice would break and fade away. Then he would rouse again. 'Water! For Christ's sake – water!' The doctor said too much water would make him vomit again, and he was too weak; he couldn't stand the vomiting. At last we couldn't bear it. They would only allow a quarter of a glass. Sammy took it in two gulps, and sank back begging for more.

Sometimes he cried for cigarettes and we reached hurriedly for one. But the doctors shook their heads. It would be bad for him to smoke too much, they said. No morphine, no water, no cigarettes, no blood transfusion – nothing but the hell of suffering. It was like that for three hours, until they got his leg re-bandaged and the rest-machine fixed under his broken hip. That was to ease the jolts on the road. They said he would have to go all the way back to Yannina, four or five hours on the road, without any rest, so he could get a blood transfusion tomorrow. The thought of that ride churned me up inside. I couldn't feel right about it. I didn't see how Sammy could stand it, weak and pain-racked as he was. But what could we do? Hickey would have their own RAF surgeon waiting on the other end. That was the only thing he could be hopeful about.

Sammy was quieter now, but with the quietness of exhaustion. He had had nearly eleven hours of this without a minute's sleep. They got him back on the stretcher, and we had to tell him he still had to ride a little farther. A little farther – that was the most damnable lie of all, but how could anyone say five more hours? It helped that he seemed resting a little. Just the same, I didn't feel right about it. I didn't like the idea of carrying him out into the cold night and into the ambulance again, but it seemed the only thing to do. The doctor must know if he couldn't stand the morphine. But if only they would let him sleep a little first – if only he could lie still and sleep for an hour or two.

Up the cobbled road in the darkness the soldiers carried Sammy as gently as they could. I lit another cigarette and put it between his teeth. He pulled and pulled. He couldn't use his hands, they were under the blanket, so I had to watch for fear he would pull the fire all the way down on to his lips. I kept my hand on his shoulder and kept talking cheerfully, as if everything was all right now.

Inside the ambulance Hickey, Steve, and I tucked heavy blankets around and around him, and one around his head so there would be no draughts on his neck. We gave him a tangerine, a piece at a time, and that helped. 'I feel much better now,' Sammy said. We fixed another blanket and left another tangerine for him and the CO said: 'You'll be all right, and back with the squadron any day, Cooper. Just take it easy, old chap.' We had to keep saying something. 'Don't steal all the good-looking nurses down in the hospital, you damned heart-breaker,' we said. Then: 'We'll be down in a few days. We'll be in to see you, Sammy.'

He seemed to be half asleep and we crawled out, not liking to do it. The door of the ambulance was shut. It backed up the hill and then pulled round the corner and down. We stood watching it disappear and thinking and praying in our own way. Then we stumbled through the darkness and down to the hotel. Hickey was up until after two in the morning. It took that long to get a call through so as to have Doc Astbury up and waiting for Sammy when they brought him in. We gave Hickey a room, but with the windows blasted out, all the rooms were frightfully cold. I slept little and badly. Mostly I shivered and tossed around, thinking about Sammy, wondering whether he was at the hospital by now and whether he got through? I couldn't get Sammy out of my mind. At daybreak Hickey came in. I think he had been too cold to sleep much, but he came in to say good-bye and thank us for the too little we had been able to do. We said we'd be back in three days now. We'd have dinner with him at Yannina. He must give our best to Sammy.

The 24-year-old Cooper from Oxfordshire died in the ambulance on the way to Yannina.

At 1000 on **20 December**, Flt Lt Pattle was off at the head of nine Gladiators to meet Blenheims of 211 Squadron returning from a raid, and to carry out an offensive patrol over the Tepelene–Kelcyre area. The squadron flew in three sections of three at 10,000ft. The Blenheims were late and at 1040 a reported nine SM79s were seen. There were actually six aircraft drawn equally from the 252ª and 253ªSquadriglie escorted by 18 CR42s flying at 20,000ft. Pattle at once attacked one of the SM79s from 253ªSquadriglia, flown by Tenente Andrea Berlinghieri, and shot it down in flames, the crew of four being seen to bale out before it crashed into the mountainside about five miles south-east of Tepelene, where it blew up. A second 253ªSquadriglia machine (flown by Tenente Torazzi) was badly damaged. On returning to Tirana the crew reported that a Gladiator had collided with them and had been seen to crash, minus its propeller. In another SM79, Tenente Vivarelli's crew claimed a second Gladiator shot down. The Gladiators flown by Casbolt and Richens were, in fact, damaged during this engagement but were able to return to Yannina. Tenente Vivarelli recalled:

I almost ended like Berlinghieri. I was attacked by fighters from all sides and one engine was hit, so that I remained slightly behind

Torazzi. I was not sure to be able to make it back, in particular when I saw some planes that instead of attacking me from the stern, attacked me frontally, hitting me in the fuselage and wings. One of those planes jumped Torazzi and, seeing that they were colliding, zoomed and the fighter hit its belly.

The remainder of the 80 Squadron formation, still led by Pattle, continued its patrol, soon spotting another formation of tri-motors – this time six SM81s from the 38°Stormo BT, escorted by 24°Gruppo G.50s. The escort had no chance to intervene as Pattle bored in to attack the middle aircraft of the leading section and shot down one bomber. Meanwhile, Bill (N5784) claimed a second SM81 shot down. In fact one aircraft, carrying the Stormo commander, Colonello Domenico Ludovico, was badly damaged and landed at Berat with three dead, including Capitano Giulio Beccia, the pilot, and three wounded. The survivors just managed to get out before the aircraft with all its bombs still aboard, blew up. A second SM81, piloted by Tenente Croci, limped back with all its crew wounded. The British pilots reported that throughout the engagement the G.50s patrolled overhead without attacking the Gladiators. Bill now had five victories to his credit including two shared. Of the fight, Pattle reported:

> The bombers approached very rapidly and they were almost on top of us before I was able to identify them as SM79s. I dived at the first three followed by my section in line astern but realised they would pass me before closing into effective range. I therefore swung round and attacked the section of three from ahead and slightly to one quarter. As I closed I opened fire and maintained the fire as I swung through the beam and ended my attack from quarter astern and only about 50 yards from the SM79 on the right of the formation.
>
> Just before breaking away I saw a puff of black smoke steam from the starboard engine and the airscrew immediately slowed up. The e/a, once disabled, fell behind the remainder of the section, jettisoned its bombs and turned right towards Tepelene. I then fell in dead astern of it at about 100 yards range and fired short bursts at the fuselage in an attempt to disable the crew and pilots. The remainder of my section and No. 2 section carried out quarter tacks on it from both sides. A fire broke out just in front of the bottom turret but did not spread appreciably. After a good deal of lead was pumped into myself and others, the SM79 finally dropped its nose and dived straight into the top of a mountain about five miles south-east of Tepelene, where it exploded with a terrible sheet of flames.
>
> I [again] spotted fighters, about 18 of them. Throughout the engagement they had not attempted to engage us. It seemed impossible

that they had not seen us. I repeated the attack on No. 2 of the leading section. The SM81, being slower, afforded an easier target and I closed right up to it before breaking away. The bombs were jettisoned right in front of my airscrew. On my first attack I managed to hole the starboard petrol tank and damage the engine. Unfortunately, I had no incendiary left as only the fuselage guns were still operating.

The SM81 turned towards Albania and, getting dead astern, I fired my remaining few rounds into the port engine. Petrol streamed from the tank and smoke started coming out in short puffs from the engines. Having no further rounds I formatted above it hoping another Gladiator would come and finish it off. The remainder of my flight however were busy elsewhere. After flying about five miles the starboard engine packed up while I could see the port engine was running badly. The e/a slowly lost height and finally crash-landed in a valley about 15 miles north of Kelcura. The aircraft landed on bad ground and finally ended up against a tree.

I then returned to base. On landing I discovered that P/O Vale had brought down another SM81, which was destroyed.

80 Squadron departed Yannina at 1030 on **21 December**, to undertake a patrol over the front lines. They were led by Sqn Ldr Hickey and flew in three sections. The first comprised four aircraft and was led by Hickey, the second of three was led by Pattle and the third trio by Linnard. Near Argyrokastron three Italian tri-motor bombers were seen and were identified as SM79s. Three more aircraft with twin tails were observed following behind the first flight and recognised as BR20s. All six were in fact Cant Z.1007bis from the 47°Stormo BT from Grottaglie.

The bombers were immediately attacked by the Gladiators and Pattle believed that he hit one before CR42s of the 160°Gruppo appeared on the scene. Maggiore Oscar Molinari, the Gruppo commander, was leading the Fiats on an offensive reconnaissance over Yannina, Paramythia and Zitsa, when he sighted the bombers under attack by an estimated 20 Gladiators. The Fiats waded into the Gladiators, joined by more fighters from 150°Gruppo so that the 80 Squadron pilots assessed the number of their opponents at 54! After 25 minutes the air battle broke up and eight of the Gladiator pilots returned to claim eight confirmed and three probables. Bill claimed three, one of them in flames. Pattle witnessed one of Bill's victories:

Another Gladiator flaming furiously just missed the port wing of his plane, and Pat could see the still figure in the cockpit slumped forward across the control column. It was Flying Officer Ripley. He had only been with the squadron for a few weeks. Pat looked upwards, searching for the CR42 that had got Ripley, and saw the Italian fighter winging away, with Cherry Vale's Gladiator going after it. Cherry closed in right behind the Fiat, and clung to it like a leech, pouring burst after burst into the fighter, until it finally began to burn.[5]

Bill's official report revealed:

At 1050, then Gladiators took off from Yannina on an offensive patrol, flying in three flights of four, three, and three aircraft. I was flying in No. 3 in the third flight led by F/O Linnard.

On reaching the patrol line 'Tally-ho!' was immediately given for three bombers seen going from west to east. The leading flight led by S/L Hickey immediately went into action. At the same moment three more bombers were seen approaching from our port beam. The leader of the second flight, F/L Pattle, immediately turned left and carried out a head-on attack, and my flight leader followed.

I was able to get in a short burst before breaking away. On turning to follow, I observed a large formation of CR42s diving down from above. We immediately climbed to attack and a general dogfight started. I singled out one enemy aircraft who tried to dive away and dived down firing a burst at long range. He pulled up and I got in a full deflection shot from underneath and noticed flames coming from underneath his engine. The enemy aircraft went down out of control and finally hit the ground in flames. I then noticed a single Gladiator low down in a valley being attacked by five CR42s. I dived down and engaged two of them and managed to get behind one and fire a long burst until it suddenly spun out of control and crashed into the valley.

I was then attacked by more CR42s who carried out frontal quarter attacks on me with the superior speed that could out-climb me. I carried out one evasive action and noticed that the Gladiator below me was on fire and spinning down out of control [this was Sqn Ldr Hickey's aircraft]. I dived down towards it and saw the pilot leave the aircraft and use his parachute. I was again fired at by a CR42 from above who carried out his attack and then headed away north. When I again looked down I saw the Gladiator in flames on the ground with the pilot going down in his parachute. At the same time I saw a CR42 dive on the pilot and twin streams coming from behind his aircraft. I dived down and managed to get in a surprise attack as he pulled away from the parachutist. I got on his tail and fired a long burst from a single fuselage gun until he turned over out of control and went straight down to crash in the valley.

As I pulled up another CR42 came down very close to my machine, out of control, and crashed quite near to the burning Gladiator. I gained altitude and saw another Gladiator circling above me, and as I was short of ammunition I joined formation and found the other pilot to be F/S Richens, who had shot the CR42, which went past me. I noticed the position of the crashed Gladiator in respect to Argyrokastron and then returned to base.

On landing I inspected my aircraft and found that my lower and upper starboard mainplanes had been hit twice by explosive bullets, one of which had entered the wing ammunition tank and had exploded inside but had done no apparent damage to the structure of the mainplane. The fuselage was hit in several places but with no structural damage.

Casbolt claimed one, which blew up and another that spun down (later down-graded to a probable). Gregory claimed another two, again one in flames, but his own aircraft was badly shot up and he was wounded in the right eye. He managed to return to Yannina, where he reported:

Turning round in a stall turn I observed the leader [of the 42s] diving vertically whilst the remaining two had split, No. 2 going up, No. 3 down. As I had the advantage over the lower aircraft I decided to attack this first. He attempted to come up under me but as I was near to stalling, I had no difficulty in bringing my sight round to get in a deflection shot and then turn astern on him. Followed him down. At the same time I observed the leading aircraft crash on a hill and burst into flames. This dive was very steep, so much so, that I very nearly hit the ground with the 42. When I pulled up sharply out of this dive the third 42 came past and then pulled up underneath me into such a position that we could both get in quick deflection shots.

This happened three times and each time we missed colliding by inches, so that after each attack I had to find him again. Quite naturally this developed into a head-on attack, the first of which I slid out of. As the following attack was also head-on I became rather worried. I brought him into my sights, fired, ducked down behind my engine for cover, at the same time pulling back on the control column.

Immediately after this my right eye became warm and I found I had lost my sight in this eye. It took me some seconds to get used to this, as I would try to look towards the rear on the right side, but all I saw was the extensive damage to the centre section, starboard lower plane and a flying wire that had broken. I seem to remember at this point that he came at me from below and we had another deflection shot at each other, but as I had seen him so often in this position it may have stuck in my mind. However, I do remember I decided that my position was desperate and I weighed up the ground that was to receive me below. When I was overcome by a wave of determination, possibly due to the fact that when I was hit and saw the blood I turned my oxygen on at full strength. I pulled up in a loop and rolled off the top into a tight turn back into the direction I had come from. I looked at my compass but it seemed blurred. Although I could see the sun, I could not convince myself which direction to fly.

Diving down into the valley seemed to be the only means of escape. I was unable to look behind, as this brought on pain in my eye. At one period my sight was so blurred that I could not decide whether I was being chased by CR42 or if it was AA fire. Fortunately it was the latter. I discovered my position to be ten miles north of Valona at four thousand feet. As I could use only sixteen hundred revolutions due to damage to the rocker arm, causing excessive vibration, it took forty minutes to return to base where a landing was made under difficulties due to damage to eyesight and to undercarriage.

Gregory was recommended for an immediate DFM. Pattle and Richens also claimed a CR42 apiece, Pattle reporting that his victim fell in flames, while Hosken and Price-Owen (attached from 112 Squadron) claimed probables. Apart from the loss of Flg Off Henry Ripley,[6] Sqn Ldr Hickey also failed to return. He was seen to bale out but sadly his parachute caught fire, and he died from injuries soon after reaching the ground. Of Hickey's death, Bill later recalled:

The Gladiator was flat spinning too. Suddenly the pilot hurled out of the cockpit like a black ant and the white burst of his parachute spreading in a puff . . . the parachute burst into flames and the sudden black smudge as its slow speed became a lightning streak of charred smoke and the black figure of the Gladiator pilot hurtling two thousand feet down to the black earth.

Linnard's aircraft was also badly damaged and he was hit in the left calf by an explosive bullet and was taken to hospital after landing at Yannina. It had been a disastrous mission, with two killed including the CO, and two wounded. The Squadron Diary records:

On landing, all pilots attended Cooper's funeral [who had died from his wounds during the evening of 19 December]. Six pilots were coffin bearers and our own troops provided a firing party. A report from the Greek forward troops said the CO and F/O Ripley had been killed.

Greek troops recovered the bodies of both Hickey and Ripley. The pilots of 160°Gruppo claimed six Gladiators, two each by Maggiore Molinari, Tenente Edoardo Crainz, Tenente Eber Giudici and Capitano Paolo Arcangeletti.

The 150°Gruppo pilots claimed two more Gladiators in collaboration, while 47°Stormo gunners claimed one more and a probable. Actual Italian losses totalled only three aircraft, Tenente Mario Gaetano Carancini and Tenente Mario Frascadore of 160°Gruppo being lost, while Maggiore Molinari was wounded in the right foot and force-landed near Tepelene with a damaged engine.

The Squadron Diary for this pre-Christmas period reveals:

21 December 1045 Air raid alarm followed immediately by bombs from three aircraft flying very high. About eight or nine bombs fell in or near the town (Larissa), four of which fell in or near the square. One fell less than 50 yards from the Officers' Mess, breaking many windows in the house. The warning was too late and many people in Larissa were killed or wounded.

Two American reporters [Stowe and Stevens] came down from Argyrokastron that evening and told us of the amazingly courageous effort made by the CO in evacuating Cooper two days before. Through his courage and leadership the rescue party carried on in the face of heavy artillery fire and brought Cooper back to Argyrokastron.

22 December No ops due to bad weather and poor serviceability. Four aircraft serviceable only in the morning but by evening nine were OK. Magnificent effort by the ground crews.

23 December Bad weather kept the enemy on the ground, and no enemy aircraft were sighted. Our relief, 11 Gladiators from No. 12 Squadron [*sic* – should be 21 Mira] of the Greek Air Force arrived at 1600.

24 December Preparations for Xmas. Bad weather prevented the detachment from returning from Yannina.

Local collection of 45,000 drachmas in order to give the troops and officers an advance of pay to see them over Xmas. Ration supply ran out but the Greeks, as usual, helped out.

25 December The airmen's dinner was great success. The officers remaining were invited to dine with the Greek group captain at the Greek Officers' Mess. A thoroughly good evening.

Xmas morning was quiet. At 1700, a banquet was held in the local restaurant for officers and men. Arrangements made by Sgt Battle were excellent, and even the precious beer was supplied in sufficient quantities. Afterwards, all ranks were invited to the Xmas tree organised by the Greek Youth Movement. We all received a small souvenir and wine was liberally supplied. The party ended in high spirits at 2200 hours.

It is assumed that Bill, stranded at Yannina with the detachment, was able to find solace with Janina. According to sources, Bill proposed marriage despite the overwhelming problems facing both. The future was so uncertain. However, the romance was interrupted on 27 December when Bill was ordered to fly back to Larissa.

The war was never far away and, on 30 December, three Gladiators from the detachment at Larissa were scrambled at 1040, but one had to land early due to engine problems. Another raid was reported approaching from the north-west. At this point ten Gladiators en route from Athens arrived overhead. They were signalled to look out for these raiders, whereupon Ape Cullen spotted a three-engined aircraft out to sea. He went to investigate and found it to be an SM81, which he attacked and claimed to have brought down into the sea to the west of the Kassandra peninsula.

During this month the AOC talked to the war correspondents about the war in Greece. In a long and informative discussion he declared:

> Flying conditions in Greece are more difficult than anywhere in Europe. The weather changes with great rapidity, making accurate forecasts impossible, and the nature of the country does not always allow landings when pilots are unable to regain their bases. Ice formations are another difficulty – instruments freeze, and airscrews get a covering of ice, which makes it difficult to maintain sufficient altitude to clear the mountains. The temperature is never more than minus 28°C, and sometimes goes to minus 50°C.

Because of these conditions, as well as the restricted number of air bases available to the RAF, he considered the operation of a large air force in Greece during the winter to be impracticable, but he expressed the belief that the RAF would be greatly reinforced when the weather improved.

Chapter 6

BILL'S MYSTERIOUS ADVENTURES

At a meeting with British Commander-in-Chief Middle East, General Archibald Wavell, in January 1941, Greek Commander-in-Chief Papagos requested nine fully equipped divisions for the Greco-Bulgarian border. When Wavell answered that he could dispose of only two to three divisions, the offer was turned down, as the force was totally inadequate, and would only hasten German intervention. Churchill, however, by now hoped to re-create the Balkan Front of the First World War with the participation of Yugoslavia and Turkey, and sent Foreign Secretary Anthony Eden and Sir John Dill for negotiations to the region.

At a meeting in Athens on 22 February between Eden and the Greek leadership, the decision to send a British Commonwealth expeditionary force was taken. Already German troops had been massing in Romania, and on 1 March Bulgaria joined the Axis. As German forces began crossing the Danube into the country, the German invasion was now imminent. A detachment of 58,000 British, Australian, and New Zealand troops were sent to Greece in March 1941, comprising 6th Australian Division, New Zealand 2nd Division, and British 1st Armoured Brigade Group. The three formations later became known as 'W' Force under the command of General Henry Maitland Wilson.

The New Year of 1941 found a situation of stalemate fast developing along the front line. The weather had clamped down hard, making movement on the ground difficult, and in the air on many days well nigh impossible. The early part of January was marked by continuous rain, airfields becoming seriously waterlogged and operations rare. The Greeks were practically exhausted by the tremendous exertions of their autumn counter-attacks, and were still desperately short of transport, clothing and anti-tank and anti-aircraft artillery. The major part of their armed forces and most of their air power were involved at the front, leaving only four weak divisions on the frontier with Bulgaria. Should any threat from this area develop, it was considered that nine more divisions and associated air support would be required to defend Eastern Macedonia and Salonika.

RAF units were allowed to operate only in the west and south of Greece, no squadrons being based in the Salonika area. During January, RAFME Command decided to send two more squadrons to Greece, one of fighters and one of bombers, while planning at the same time to capture the Italian Dodecanese Islands – particularly Rhodes – to secure the Aegean and Eastern Mediterranean.

Nothing, however, was to be allowed to alarm the Germans, and still no British land forces were to be accepted for service in Greece unless the Germans crossed the Danube and entered Bulgaria. The threat of German intervention was a real one, for early in the month Hitler decided to send a strong contingent to Albania to bolster the Italians, but the end of the Greek counter-offensive and reinforcement of the Italian forces brought a halt to these preparations.

* * *

The start of the month brought three replacement pilots and Gladiators for 80 Squadron, one of which was flown by Flt Lt Timber Woods DFC, who had served with distinction at Malta. The other two were flown by Rhodesians Plt Offs Eldon Trollip and Cecil Tulloch. The squadron now made various moves. The detachment at Larissa moved to Yannina and was settled in by the 18th, although the weather conditions still prevented any flying. An idea of just how atrocious weather conditions were at this time can be judged from the Squadron Diary entries. The new CO, Tap Jones, had been ordered to transfer the whole squadron to Yannina 'as soon as possible'. Many of the vital ground personnel were to be flown from Larissa aboard a Greek G.24:

> **8 January** Air raid [Larissa] 1220 and ending 1400 resulted in the disappearance of the Greek pilot of the Junkers so that ten NCOs and men ready to leave for Yannina were unable to do so.
>
> **9 January** NCOs and men left for Yannina by Junkers. The Medical Officer and P/O Rolfe [Adjutant] and eight NCOs went in the afternoon. A third trip by the Junkers took stores and luggage. Four Gladiators [including Bill in N5784] also left for Yannina in preparation for transfer of the whole squadron.
>
> **10–11 January** Weather still very bad. Continuous rain. Aerodrome u/s.
>
> **12 January** The weather cleared, drome serviceable. Some aircraft took off for Yannina in the afternoon but could not get through the pass owing to bad visibility. At Yannina the Adjutant spent this and the following six days in finding billets. Valuable assistance was rendered by General Dragoumis and Captain Melas of the Greek Army in finding suitable houses and carrying out repairs. Drome at Yannina u/s.
>
> **13 January** Heavy fall of snow during the night. Drome u/s.

14 January Continuous snow and rain. Instructions received from HQ British Forces in Greece for this unit to move to Yannina with all possible speed.

15 January Rain and snow. Party of vehicles and men left for Yannina at 0700.

16 January The convoy at Trikkala was ordered by the CO to remain there. The mountain pass was blocked with snow. Nine Gladiators led by F/L Kettlewell left Larissa for Eleusis, near Athens, landing there at 1330. Aircraft were serviced by 30 Squadron personnel. The reason for leaving Larissa was because another squadron was due to arrive, and Yannina was still u/s due to heavy rains and snow.

17 January The convoy at Trikkala left for Yannina at dawn. The main convoy left Larissa for Yannina at the same time. Unfortunately, on approaching the snow region in the mountains, a snowstorm began and the vehicles were unable to proceed. When it was realised that the convoy would have to remain in the mountains indefinitely, arrangements were made to evacuate the troops to a village below the mountains approximately eight miles away. The local villagers received the men with open arms, provided them with rugs in front of a fire and made them as comfortable as possible. This was badly needed by the men owing to the intense cold. Arrangements were made for a party to remain with the vehicles. Efforts were made to dig the vehicles out of the snow, and with the assistance of a snow plough, a few made a little headway, but had to give up owing to the raging snowstorms. During the night, the temperature dropped to 32° below freezing point, and the radiators of the vehicles were drained.

On 18 January, the Officer i/c Convoy decided to return by himself to Trikkala to get in touch with the CO and obtain instructions as to the disposal of the troops, the snowstorm having abated somewhat during the day.

Three Gladiators led by Sqn Ldr Jones arrived at Yannina from Larissa at noon on 19 January. Meanwhile, orders were received by the detachment at Eleusis from HQ Athens that all pilots would be required to stand by with their aircraft at Eleusis from dawn to dusk to defend a convoy in the dock.

One of the two sections at Eleusis was ordered up next day (**20 January**) to protect the convoy as it was being unloaded. Blenheims from 30 Squadron were also in the air at this time to provide additional protection. Four Italian bombers attacked Athens at 1330 from around 13,000ft and were able to escape without being intercepted. A second formation was not so fortunate and was met head-on by the three Gladiators. Plt Off Stuckey closed to very short range before opening fire. Unfortunately he was hit and broke off the attack and attempted to land on a small strip to the south of Athens. As he was coming in to land another aircraft came in to land and Stuckey had to go round again. As he came in for his second approach flames were seen coming out from the bottom of the Gladiator, which then exploded and crashed, killing him.

Meanwhile, the other section of Gladiators arrived on the scene and attacked the bombers, along with a Blenheim 1F from 30 Squadron. Flt Lt Timber Woods latched on to a straggler, which had been damaged by the Blenheim. After several passes the bomber fell blazing into the sea; four of the crew were able to bale out. The bomber was later identified as a Cant Z1007bis. A second Cant was reported to have crashed as well (although this report was incorrect) and this was credited to Stuckey.

On **27 January**, the Eleusis detachment flew up to rejoin the squadron at Yannina. During the afternoon of the following day, 15 Gladiators took off to fly an offensive patrol over the Kelcyre–Premet area, where they encountered four 37°Stormo BR20s and five 35°Stormo Z.1007s. Flt Lt Pattle's section took on one of the Cants, which fell in flames, from which only two parachutes were seen. Pattle and his No. 2, Eldon Trollip, then went after the BR20s, one of which they claimed as probably destroyed. Casbolt also attacked the formation of Cants and claimed damaging strikes on two. Cullen claimed another, which he reported blew up in the air, while it seems that Bill attacked the same aircraft. Bill's report of the action revealed:

> I was leading No. 3 flight [of five aircraft] and after reaching the area at 1415 'Tally-ho!' was given and No. 2 flight went into attack on four enemy bombers in vic formation. I carried out an umbrella [cover] until I sighted five enemy bombers approaching from the north. I gave 'Tally-ho!' and put my flight into line astern and carried out a head-on attack on the right-hand aircraft. I pulled up and followed the aircraft until they turned towards the south. Another Gladiator carried out a head-on attack on a damaged aircraft, which had turned away from the formation. I carried out a head-on attack on the same aircraft. I pulled up and saw a Gladiator in the astern attack position, and another one approaching. The starboard engine caught fire and the e/a started to go down in flames. Two Italian crew jumped by parachute before the e/a blew up in flames in the air.
>
> I found out later that the pilot who carried out the head-on attack was F/L Pattle, who also carried out the stern attack later.[1]

From Yannina at 1430 on **31 January**, six Gladiators led by Flt Lt Pattle took off for an offensive patrol over the Corfu area. No enemy aircraft were seen and the patrol landed at 1620. Unfortunately on landing Flt Lt Kettlewell's machine turned over on its back having struck a soft patch, resulting in considerable damage to the aircraft. He was shaken, but not hurt.

Heavy rains had prevented any flying in the first week of February, but the second week saw some of the heaviest fighting yet encountered. A lone SM79 made an abortive attempt to bomb the airfield in the early morning of **9 February**. Thirteen Gladiators were on patrol over Tepelene when a trio of SM79s were seen, then lost in cloud, but not before Bill (N5784) had claimed damage to one. Two Gladiators suffered engine problems and the pilots were forced to return to Yannina. Flt Lt Pattle took over the flight and a little while later an estimated 30 to 40 CR42s were encountered. In fact, there were just 16 fighters of the 150°Gruppo, led by Capitano Edoardo Travaglini, the new commander of the 365ªSquadriglia. The Italian pilots also overestimated the opposition, identifying the 11 Gladiators as 20 strong.

A fierce mêlée took place between Tepelene and Argyrokastron. Pattle hit one Fiat and saw it crash in the outskirts of Tepelene, while Cullen fired four short bursts into another and saw it crash into a hillside. When the pilots returned to Yannina they submitted claims for four destroyed and three probables. The three probables were 'confirmed' the next day when the wreckage of seven Italian aircraft was found. The victors in addition to Pattle and Cullen were Kettlewell, Gregory and Casbolt, newcomer Tulloch, and Bill, who reported:

> I was slightly behind the main formation . . . I observed about six or more formations of five CR42s [each] above us and so I gave 'Tally-ho!' and I immediately climbed. A dogfight started and from my position the policy of the e/a seemed to be diving attacks and gaining height straight away. One CR42 dived on me from above but I managed to evade his fire by pulling round and up towards him. I fired a short burst, which seemed to scare him away. I then saw a CR42 diving down on another Gladiator and so carried out a diving quarter attack and he pulled away, which left me in an astern position close in. I carried on firing until the e/a turned over on its back and the pilot left the machine. I saw his parachute open and so gained height and fired a long burst at a CR42, which dived down on me from above. I then broke away from the combat and owing to shortage of ammunition and fuel returned to base with F/O Cullen, who came up and formatted with me. We landed at 1240 and on inspecting aircraft found no damage.

Two Gladiators failed to return. Hosken had to bale out of his aircraft when the controls were shot away and Kettlewell landed 50 miles away from base, although his aircraft was relatively undamaged. Both returned to Yannina aided by the Greek Army. The Italians in fact lost four fighters, Sottoten

Romano Maionica and Sergente Birolo were both killed, while Tenente Rovetta was wounded and crashed on landing. Capitano Travaglini put his aircraft down near Turano. Four Gladiators were claimed shot down by the Italians and a further nine damaged. Within the hour Bill, and others, were off again, escorting Blenheims to Tepelene, a two-hour flight.

The day was brought to a close by the announcement of a long overdue DFC for Flt Lt Pattle, whose score now stood at over 15. Further reinforcements arrived in the form of five 112 Squadron Gladiators and their pilots on detachment.

Gladiators from both squadrons were up on defensive patrols against further raids by Italian bombers next day (**10 February**). Italian bombers of all types made sustained attacks on Yannina. Fighters of both the EVA and the RAF patrolled and intercepted in a series of rather confused engagements. During the morning three formations of 47°Stormo Z.1007bis and five SM79s from the 104°Gruppo attacked Yannina. The latter formation was escorted by 24°Gruppo G.50s, led by Maggiore Eugenio Leotta. This formation was intercepted by a trio of 21 Mira Gladiators, but the escort were on them in a flash, Leotta claiming one shot down and his pilots a second in collaboration. The Greek unit lost only one aircraft.

Three Gladiators of 80 Squadron (Pattle, Graham and Dowding) had chased five Z.1007bis during mid-morning (probably a formation from 47°Stormo), but could not gain sufficient height to make an effective attack. Nevertheless they saw their fire strike two of the bombers, Pattle claiming one damaged. During these morning raids bombs fell on the west and north sides of the airfield, but little damage was caused other than to one staff car. Bill's flight failed to make an impression:

> Thirteen Gladiators in three sections of three and one of four. Five SM79s [presumably the 104°Gruppo flight] observed but owing to lack of speed it was impossible to attack e/a again after head-on attack. Tried to overhaul e/a but distance increased. No apparent damage done to enemy aircraft, which proceeded on course after carrying out bombing.

The afternoon was practically a continual air-raid alarm. Four SM79s of 104°Gruppo attacked under escort by a dozen 154°Gruppo G.50s, the escort claiming a Gladiator shot down, while 47°Stormo Z.1007bis crews reported being attacked by ten Gladiators and seven PZLs, claiming four Gladiators shot down. Seven of the bombers were hit, one of them badly, and a number of aircrew were wounded. Fourteen RAF Gladiators, a dozen from 80 Squadron and two from 112 Squadron, undertook defensive patrols, during one of which Cullen chased away one formation of five trimotors, then attacked five more head-on (identified as SM79s) and chased these out to sea, claiming to have shot one down south of Corfu. Another formation identified as BR20s, but almost certainly the 47°Stormo Z.1007bis, was intercepted by Pattle, Woods and Casbolt, each of whom claimed one damaged. At least five formations raided the airfield during the afternoon, an estimated 150 heavy bombs falling on or near the base. Three 80 Squadron Gladiators were damaged and one 21 Mira fighter was destroyed. In the nearby town much damage was caused and many civilians killed or injured.

Further raids were carried out against Yannina on **11 February**. The first was a strafe by 17 CR42s. A Gladiator from the Greek unit 21 Mira was shot down as it tried to take off, and three of 80 Squadron's Gladiators were slightly damaged. It was thought that the AA guns had shot down one of the Fiats, as an aircraft was reported to have crashed into the hill not far from the airfield. Standing patrols were initiated for the rest of the day and no further attacks developed. During the night three CR42s carried out a strafe, but only one aircraft was slightly damaged.

The Gladiators were in the air for most of **13 February**, escorting various formations of Blenheims. During one mission in the afternoon the bombers came under attack but the Gladiators did not see the enemy fighters so continued on their way to strafe Italian positions at Tepelene. Ground fire was intense and Barker's aircraft was hit in the engine. He made a forced landing 40 miles north of Yannina, the Gladiator being written-off in the crash. He was unhurt and returned to the unit that night. Although not recorded in the squadron ORB, it would seem that this was also the occasion when Bill was apparently shot down by Italian fighters, captured and temporarily imprisoned.[2] He later recounted:

> I was shot down and taken prisoner by the Italians. I was taken to the officers' mess on an Italian-occupied airfield [it seems that this was Argyrokastron, about 15 miles south of Tepelene, which housed CR42s of 365ªSquadriglia] and, having given my word that I would not try to escape, I was paroled by them and lived in their mess for about a week, sharing their slit-trench when the airfield was attacked by units of the RAF. I committed this particular layout to memory, and then after about a week succeeded in escaping and joined up with Greek partisans and was with them for a time. We went in a village café or wine-shop and there, well behind the lines, saw Richard Dimbleby,[3] who was a war correspondent at the time. I had previously met him so was not mistaken. He was sitting with Italian officers, talking and drinking in their company. It puzzled me as to what particular role he was playing – and was he in fact an agent? I kept a low profile since I was in partisan clothes, having discarded my uniform for the journey back through enemy-held territory.[4]

Meanwhile, Kettlewell had been sent to Athens with a party of five other pilots to test a number of Hurricanes that had been promised for the squadron. Frequent patrols were flown from Yannina but little was seen of the enemy for several days. On **14 February**, five more pilots (Woods, Graham, Wanklyn Flower, Acworth and Casbolt) were sent to Athens to collect some of the Hurricanes. Six of these aircraft arrived at Paramythia on the 17th, where they were to stay as the airfield at Yannina was virtually under water. Rain continued for several days and the Hurricanes remained on the ground until the 20th.

Thirty miles south-west of the Albanian frontier and midway between Yannina and the island of Corfu was the narrow valley hemmed in by a ridge of mountains which contained the aerodrome at Paramythia. Aerodrome, in actual fact, is hardly the right term, since it contained no runways, no control tower, and no permanent buildings of any kind; landing-ground would describe it better, for it was merely the large, flattish floor of the valley. Its surface was stony and well drained, and in the early spring encouraged the growth of thousands of alpine flowers, indescribably beautiful, particularly at dusk, when the failing light of day blended the hues of the rocks and flowers in delicate harmony.

As a direct contrast, the tremendous range of mountains to the east stood out in stark silhouette against the background of puffy white clouds reflecting the glory of the setting sun and the glow of the rising moon. High up in those mountains lived the wolves and bears, which had thrived in the early days of the war on the bodies of the Italians, rotting there after the blood-thirsty guerrilla attacks of the tough Greek farmers, armed with an assortment of pitchforks, plough shares and pruning knives.

The camp, consisting of a dozen tepee-styled tents, was some way up the mountainside, close to the olive groves. Through the middle of it a fast-moving stream poured its waters into a shallow depression, which had been blocked at one end by the pilots to form a miniature lake, in which they could bathe or soak at will. A bath in that water, however, was more of a necessity than a pleasure, for the water, descending from the snowy regions towards the top of the 5,000ft-high peaks, was icily cold.

Farther down the mountainside more tents were pitched closer to the landing-ground. They were the homes of the ground crews. Near to these were the station wagons, trucks, bowsers and other vital equipment, which had taken seventeen days to travel by road from Athens. The men who operated this equipment had flown up in the Bombay in just over an hour.[5]

Sqn Ldr Tommy Wisdom, the RAF press officer, was already at Paramythia covering the activities of 211 Squadron's Blenheims. Of his arrival at Paramythia aboard a Blenheim, he wrote:

> We struck north over the mountains – snow-capped Olympus could be seen in the far distance – and crept between two towering peaks. What a view opened out before us! Five thousand feet below, down cliffs that fell sheer from those peaks, was a narrow valley, almost surrounded by mountains. It was an unforgettable scene, so much wild beauty crammed into one valley.
>
> This was Paramythia – its ancient Greek name means 'the place of fairy tales' – south of the Albanian frontier, and almost midway between Yannina and the island of Corfu. The Greeks had at last responded to the pleadings of RAF Headquarters and had allowed us to occupy a landing-ground within reasonable distance of our targets. There was no aerodrome there – we circled the valley and came down on the stony, flower-covered bed of the valley, just south of the little village perched perilously on the side of the mountain.[6]

On the arrival of the Hurricanes, he added:

> Out of the evening sun came a sound as of the buzzing of angry hornets – an old and familiar note, but the first time we had heard it in Greece. A moment later six Hurricanes, in perfect formation, swept low over the aerodrome, and then proceeded to give us a Hendon flying display. It was good to see those Hurricanes. When they landed we went over in a body and examined them, and patted them as if we had never seen an eight-gun fighter before. The boys of 211 were overjoyed – now we could have a fighter escort. The Ities were in for a bad time.
>
> Then, to support the Hurricanes, there arrived five Wellingtons. The messing arrangements and our tentage were tested to capacity. We ran out of beer, of course, but the chaps were content to eat bully and biscuits, drink the throat-tearing Greek wine presented to us by the Mayor of Paramythia, and sleep under a pile of flying suits in their aircraft.

Wisdom continued:

> Next day I went as observer on a job with Pip Cox [in his Blenheim]. By this time I was regarded as a member of the squadron. Pip was a great big chap from Rhodesia, a fine pilot and a charming companion. We were No. 2 in the second flight. The Hurricanes were above and behind us – and most satisfying it was to see them now and again through gaps in the cloud.

On this occasion no enemy aircraft were sighted.

In the afternoon of **20 February**, the weather cleared sufficiently for 17 Gladiators, 8 from 80 Squadron and 9 from 112 Squadron, to escort 2 Wellingtons and a Greek Junkers G.24 that were to drop food and other supplies to Greek troops at the front line. The Hurricanes, meanwhile, were escorting 18 Blenheims due to strike Berat airfield in Albania. Over the target a number of G.50s attacked the bombers, damaging one before the Hurricanes could intervene. The Hurricane pilots quickly claimed four of the fighters shot down, two by Casbolt and one each by Flt Lt Pattle and Timber Woods. The withdrawing Blenheims and escort were followed at a distance by the remaining Italian fighters, which were joined by a number of CR42s, only to run into the Gladiators north of Klysoura. Cullen claimed one of each, with Kettlewell and Trollip each claiming a G.50 as a probable. Cullen's Gladiator was damaged in these combats and his right hand grazed by a bullet:

> The leader came into close range and then flicked over on its back and dived down. I did a half-roll and got into position dead astern. Four long bursts and the enemy caught fire and crashed into a snow-covered hill. Then engaged another G.50 and got in some good deflection shots. Saw two formations of biplanes, thought they were Glads and went to take a look at them. They were CR42s. Got on the tail of one, gave him a burst, and he went over on his back, and the pilot baled out. The others made off at once. Just as well – I hadn't any ammo left.

Of this action Sqn Ldr Wisdom wrote:

> In the rush to go on the aerial armada I failed to get a ride. I waited, as so many times I had waited, for the chaps to come back. And they had a grand story to tell. The Hurricanes had shot down four monoplane fighters – every one off the wing tip of a Blenheim. The rear-gunners in the bombers had a front-seat view of the whole affair. Plt Off Arthur Geary said: 'A G.50 came for us and in a flash a Hurricane just shot it off our wing tip. It simply rolled over, went on fire, and dived into the mountain. It was wizard.'

It appears that only two Fiats were actually lost. Tenente Alfredo Fusco was killed and Tenente Livio Bassi was wounded. While attempting to land at Berat his G.50 flipped over and caught fire. Bassi later died in hospital from his injuries. At the time he had seven victories to his credit and was awarded a posthumous *Medaglia d'Oro*.

Bill had by now returned to the fold, and had apparently discussed with Flt Lt Pattle the possibility of paying Argyrokastron a visit. Pat agreed and the pair set out on this unauthorised sortie; Bill later recalled:

I suggested to Pat that it would be worth an unscheduled visit to the airfield in view of the information of its layout that I had memorised. We paid the airfield a visit under the guise of a patrol, paying particular attention to the slit-trench area around the Italian officers' mess. We shot up the whole area around the mess. I felt sure that we had wiped out the opposition.[7]

The persistent rain continued for most of the following week. There was very little flying done by either side. The only action of note was on **23 February**, when Cullen was ordered to search for a seaplane reported on the sea south of Praga. The aircraft was finally located to the south of Antipaxoi Island, attempting to take off. As he carried out his attack a white flag was seen being waved by one of the crew members. He circled the aircraft, which started to move again still with the white flag flying. As Cullen flew over it he was met by gunfire so he continued his attack and eventually the aircraft, identified as a Cant Z.506B, appeared to sink. In fact, the wreck drifted ashore, where Greek troops captured the survivors.

The floatplane had been attempting the rescue of the crew of a downed Z.1007, which had been damaged by AA fire a day earlier during an attack on Preveza harbour before being shot down by two Blenheim fighters of 30 Squadron. One of the crew baled out and was drowned, while three of the remaining four suffered injuries. All survived the night by clinging on to parts of the floating wreckage, and around midday a Z.506B finally arrived and alighted nearby. Two of the crew were hauled aboard before the floatplane hit a submerged object, causing a leak, whereupon the pilot pulled away and attempted to take off, but failed. At that point, Cullen arrived and attacked the machine, his gunfire fatally wounding its pilot and one of the two survivors.

Towards the end of February all Gladiators from 80 and 112 Squadrons were moved to Paramythia. More reinforcements from Egypt had arrived in the form of 33 Squadron, Bill's old unit but now flying Hurricanes. Some of these were passed over to 80 Squadron including V7589, in which Bill undertook a 30-minute familiarisation flight on 26 February, and next day carried out mock dogfighting with other Hurricanes to help hone his skills.

33 Squadron's Hurricanes were soon in action, on **27 February**, escorting Blenheims to Valona airfield in Albania. Italian fighters rose to meet them and the Hurricanes of 33 and 80 Squadrons claimed seven shot down, while two more were seen to collide. Flt Lt Pattle claimed one, Hewett two, Cullen one, Dicky Acworth one, and Wanklyn Flower one shared with a 33 Squadron pilot, the seventh also claimed by 33 Squadron. Only two CR42s were reported lost, both pilots baling out, wounded. Sottoten Egidio Faltoni survived, but Sergente Osvaldo Bartolaccini died. 211 Squadron's Plt Off Arthur Geary, the CO's air gunner, recalled:

I had a grandstand view of the whole affair. It was lovely bombing – direct hits all over the aerodrome and on buildings. A large formation of CR42s took off to intercept us. One got on my tail, so I put a burst into him, and he fell away. Then two Hurricanes appeared in a flash, and, well, he just fell to pieces. The Hurricanes wheeled and proceeded to deal with the others. The sky was full of crashing aircraft – and they were all enemy. The Hurricanes shot down seven, all of them in flames, and two others evidently got so fuddled with what was going on that they collided and went down too. We had a most pleasant tour home, and the scenery looked more lovely than ever.

The weather cleared up on **28 February** and in the afternoon a large formation of Gladiators (8 from 80 Squadron and 11 from 112 Squadron) and Hurricanes (5 and 4 respectively) took off for an offensive patrol over the Tepelene–Dukati area. An escorted formation of ten BR20s of 37°Stormo was soon encountered and the Hurricanes dived into attack. Pattle claimed two shot down, while Cullen and Wanklyn Flower each claimed one. At this point the escorts intervened, and Pattle, whose windscreen was covered in oil, was only able to escape after much twisting and diving. He returned to base and immediately took off in another Hurricane and headed back towards the fray. Over Valona he came across three CR42s and after a brief skirmish he claimed two shot down and the third a probable. Further formations of Italian aircraft were seen and Cullen claimed another two SM79s and two CR42s.

The battle extended right across Albania. First I found four Breda 20s. I got one, which went down in flames. Then we found three formations of SM79s. I took on one and aimed at the starboard engine. It caught fire, and crashed in flames. I climbed and dived on the next – and he too crashed in flames. Then we attacked ten CR42s, climbing to get above them. I got behind one, and he caught fire and went down in flames. Up again immediately, dived, fired into the cockpit, and another took fire, rolled over and crashed. I had to come home then – no more ammo.

Bill (flying a borrowed 112 Squadron Gladiator, N5829/RT-Z) claimed an SM79 and one G.50:

At 1530, eight Hurricanes and 19 Gladiators took off from Paramythia on an offensive patrol over the Hilmara–Tepeline area. I was leading No. 3 Flight of Gladiators at 13,000 feet. At approximately 1545, I observed a formation of enemy bombers away to starboard and gave 'Tally-ho!' but as they were a long way off no action was taken.

'Tally-ho!' was then given for bombers approaching from the sea and also to our starboard. The front formation of Gladiators went into attack the ones to port and the last three sections went to starboard. I observed five bombers approaching from starboard and put my flight into line astern and carried out a head-on attack, which did not bring anything down. I carried out a rear quarter attack but the cross fire was thick, so I left the bombers. I then saw a G.50 coming south in a valley, and so half-rolled down onto it but it put its nose down and got out of range. Another Gladiator dived down onto it and I last saw it with small bursts of smoke coming from it, diving down at the side of a hill. I then observed another G.50 pulling up under the other Gladiator and so I carried out a quarter attack and at very short range. It pulled round and after another burst from astern went down out of control into the valley.

I pulled up and saw enemy bombers coming from the coast and carried a quarter head-on without any effect. Another enemy bomber had broken away from the formation and was losing height and heading north, so I carried out a vertical downwards attack and finished close up in astern, firing at the port engine until the e/a started to turn to port, put its nose down and went down into the sea about three or four miles south of the point. I climbed up and observed one more Gladiator heading for base and so I followed and landed at 1755. My aircraft was not damaged.

Two more CR42s were claimed by Tap Jones. The commander of Western Wing, Wg Cdr Paddy Coote, had borrowed an 80 Squadron Gladiator and went along on the mission. At the end of the day he put in a claim for a CR42 shot down. Pilots of 80 Squadron made further claims for three CR42s and two G.50s. When the 112 Squadron pilots added in their claims the total stood at 27 shot down and 9 probables. All this for the loss of one 112 Squadron Gladiator, the pilot of which, Flt Lt Dicky Abrahams, baled out:

The old Glad suddenly went all soft. Nothing would work. I sat there and then decided I had better get out. I couldn't, so I sat there with my hands on my lap, the aircraft spinning like mad. Then, eventually, I did manage to get out. It was so pleasant sitting there in the air that I damn nearly forgot to pull the ripcord. I reckon I did the record delayed drop for all Albania and Greece. I landed, and no sooner had I fallen sprawling on the ground than I was picked up by Greek soldiers, who cheered and patted me on the back. I thought I was a hell of a hero until one soldier asked me. 'Milano, Roma?' and I realised that they thought I was an Iti. They didn't realise it was possible for an Englishman to be shot down. So I said 'Inglese', and then the party began. I was hoisted on their shoulders, and the 'here the conquering hero comes' procession started. We wined and had fun. Jolly good chaps.

Chapter 7

HURRICANES AT LAST

With the passing of the Gladiator, Flg Off Dixie Dean's personal reflections of combat against the Fiat CR32 and CR42 were that:

> The CR42 and the Gladiator were fairly evenly matched. The CR42 pilots were better too and were much more of a match for the RAF pilots. The CR42 had a constant speed airscrew whilst the Gladiator had a fixed pitch screw. This gave the CR42 a much better rate of climb and a higher flat out diving speed. But the Gladiator had slightly better manoeuvrability and the four Browning machine guns were superior to the 12.7mm cannon in the CR42. The Italians used explosive ammunition, which tended to explode on impact with little penetration. The Hurricane was greatly superior to the CR42 in speed and armament and also had armour plating. But the manoeuvrability of the CR42s compared to the Hurricane made them difficult to shoot down once they had seen you.

Dean had the following impressions of the Hurricane:

> Having been trained at No. 11 FTS, Wittering, in 1937 on the Hawker Hart trainer, then the Audax and the Fury, I had formed a great affection for the Hawker stable, particularly the wonderful Fury. My love for Hawkers had re-blossomed.
>
> Later, after I had flown with 33 Squadron from the outbreak of the war in the desert and had had a successful time with the Gladiator, we were re-equipped with the Hurricane 1, much to my delight. One felt immediately safer in this well-constructed all-metal machine with the pilot's back protected by thick armour. It was larger overall than the Gladiator and much more aerobative and manoeuvrable. The powerful cone of shot from the eight Brownings was very impressive.
>
> Some time later, when the desert seemed to be full of fighter squadrons, we were converted to fighter-bombers. The idea was that we would roam far into the desert and bomb a map

reference where the presence of enemy troops or vehicles had been reported by returning bombers or recce aircraft. The Hurricane behaved very well in the high-speed dive and getaway. But its tactical use in this role was flawed because the desert is an extremely difficult place in which to navigate and, all too often, the intended target was either not there or too well camouflaged.

The Hurricane was a very effective ground-strafing weapon with its speed and powerful guns. It was also adapted an effective anti-tank weapon fitted with two heavy cannon. The other advantage it had, according to the ground crews, was that it was remarkably adaptable to transplanted parts and thus had a good serviceability record.

* * *

On **3 March**, two Hurricanes from 80 Squadron flown by Bill (V7288) and Cullen were sent off to patrol at 1025, while a third, flown by the attached 112 Squadron pilot Dicky Acworth, was sent up on an air test. As these got into the air ten Z.1007bis bombers of 50°Gruppo from Brindisi approached the area in two formations of five each, while other such aircraft from 47°Stormo BT were also over Greece at this time. The 50°Gruppo aircraft bombed the earthquake-shattered town of Larissa, and were on their way home by the time the Hurricanes were vectored onto them. Acworth was first on the scene, soon joined by the other pair, and he reported:

> Took off to test aircraft. Before leaving heard that ten enemy aircraft heading towards Preveza. I flew in that direction and saw bombing in progress, and although I had not enough speed to catch the first section of bombers, I finally got near enough to second section – attacked No. 5 and shot it down in flames – witnessed by Flg Off Cullen, who shot down No. 4. I saw one crewmember leaving No. 5 but afterwards, apart from an empty chute floating down, no trace of him was found. Both mine and Cullen's first bomber crashed into the sea five miles south-west of Corfu.

Cullen continued to attack and returned to claim a total of four Cants shot down and one probable, although his Hurricane was badly damaged by return fire, one bullet passing through his flying boot and grazing his shin; he reported seeing 18 parachutes in the air at one time. Bill also claimed a bomber shot down, but identified his victim as an SM81. It was his first kill while flying a Hurricane, and his eleventh in total.

During the morning on **4 March** five Italian warships identified as two cruisers and three destroyers, sortied down the Albanian coast and commenced shelling the coastal road near Himare and Port Palermo, under cover of a fighter escort of 15 G.50s and CR42s. The flotilla actually comprised the destroyer *Augusto Riboty*, the torpedo boat *Andromeda* and three MAS boats.

An immediate strike was mounted by RAF units, 15 Blenheims being ordered off, with an escort provided by 10 Hurricanes, followed by 17 Gladiators, 14 from 112 Squadron and 3 from 80 Squadron. Four 80 Squadron Hurricanes led by Flt Lt Pattle flew on the starboard flank of the bombers, with four from 33 Squadron to port, and two more above as weavers. At 1500, the warships were seen ten miles south of Valona, and the Blenheims went in to bomb in line astern; several near misses were seen, but no hits were recorded.

At this point six G.50s dived on the Hurricanes, shooting down Wt Off Harry Goodchild DFM (won in Palestine), who was killed. It seems that the Italian fighters did not see the bombers, for they reported only single-engined types – 10 'Spitfires', 3 'Battles' (obviously Hurricanes) and 20 Gladiators. Once the Blenheims had completed their run and were on their return flight, Pattle ordered the Hurricanes to hunt in pairs over the warships, where a number of Italian fighters were seen. At once a lone G.50 attacked Pattle and his No. 2 – on this occasion Cullen – but Pattle promptly shot this down and watched it spiral into a mountainside just north of Himara. At this moment a second Fiat jumped Cullen and he was not seen again; his aircraft crashed near Himara, and the Australian ace was killed.

Pattle flew on towards Valona, and was attacked by another lone G.50, which he reported went into the sea after a brief combat. He then became involved with a third such fighter over Valona harbour and claimed to have shot this down into the sea in flames. Nine CR42s were then seen below and he dived on these, reporting that one went into a spin with smoke pouring from its engine; he claimed this as a probable. Hewett was also heavily engaged, claiming one G.50 shot down near Himara and three of eight CR42s near Valona. The only other claim by a Hurricane pilot was made by Bill, flying V7589, who claimed another G.50. Meanwhile, the Gladiators claimed a further two victories, plus four probables, for no loss.

In return, 24°Gruppo pilots claimed four Gladiators, one 'Spitfire' and one 'Battle' shot down. Sottoten Nicolo Cobolli Gigli of 355ªSquadriglia and Sergente Marcello De Salvia of 354ªSquadriglia were both shot down and killed, while Tenente Francesco Rocca of the latter unit was wounded. This was virtually the last operation over the Albanian front for 80 Squadron; on **6 March** the pilots at Yannina withdrew to Eleusis to complete re-equipment with Hurricanes. They were followed next day by four Hurricanes from Paramythia. On arrival at Eleusis a number of pilots were flown to Egypt to collect new aircraft. The 33 Squadron Hurricane detachment joined forces with 112 Squadron's Gladiators and flew to Paramythia to take over 80 Squadron's role.

Bill, as did several other 80 Squadron pilots, spent most of the month practice-flying Gladiators and the station's Tutor, in which he made seven flights providing dual instruction for two ground staff officers. He also had some leave and obviously spent time with Janina, who was now back in Athens with her parents.

Six new Hurricanes duly arrived for 80 Squadron from Egypt, two flown by replacement pilots Flt Sgts Pierre Wintersdorff and Jacques Rivalant, Free French volunteers. During the month a number of awards were announced for 80 Squadron pilots, Pat Pattle – who was now promoted and posted to command 33 Squadron – receiving a Bar to his DFC, while Sqn Ldr Tap Jones, the missing Ape Cullen, and Bill each received the DFC, and Sgts Ted Hewett and Don Gregory were awarded DFMs. The recommendation for Bill's DFC revealed:

> *This officer prior to the outbreak of hostilities was with 33 Squadron on active operations during the disturbances in Palestine 1938/39. He was mentioned in dispatches by the GOC Commanding British Forces in Palestine.*
>
> *Whilst with this squadron [80] he has carried out numerous patrols over enemy territory both in Libya and Greece and has seven confirmed victories to his credit. He is a skilful and courageous pilot always keen to engage the enemy; very cool, observant and fearless in action. On 23/11/40, with two other Gladiators, he carried out a daring ground strafing attack on three different enemy MT and animal convoys deep in enemy territory, inflicting severe damage in spite of heavy opposition from the ground.*
>
> *His outstanding engagement was when patrolling with eight other Gladiators over Argyrokastron in 21/12/40. The patrol became engaged with a formation of over 50 enemy aircraft. This officer, in this action, had three confirmed victories, and also distinguished himself by his covering action in helping other Gladiators out of difficulties.*

Chapter 8

THE GERMANS ARRIVE

On 6 April 1941, the German Army invaded northern Greece, while other elements launched an attack against Yugoslavia. The Metaxas Line was defended by the Greek Eastern Macedonia Army Section under the command of Lt Gen Konstantinos Bakopoulos, comprising 7th, 14th and 17th Infantry Divisions, all under strength. The line ran for about 120 miles along the River Nestos in the east, and then along the Bulgarian border as far as Mount Beles near the Yugoslav border. The fortifications were designed to garrison an army of over 200,000, but were manned only by about 70,000 soldiers to face the German threat due to lack of manpower. As a result of the small numbers, the line's defences were spread thin. Furthermore, there were severe deficiencies in anti-aircraft and anti-tank guns, as most had been sent to Albania, and Bakopoulos's only reinforcements were the units of the Central Macedonia Army Section, 19th, 12th and 20th Divisions, which were severely under-manned and equipped with obsolete or captured weapons.

Initial German attacks against the Metaxas Line by mountain troops (5th and 6th Mountain Divisions) encountered extremely tough resistance and resulted in limited success. A German report at the end of the first day said that the German 5th Mountain Division 'was repulsed in the Rupel Pass despite strongest air support and sustained considerable casualties'. After one day of fighting, out of the 24 forts that made up the Metaxas Line only 2 had fallen and only after they had been destroyed.

However effective the resistance of the Metaxas Line was, the Germans found alternate routes of attack. Yugoslav resistance in the north quickly collapsed and German forces poured into Greek territory via Yugoslavia by 7 April. The line was quickly outflanked by German Panzer forces (2nd Panzer Division), which invaded through southern Yugoslavia and advanced down the Vardar Valley where they rapidly defeated the sporadic resistance from the Greek forces. On 9 April, elements of 2nd Panzer had reached Thessaloniki, and the remaining Greek forces were reluctantly forced to surrender. Even after Gen Bakopoulos surrendered the Metaxas Line, the soldiers manning the frontier forts and some of the field troops continued to fight on and as a result of this ongoing resistance about half of the soldiers of the Metaxas Line were able to evacuate by sea.

* * *

As German forces streamed through the Rupel Pass, the Royal Air Force waited tensely for news. Plt Off Bill Winsland of 33 Squadron later recorded:

> We heard the news before dawn, got up, washed in freezing water and dressed. Everyone was tense; our feelings and thoughts were confused – what was going to happen now? Our army was on the retreat in Egypt; the Greeks were only just managing to hold the Italians back in Albania; had we sufficient British troops to hold the Germans in Greece? What was going to happen in the air? While we had sufficient to cope with the Italians, surely we were going to be hopelessly outnumbered by the Germans? For weeks past we had heard of colossal German air forces forming up in Bulgaria. What were we in for? Little did we know! In the afternoon (having been on instant readiness all morning, with all available Hurricanes parked at the end of the runway, facing into wind, ready for take off) all available Hurricanes (12) took off for an offensive patrol over Bulgaria. I had the good fortune to be flying next to Sqn Ldr Pattle. Suddenly we spotted eight Me109s and dived to attack. This was my first really good look at a Hun from close quarters. I saw the CO beside me shoot down two of them in a few seconds. What a sight. I shall never forget it. What shooting too. A two second burst from his eight guns at the first enemy machine caused a large piece to break off in mid air, while the machine turned over vertically onto one wingtip as the pilot baled out – his parachute opened while his feet were still in the cockpit but he got clear in spite of the chute opening so soon. A similar fate awaited the second enemy machine, which went spiralling down in flames. I did not have time to see what happened to its pilot.

The Bf109s were bomb-carrying aircraft of 8./JG27, led on patrol over the Rupel Pass area by Oblt Arno Becker; Becker was one of those shot down and killed, his aircraft – Black 2 – crashing in flames. He was possibly Pattle's second victim; the first was undoubtedly Ltn Klaus Faber, who baled out to become a prisoner. Cottingham claimed a third Bf109 shot down, from which he saw the pilot bale out. As the German pilot floated down, another Messerschmitt circled round to give protection, and Cottingham promptly attacked this aircraft. It would seem that this was the fighter also engaged by Winsland, who added:

While all this was in full swing and machines were twisting and turning in all directions I found myself directly on the tail of another Hun at whom I let off burst after burst, but either he was made of cast iron or possibly my shooting wasn't so hot! I fear it was the latter as I have had cause to discover several times since. However, I do know the cause – excitement – which is something. I start firing with the centre of the gunsight dead on target, then find myself a few seconds later aiming purely by my tracer – looking round the edge of the sight instead of through it! On this occasion the enemy plane merely 'vibrated' all over and started a diving turn to the left. I continued to chase it but still could not get it down. Luckily another Hurricane [Cottingham] suddenly came diving at it as well as myself and at last the enemy bought his packet.

The two pilots claimed a half share each, while Wickham claimed one more shot down out of a trio he engaged. Apart from the loss of Becker and Faber, Obfw Gerhard Frömming was wounded and crash-landed his badly damaged Black 8, while a fourth pilot baled out of Black 6 and returned to his unit on foot, unharmed. A fifth crashed on returning to base. A resounding victory for the Hurricanes. Meanwhile, further south, Keg Dowding of 80 Squadron had been scrambled at 1500 as a reconnaissance Ju88D from 2.(F)/123 (4U+EK) approached Athens. Sighting the intruder, he chased it out over the Gulf of Corinth, exchanging fire with the gunners. The Hurricane received a few minor hits before he delivered the mortal blow, the German machine falling into the sea off Patras, with the loss of Uffz Fritz Dreyer and two of his crew.

Back at Larissa, 80 Squadron was not directly involved in the action though Hurricane patrols were flown in defence of Athens and the ports, Bill making two such sorties without any enemy aircraft being sighted. A raid by Ju88s of 7./KG30 on the major Greek supply port of Piraeus that night achieved an unexpected success when three bombs scored direct hits on the freighter *Clan Fraser*, which was carrying 250 tons of TNT. The resulting explosion destroyed a total of 11 vessels one of which had crated Hurricanes on board, and caused a temporary closure of the port. Even when the port was reopened, the damage was so severe that it was unable to function efficiently.

On the ground all was far from well for the Allies. While the Greeks had again attacked on the Epirus Front on **9 April**, that same day armoured units of the German XVII Armee Gruppe had entered Salonika despite sustained resistance by three Greek divisions under Gen Bakopoulos, and next day all fighting in Eastern Macedonia would come to an end. In Yugoslavia the Panzers were slicing through the defences everywhere; with no news forthcoming of events within that unhappy country, an RAF Blenheim had been flown to Sarajevo, carrying a Greek general to try and ascertain the position and see if any concerted action might be possible. It was not.

Bad weather again prevented any worthwhile bomber operations and restricted fighter activity. 80 Squadron sent out a Hurricane patrol, but these planes became lost in the mountains in conditions of heavy cloud and were obliged to return to Larissa. Later, a pair of Hurricanes from 33 Squadron were scrambled from Larissa and Sqn Ldr Pattle sighted a twin-engined aircraft in the murk. He managed to get in a telling burst at what he thought was a Ju88 before it disappeared. Shortly thereafter he was advised that it had crashed nearby and he drove over to inspect the remains. His victim was a Do17, U5+BT of 9./KG2 in which Uffz Ulrich Sonnermann and his crew were lost.

Weather yet again prevented much activity on **10 April**, although during the early afternoon, Blenheims escorted by 33 Squadron set out to bomb and strafe German transport along the Prilep–Bitolj road, while four Hurricanes from 80 Squadron made for Bitolj itself. The main formation was attacked by a number of Bf109s and Bf110s. Cloud provided cover which prevented losses being suffered, while Pattle got a burst into a Bf110 which he reported crashed in flames; he then attacked a Bf109, seeing the pilot bale out before the aircraft spun down.

Meanwhile, the 80 Squadron quartet strafed vehicles and troops, and a small ammunition dump south of Bitolj. Heavy return fire was encountered and the engine of Timber Woods's Hurricane was hit, seizing up immediately. Woods was able to locate a level field and put his aircraft down on its belly at once, recalling:

> As I clambered out the aircraft went on fire. One of the others – Ginger [Plt Off John Still] – circled round with his wheels down as if about to land. I realised he would never make it and waved him away. The field was much too rough for a Hurricane landing, though I would have liked to have ridden back with him. The Jerries were about a mile away and a patrol was after me, so I sprinted away as hard as I could go in the direction of our lines. I should think that I ran for about a quarter of an hour when a patrol of Aussies picked me up. I was just about dead beat. They quickly got into position and put a few shots in the direction of the advancing Jerries, who at once pushed off. The Aussies said they had seen me land and had come out at once, for they could also see the Germans making towards the aircraft. We continued back to their position in some hills, where they fed me and then sent me back in a car.

The collapse of Greek resistance in Eastern Macedonia now allowed the Germans to begin moving southwards, and over the next five days the British forces facing them began withdrawing to the partly prepared Servia line. Early in the morning of **11 April**, Fliegerkorps X bombers from Sicily approached the Greek coast. Sqn Ldr Pattle, who had taken off after breakfast to fly to a satellite airfield, was vectored onto a number of unidentified low-flying aircraft near Volos. He identified these as Ju88s and He111s, which were attempting to lay mines in the sea at the entrance to Volos harbour. Attacking at once, he claimed one of each shot down. It would seem that both his victims were Ju88s, however, III/KG30 losing Oblt Hans Schaible's 4D+JR of 7 Staffel and Ltn Wimmer's 4D+FS of 8 Staffel, with their respective crews.

On the ground the fighting was intensifying, as noted by Brig Howard Kippenberger, OC 20th Battalion NZ Rifles:

> The war at last reached us and we had our first casualties. Through the Castle gap we saw German planes bombing and machine-gunning transport in Kozani, some miles to the north. Then the stream of refugees thickened and began to include Greek and Yugoslav soldiers, including a dignified General and a beautifully equipped Yugoslav heavy anti-aircraft battery, which settled in unpleasantly close to my headquarters. German planes came over us, bombed Servia, and some tackled Upham's platoon and wounded two men. A nice little red-headed boy named Kelly was killed by a bomb – our first killed in action.

RAF Blenheims and Hurricanes were out over the Bitolj–Veles road during the morning of **12 April**, while in the afternoon Sqn Ldr Pattle led a formation of 33 Squadron Hurricanes on a sweep up the Struma valley. East of Salonika a lone aircraft identified as a Do215 was intercepted and this was at once claimed shot down by Pattle. As the squadron returned towards Larissa they were warned of hostile aircraft in the vicinity and almost at once encountered a reported three SM79s some 3,000ft below, apparently escorted by Bf109s. Ordering three sections to take on the fighters, Pattle led Flg Offs Holman and Starrett down on the bombers, reportedly sending one down in flames, while the other pair claimed a second. Pattle then engaged the Messerschmitts, reporting hits on one, which caused a panel to fly off the starboard wing and the wheels were seen to drop down.

As the invading Germans advanced deep into Greek territory, the Greek First Army operating in Albania against the Italians was reluctant to retreat. Gen Maitland Wilson described this reluctance as 'the fetishistic doctrine that not a yard of ground should be yielded to the Italians'. Because of this reluctance to yield ground to the Italians, the Greek retreat did not materialise until **13 April**. The Allied retreat to Thermopylae uncovered a route across the Pindus Mountains by which the Germans might take the Greek Army in flank and rear. An SS regiment was given the mission of cutting off the Greek First Army's line of retreat from Albania by driving westward to the Metsovon Pass, and from there, to Ioannina (Yannina).

An improvement in the weather allowed the air forces out in greater strength. From Bulgaria and Eastern Yugoslavia, the Luftwaffe now began to intrude more forcefully into Greek airspace, and during the morning some 70 bombers attacked Volos, the port being devastated. One raid by 20 Ju88s of I/LG1 was intercepted by seven 33 Squadron Hurricanes, the German unit reporting the loss of L1+UH flown by Ltn Gert Blanke, possibly shot down by Pattle. He may also have accounted for L1+EN (a machine of II Gruppe operating from Sicily) that ditched in the sea off Crete, in which Fw Hans Garz and his 5 Staffel crew were lost. Later, Wickham caught a reconnaissance Bf110 – L2+HR from 7.(F)/LG2 – over Mount Olympus and shot it down in flames. Ltn Georg Lange and his observer were lost.

RAF Blenheims were very active throughout the day, but their apparent immunity was to come to a tragic end as the Luftwaffe finally managed to intercept an unescorted raid. Even then it was a chance encounter. Three Bf109s from 6./JG27 had been ordered to fly to Bitolj as the Germans pushed ever forward into Greece. En route, they encountered six unescorted 211 Squadron Blenheims and, with ruthless efficiency, shot down all six, two each being credited to Hptm Hans-Joachim Gerlach, the Staffelkapitän, Fw Herbert Krenz and Uffz Fritz Gromotka. There were only two survivors out of the 18 crewmembers; one of those killed with Wg Cdr Paddy Coote, who was flying as an observer in one of the Blenheims.

Even as this slaughter was taking place, nine more Blenheims from 113 Squadron had set off 15 minutes later at 1515, heading for the same target, but with an escort of six Hurricanes from 33 Squadron. One of the Blenheim pilots recalled:

> We were going up the line to bomb the enemy forward troops. In the valley as we went north, we suddenly saw far more aircraft than we had ever seen in the air before, and going down the other side of the valley to attack our forward troops – later confirmed as a Luftwaffe bomber formation. I remember our Hurricanes fussing around us like bees, but obviously both formations had the same instructions 'do not leave your bombers' because although only a few miles apart none interfered with the other.

During the same afternoon, 33 Squadron's Woody Woodward carried out a lone reconnaissance to Bitolj and Vire. He was intercepted by three Bf109s, one of which he claimed to have shot down, believing that he had seen the pilot bale out. He then finished his reconnaissance and returned unscathed.

It was on **14 April**, as the British Army completed its withdrawal to the Olympus-Servia line, that improving weather allowed aerial activity over Greece to show a marked increase. Early in the day six Blenheims escorted by four Hurricanes, attacked vehicles and troops north of Ptolemais. Intense flak was experienced and two Bf109s also attacked the bombers, four Blenheims being damaged. Some five hours later at 0930, eight more Blenheims were off with an escort of ten Hurricanes, seven from 33 Squadron and three from 80 Squadron. Returning from attacking targets north of Ptolemais, Ju87s were seen dive-bombing Allied troops near Servia and one of these was claimed shot down by Bill (flying V7795); a Blenheim gunner fired at one of the dive-bombers, reporting seeing smoke and flames pouring from this aircraft, but this is believed to have been the machine attacked by Bill. It seems that this was a I/StG3 machine that was reported lost over Servia, in which Obfw Rudolf Schnurawa and his gunner were killed.

Somewhat later, over Athens, three Hurricanes of 80 Squadron and four Blenheim fighters of 30 Squadron scrambled to intercept Ju88s and Bf110s attacking Piraeus early in the afternoon. The Blenheims failed to make contact, but it seems that one Hurricane was hit and force-landed. An hour later pairs of Hurricanes were dispatched by 33 Squadron to patrol over troops in the Servia area who were now under constant Stuka attack. Woodward and Dean came across six of the dive-bombers as they were peeling off to attack motor transport, and three were claimed shot down with three others damaged, Woodward claiming two destroyed and one damaged, and Dean the remainder, although his aircraft was hit by return fire:

> After chasing some Ju87s at full throttle and maximum boost, I received a hit in the throttle connection, which fixed it wide open. The engine overheated and the exhaust pipes became red-hot. I had to switch off to cool it down and then make my way back to base alternately climbing with the engine on and diving with it off. I had to land with a dead-stick at a much steeper angle to maintain gliding speed. But the Hurry behaved perfectly and I made a very good landing.

Among those watching the air fight was Brig Kippenberger of the 20th NZ Rifles:

> At daylight we found ourselves in a complete traffic jam where the road wound out of the plain at Domokos. The reconnaissance plane came over and found us, as expected; then came some forty Stukas and bombed and strafed, also as expected. It was unpleasant, but only a few trucks were hit and not many men, and we were all greatly cheered by three Hurricanes, which suddenly appeared and downed three Stukas like pigeons. At last the block cleared, we wound slowly over the hills, stopped and bathed at beautiful Lamia, and then to our joy found ourselves amid New Zealand infantry.

Oblt Christian Banke and Fw Georg Hoser were lost from 9./StG2 in T6+KT south-west of Mount Olympus. A second 9 Staffel aircraft was badly damaged and crash-landed on its return to Prilep-West, Obfw Paul Lachmann and his gunner both having been wounded. 2./StG1, recently arrived from Libya, lost A5+EK to fighters; Fhr Walter Seeliger and Gefr Kurt Friedrich were taken prisoner, and were brought to the HQ of Col Stanley Casson, who wrote:

> A couple of young dive-bomber airmen were brought in to me in the late afternoon. The subaltern was young and dark, his companion, a Sergeant, was bullet-headed, morose and sullen – the subaltern was a Viennese dandy. He wore elegant riding breeches and field boots, an odd costume for an airman. I thrust him and his friend into a cowshed, our only available prison. After an hour there he asked to see me and complained, after many salutes and heel-clickings, that it was very cold there. I told him that he had visited Thessaly of his own volition – that no one had invited him, and reminded him that Greece in spring is very chilly in the evenings; he should have brought his overcoat. Later we sent him to Athens.

A German war correspondent, who flew a sortie in the rear seat of a StG2 Stuka, provided a graphic account of his experience:

> Now it was our turn to take-off. As we climbed I could make out those behind us – small dots trailing long banners of dust behind them as they accelerated across the surface of the field. As they gained height to formate on us they looked like dark fishes swimming through the morning haze. Closing up in *Ketten* formation, we continued to climb. Spread out ahead of us were the mountains of Macedonia. We set course for Fortress Moumain. Rising from it, a long grey-blue column of smoke was spreading northwards, blown by the wind. Large fires were burning in the enemy positions and a bright red wall of flame was eating through the thick undergrowth on the Greek side of the mountain.
>
> I did not have time to notice much else. 'Dive', yelled the pilot. I quickly grabbed the cabin cross-struts in both hands and braced my feet. The aircraft was already standing on its nose, the tail pointing up into the blue sky. For a second we seemed to hang there in space. Then the force of the dive pressed me hard into the seat. In front of us, framed in the windscreen and growing larger every second – Fortress Moumain!
>
> We hurtled downwards towards some small grey squares. These must be the bunkers. My whole body was quivering, the wings of the aircraft vibrated with a noise like ghostly metal drums, and my ears were filled with a high-pitched screaming and whistling. Suddenly, a tremendous jolt and I felt a wave of dizziness – the pilot was pulling

out of the dive. The pressure in my head and ears slowly eased – I could breathe freely again. Below us the bombs streaked towards their target. We were already several hundred metres away when they exploded, sending huge fountains of earth and debris high into the air between the bunkers.

Late that evening another pair of 33 Squadron's Hurricanes were returning to Larissa from a fruitless 1½-hour patrol when they became separated in heavy cloud. Winsland recalled:

> I sighted what I thought to be a friendly Greek or British fighter. However, after circling round it I identified it as a Henschel 126. What a gift – or so I thought. But again I had the old trouble – excitement! To make things more difficult the enemy put down his flaps and cruised at about 70mph so that I had to shoot past him after each attack. He also used his camouflage to his best advantage by flying low – 500 feet – thereby giving me no room to dive away downwards after attacking. All this was, of course, very much to his credit and courage. However, all that was no excuse for my not having blasted him out of the sky with the first attack. After my last burst at him I could no longer see him flying, yet neither could I find the machine smashed up on the ground. However, I can at least say that a report came in next day from Field HQ that a Henschel 126 had been found wrecked near Katerine and that it crashed at the very time and place I claimed to have been attacking it – but with this difference – the Greeks claimed having got it by ack-ack!

Nonetheless the Hs126 – believed to have been a machine from 2.(H)/10 – was credited to Winsland; the crew survived, although Oblt Hans Wiedemann, the observer, was wounded. II/KG51 lost two Ju88s on this date, one shot down during a raid on Illidza, the crew baling out unhurt, while the second crash-landed at Pecs airfield on return, after suffering battle damage. These would seem to have been the opponents of 33 Squadron either during the morning or evening raids. Sqn Ldr Pattle apparently made five claims during the day, including two Ju88s and a Bf109. The only Bf109 recorded as lost on this day was that flown by Hptm Hans-Joachim Gerlach, Staffelkapitän of 6./JG27, who was taken prisoner when his aircraft was allegedly hit in the engine during a strafing attack.

At Larissa six more replacement Hurricanes arrived from Egypt for 80 Squadron. One of these was flown by Plt Off Roald Dahl, who had only just regained his flying status following his crash six months earlier. With just seven hours' flying experience on the Hurricane, he was ordered to fly to Greece to rejoin 80 Squadron:

I took off from the bleak and sandy airfield of Abu Sueir, and after a couple of hours I was over Crete and beginning to get severe cramp in both legs [he was 6ft 6in tall]. My main fuel tank was nearly empty so I pressed the little button that worked the pump to the extra tanks. The pump worked. After four hours forty minutes in the air, I landed at last on Eleusis aerodrome, but by then I was so knotted up with terrible excruciating cramp in the legs I had to be lifted out of the cockpit by two strong men.

The squadron leader had a DFC ribbon on his chest. 'Oh, hello,' he said, 'We've been expecting you for some time.' 'I'm sorry I'm late,' I said. 'Six months late. You'll start flying tomorrow like the rest of them.' I could see that the man was preoccupied and wished to be rid of me.

Dahl's tent mate was another newly arrived pilot, Flg Off The Hon David Coke, who had seen some action during the Battle of Britain. They became good friends:

I asked him: 'Are things out here really as dicey as I've been told?' 'It's absolutely hopeless,' he said, 'but we're plugging on. The German fighters will be well within range of us any moment now, and then we'll be outnumbered by about 50 to one. If they don't get us in the air, they'll wipe us out on the ground.' 'Look,' I said, 'I have never been in action in my life. I haven't the foggiest idea what to do if I meet one of them.' David stared at me as though he were seeing a ghost.

In eastern Greece on **15 April**, the Allied airfields suffered another bad day. Bill Winsland of 33 Squadron at Larissa's satellite airstrip recorded:

What a day! Reveille 5am. Cold, dark morning. Rough, bumpy journey with a dozen other pilots in the back of a lorry through the almost deserted and ruined town (Larissa) over broken roads, over hill and dale to our satellite airfield (Churton's Bottom)[1] – well away from the main aerodrome (Larissa) and safer from bombing. An hour or two later we were in our cockpits, engines warming up and ready to take to the air at a moment's notice when the orders came through on our radios. At about 7am the first alarm was sounded. A few seconds later (we were already lined up into wind and engines running) six Hurricanes roared into the air. We had reached some 10,000 feet in cloud, when suddenly my machine shook violently and tremendous vibration set up. I thought at first that I had been jumped and hit by an enemy fighter and so took evasive action by half-rolling onto my back and diving. However, there was no response from my throttle – and nothing behind me either.

What had actually happened was that my crankcase had fractured causing oil to stream out and so seize up the engine. The speed of the machine forced the propeller to keep turning much against the will of the engine, so causing friction and tremendous vibration. I was lucky considering the situation – the main aerodrome was in sight and it looked as though it might be possible to reach it in a long glide from about 7,000 feet. I had to use hand-pumping emergency devices to lower flaps and the undercarriage – but judged everything OK, thank God, and reached the main aerodrome (Larissa) without any further damage to the aircraft. I was lucky again that I came across no enemy fighters on that glide! On stepping out of my aircraft I learnt that nine Messerschmitt 109s had only 20 minutes previously shot down two of our machines on their take-offs and afterwards strafed all our other machines on the ground – two were still burning after I had landed. I had seen the flames and smoke during my forced-landing.

This attack on Larissa had occurred at 0650, when the stand-by flight – Hurricanes flown by Flt Lt John Mackie, Plt Off Charles Chetham and Sgt Chico Genders – was scrambled just as Bf109s of II/JG77 – an estimated 15 in number, but actually only 8 strong – swept over the airfield in threes. The first trio narrowly missed the barely airborne Hurricanes, but the next three caught them at 1,500ft, Ltn Jakob Arnoldy obtaining hits on Chetham's aircraft. Onlookers saw the latter come down in a seemingly controlled glide and disappear behind some trees outside the airfield boundary, but he was killed in the crash. Arnoldy now overshot the other pair of Hurricanes and Mackie immediately latched on to his tail and managed to put a few shots into the Messerschmitt before Fw Otto Köhler engaged him from astern. The Hurricane flipped over, caught fire and exploded on crashing, killing the Canadian pilot.

Arnoldy had been hit in the chest by Mackie's quick burst and struggled to bale out at 1,000ft. As he floated down over the airfield Greek soldiers fired on him. It is not known whether he was hit again, but he died within a short time, in the medical officer's tent. His aircraft – White 5 – made an almost perfect belly-landing and was virtually undamaged; just two bullet holes below the cockpit hood, in line with the pilot's chest. The one remaining Hurricane, piloted by Chico Genders, participating in his first combat, managed to evade the Messerschmitts and to get on Fw Köhler's tail; Köhler, like Arnoldy a member of 4 Staffel, was shot down and crash-landed not far from the airfield. When a party arrived to capture the pilot, he was nowhere to be seen – the cockpit contained his parachute only. Köhler evaded capture and eventually rejoined his unit.

Following the JG77 attack, Winsland was asked to carry out a flight and gun test in a Hurricane, which had just undergone a routine inspection:

I was asked to test this machine immediately – when a poor bloody lowest of the low Pilot Officer is 'asked' to do anything it's really a bloody order! I had started the machine and was taxying along the edge of the aerodrome to the take-off point when suddenly the surface of the drome to my right became a mass of exploding cannon shells and incendiary fire from a low level ground attack – there were no less than 12 or more 109s diving in formation across the drome, strafing everything they saw yet again. How they did not see me I just don't know. Not only was I in a perfectly good aeroplane – the others, most of them anyway, were already damaged – but I was bumping along the surface, the sun flickering on my cockpit hood and shiny wings and my prop was, of course, revolving – enough to have attracted every Hun's attention one would have thought. God! Was I scared!

I lowered my seat and crouched up double inside the cockpit in an effort to get some protection from the engine in front and the small bit of armour plating behind. The situation looked so awful that I felt like undoing my straps, jumping out of the cockpit and running to the nearest slit trench, but since that would have looked very bad in front of all the Greek and British ground airmen in the trenches, I seemed to have no real alternative but to take off right through the middle of it all. It was not a pleasant prospect especially after hearing of the fate of my two friends under the same circumstances.

However, in the heat of the moment I soon found myself in the air. In those particular moments I did a little thing, which again I will never forget. I behaved like an ostrich, my action only making my existence more precarious than ever and giving me no possible additional protection – I took off by instruments with my head and shoulders in a crouched position below the sides of the cockpit, believing for some amazing and unexplained reason or other that if my head was not visible the enemy would not shoot at me! Just one of those peculiar things one does in a really terrifying moment, I suppose. I kept my machine low and flew away at full throttle hoping to evade such hopeless odds. Having left the aerodrome well behind me I climbed up into the sun. Fires repeatedly appeared here, there and everywhere (on the drome). There must have been far more than just those 12 Messerschmitts on the job (afterwards I learnt that a second wave of 20 attacked the aerodrome, while I was gaining height). During that climb I suddenly heard a terrific yell over my radio from someone on the ground who was apparently watching the aircraft though they

102

did not know who was the pilot. An agitated voice shouted, 'Hullo Hurricane, look out, beat it, there are five 109s just above and behind you.' Few Hurricanes have ever dived more quickly and vertically! I had just got over that fright and was again climbing when I spotted 12 109s below me, flying south near my aerodrome.

Having the advantage of height I decided that I should at least make one attack on them, even if I did beat it afterwards! Accordingly I positioned myself between them and the sun and dived vertically down on top of the enemy formation, firing all the time (grossly out of range at first) and flattened out just above their heads and pointing in the opposite direction. I had come and gone too quickly for them to do much about me. Gone so quickly in fact that I didn't have time to observe the results of my attack!

On the airfield several aircraft had been destroyed, including one more Hurricane, a Gladiator which was still on the strength of 33 Squadron, and several Greek aircraft.

Larissa, Kalambaki/Vassiliki and Paramythia were not the only targets, however, for at 0750 waves of Bf109s attacked Niamata where six Blenheims were destroyed and four airmen wounded. Two hours later three Bf109s from II/JG27 swept over the airfield and several more Blenheims were rendered unserviceable, two more airmen being wounded. Bofors fire was fairly accurate and two of the attackers were hit, but both got back to Bitolj where one crash-landed. At 1100, four more Bf109s appeared over Niamata and proceeded to destroy four more Blenheims; they were followed by another quartet 45 minutes later, these damaging one more Blenheim and the station Magister communications aircraft. An hour later came the final attack of the day on this field, all remaining Blenheims of 113 Squadron being shot up and rendered unserviceable.

Further south at 0845, 25 Ju88s from I/LG1 and I/KG51 had appeared over Athens where they were intercepted by six Hurricanes of 80 Squadron and four Blenheim Ifs of 30 Squadron. Bill claimed two bombers shot down, Hewett one and one probable, while one each were claimed by Ginger Still and Flt Sgt Jacques Rivalant, one of the French pilots. A sixth was claimed by Dahl. On this, his first operational sortie, and with only seven hours' experience on Hurricanes, Dahl came across six bombers. Attacking from astern he was greeted by a hail of fire from the rear gunners but succeeded in getting on the tail of one:

I was just beginning to realise that I had got myself into the worst possible position for an attacking fighter to be in when suddenly the passage between the mountains on either side narrowed and the Ju88s were forced to go into line astern. This meant that only the last one in the line could shoot at me. That was better. Now there was only a single stream of orange-red bullets coming towards me. David Coke had said, 'Go for one of his engines.' I went a little closer and by jiggling my plane this way and that I managed to get the starboard engine of the bomber into my reflector-sight. I aimed a bit ahead of the engine and pressed the button. The Hurricane gave a small shudder as the eight Brownings in the wings all opened up together, and a second later I saw a huge piece of his metal engine-cowling the size of a dinner-tray go flying up into the air. Good heavens, I thought, I've hit him! I've actually hit him! Then black smoke came pouring out of his engine and very slowly, almost in slow motion, the bomber winged over to starboard and began to lose height.

I throttled back. He was well below me now. I could see him clearly by squinting down out of my cockpit. He wasn't diving and he wasn't spinning either. He was turning slowly over and over like a leaf, the black smoke pouring out from the starboard engine. Then I saw one . . . two . . . three people jump out of the fuselage and go tumbling earthwards with legs and arms outstretched in grotesque attitudes, and a moment later one . . . two . . . three parachutes billowed open and began floating gently down between the cliffs towards the narrow valley below. I watched spellbound. I couldn't believe that I had actually shot down a German bomber. But I was immensely relieved to see the parachutes.

One of these six claims was adjudged to be 80 Squadron's 100th victory of the war. Coke ranged further north and encountered a number of Bf109s – probably aircraft of I(J)/LG2 – and claimed one shot down.

One of the LG1 aircraft, Ll+JK, was flown by Ltn Georg Sattler, who reported seeing his bombs hit an 18,000-ton transport; on the return flight he believed that he saw his target sinking. This was possibly the *Clan Cumming* which had been temporarily repaired after being seriously damaged during the raid on Piraeus during the night of 6/7 April, and had been towed into the Bay of Athens; she now struck a mine and sank. Two other large merchant vessels, the *Goalpara* (5,314 tons) and *Quilloa* (7,765 tons) were both severely damaged by air attack in Eleusis Bay, and both beached. As the Ju88s overflew Eleusis airfield on their return to Krumovo, air gunners sprayed Hurricanes seen about to take off, but no damage was recorded.

Two of I/KG1's aircraft were lost in crash-landings at Krumovo as a result of severe combat damage. Two more of this unit's bombers landed at Salonika with minor damage. An aircraft of I/LG1 failed to return, Uffz Karl Stütz and his crew in Ll+SK being posted missing; a second aircraft crash-landed at Kozani with engine trouble and was completely destroyed (although the crew survived), while a third crash-landed at Salonika with reported AA damage and was written off.

With the German advance now approaching the Olympus–Servia line, and threatening to outflank the defenders, the decision had been taken to begin withdrawal of the Imperial force to Thermopylae. Following the morning attacks on the Allied airfields, Air Vice-Marshal D'Albiac was flown up to Larissa in a Lysander to see for himself the extent of the damage and losses. This was an uneventful sortie, but earlier in the day another Lysander fell victim to German fighters, as recorded by German war correspondent Wolfgang Küchler:

> The men in the Staffel [5./JG77] could not have dreamed that they would once get to know Mount Olympus as soldiers. Sharply defined, as if drawn by ruler, the contours of the snow covered lair of the Greek Gods pass below their fast Me109s. They are flying cover for the German Panzers, which are thrusting into the heart of Greece at Mount Olympus. Cloudless is the sky, excellent the visibility. As far as the pilots can see, they see column after column of German vehicles driving southwards. In an unstoppable advance they push the English ahead of them, who are desperately attempting to stop the German soldiers on the European mainland.
>
> Will Tommy show up in the air today? The men of the Staffel wish, long for it ardently, and they are lucky. Ofw P [Werner Petermann] who is in lead of the 2nd Kette, spots him first. It is single flying English high winged modern type, a reconnaissance aircraft that probably has to report back on German troop movement. 'We're going to spoil this gentleman's party,' Ofw P calls on the radio to his two wingmen. The Tommy doesn't appear to have noticed the German flyers, although he's flying at almost the same altitude as they are. Unsuspectingly, he's flying to and fro, probably pleased he can achieve his objective unhindered.
>
> Just as the Englishman turns in, apparently to start photographing, Ofw P puts the first volley in front of his nose. Up to a hundred metres he has sneaked up on the enemy aircraft and got in a good firing position. The reconnaissance aircraft turns into his adversary. The German doesn't hesitate. The Ofw, whose comrades selflessly let him 'work this case', puts in a second volley before the opposing air gunner readies his machine gun. The lad was perfect in his sight, and the volley is exactly on the adversary's wing and engine.
>
> What happens now, happens very fast, so fast that you can't write in words as fast as it takes place. A giant yellow flame shoots out of the reconnaissance aircraft's engine, then it breaks up in the air like

a rotten piece of wood. Burning, it falls down in two pieces, crashing into a snow-covered mountaintop. Shortly the flames leap up, but then the smoking wreckage collapses like a house of cards.

Ofw P had finished the Tommy with just 20 rounds. It is his 9th aerial victory and his third during the south-eastern operation. But this short aerial combat in view of the Greek Gods, isn't the end of the fighters' mission. There is still fuel for a small detour to a Greek airfield, which lies closely behind the frontline. In a quick low level attack the Staffel dives towards the field. On the airfield machine-gunfire pours down on the aircraft and hangars, and as the Messerschmitts fly away they can clearly see that two parked aircraft have been heavily damaged and that they have effectively hit the aircraft shelters.

As a result of the ground forces' planned withdrawal and the day's air attacks, the airfields at Yannina, Kazaklar, Paramythia, Larissa, Niamata and Almyros were to be evacuated. 33 Squadron's remaining Hurricanes would join 30 and 80 Squadrons at Eleusis, while 112 Squadron's Gladiators would transfer to Hassani. The remaining Blenheims would go to Menidi, from where the Wellington detachments would leave for Shallufa. There was now just a total of 18 Hurricanes, 12 Gladiators, 14 Blenheim fighters, and 22 Blenheim bombers with which to defend mainland Greece.

By now, all was going badly for the Allies. While the Imperial forces were still managing to withdraw in good order across the Plain of Thessaly, improved weather brought them under constant and heavy air attack just at the point at which the cover afforded by the mountains ran out. To the west, the advance of the German units from Skoplje threatened to outflank the gallant but nearly exhausted Army of the Epirus. The offensive against the Italians had already been broken off, while the evacuation of the airfields close behind the front – particularly that at Paramythia – denuded the Greek soldiers of the residue of air cover that they had been enjoying. To ensure the security of these forces, a rapid withdrawal southwards was required, but to give up the territory captured with such sacrifice from the Italians would be quite unacceptable to the troops on morale grounds. All looked hopeless, and during the day Gen Papagos explained to Gen Maitland Wilson the plight of his army and suggested a British withdrawal to save the country from the full devastation of war.

For the RAF, **16 April** proved somewhat quieter as the reorganisation associated with the general withdrawal south was put into effect. During the morning two of 80 Squadron's Hurricanes were successful in intercepting a raid on Khalkis harbour by some 20 Ju88s from I(K)/LG1 and I/KG51. Shorty Graham caught one – probably 9K+FM of KG51, flown by Uffz Johannes Uhlick – and shot it down north-east of Poltika. A second bomber – L1+HL of LG1 flown by Oblt Horst Beeger – was claimed shot down by AA fire into the sea off Khalkis. This was probably the same aircraft pursued by Dahl as it lined up to bomb an ammunition ship in the harbour. He only had time to get off a short burst before overtaking it in a steep dive, and was amazed to see it plunge straight into the sea not far from its intended target. Two other Ju88s were lost in crash-landings subsequent to this sortie, possibly both having suffered damage from AA fire. One came down near Salonika with 40 per cent damage, while the other crashed at Krumovo while trying to land; the latter was a complete write-off, although all crewmembers survived in both aircraft.

During the day Hurricanes of 33 Squadron were sent out either singly or in pairs to provide cover for the convoys crossing the Thessaly Plain. During one such sortie Flg Off Charlie Dyson was ordered to drop a message bag to one convoy north of Lamia, but while attempting to do so, flying low and slow with full flaps down, a bomb exploded just ahead of him, the blast flipping his aircraft over on its back; he just managed to regain control, and returned to Eleusis badly shaken – a bomb splinter had even ripped the oxygen mask off his face! On another sortie Cottingham spotted an Hs126 observation aircraft of 1.(H)/14 'snooping around' and shot this down, Fw Richter, the observer, being killed, although the pilot survived unhurt.

At Eleusis, Sqn Ldr Pattle was now both combat fatigued and ill. Although feverish, he would barely accept medication, let alone consider hospitalisation, and insisted on continuing to fly. Eleusis witnessed the arrival of two Yugoslav SM79s and two Lockheed 10s from Paramythia during the day, all carrying government personnel. That evening a Yugoslav Do17K came in to land at Menidi from the same location, but met an unexpected reception, as AC1 Marcel Comeau, a 33 Squadron airman recorded:

> Its occupants, surviving the blitz upon Paramythia on April 15th and the two more heavy bombing and strafing attacks while their aircraft underwent repairs, did not take kindly to the volume of small-arms fire, which now greeted them from trigger-happy erks at Menidi. The aircraft circled the aerodrome for a full half hour, kept aloft by airmen pot-shooters. When it eventually landed and discharged its voluble cargo of irate, fist-brandishing Yugoslavs, the erks made themselves scarce.[2]

In the opposite direction, two Sunderland flying boats were flown up to Kotor harbour on the Yugoslav coast, ostensibly to evacuate the British Legation party, which was supposed to have made its way there from Belgrade. On arrival there was no sign of the British party, but a number of foreign diplomats and their staff were present, all anxiously awaiting some form of transport. Rather than return empty-handed, the two flying boats flew back with 44 such persons aboard, plus 4 British subjects, one of whom was a wounded Blenheim pilot.

Towards evening six 80 Squadron Hurricanes were again scrambled, this time intercepting bombers – again reported as Ju88s – which were attacking a munitions factory half a mile from Eleusis. Bill and Still each claimed one destroyed near the target, while Hewett chased another to the north and claimed this shot down. These would appear to have been Do17Zs of Stabstaffel/KG2, which lost three such aircraft – reportedly in the Larissa area. These were U5+GA (Ltn Ludwig Rohr); U5+BA (Ltn Heinrich Hunger) and U5+DA (Hptm Konrad Ebsen); all the crews failed to return.

Only one RAF claim was made on **17 April**, when Barker of 80 Squadron set off to drop a message to the 19th Australian Brigade at Katerine. Having completed his task he was intercepted by three Bf109s, apparently from III/JG77, which he managed to evade, claiming one shot down; this was confirmed by the Australian troops. The aircraft was apparently badly damaged, the pilot crash-landing at Oojransko on return. A further Luftwaffe bombing attack on Piraeus sank the Greek vessel *Petrakis Nomikos* (7,020 tons). An Australian war correspondent working for *The Times* wrote:

> For two days I have been bombed, machine-gunned and shot at by all and sundry. German Stukas have blown two cars from under me and have strafed a third . . . All day and all night there have been waves of Germans in the sky. Eighteen Messerschmitts strafed us on the road last evening. Bullets ripped the trucks, and one was destroyed, but nobody was hurt and nothing lost except the truck. Before that, the convoy I was in was attacked seven times in two hours, but not once was the convoy disorganised or broken up. The Germans are using a fantastic amount of aircraft: more than I ever saw in Norway under similar conditions of terrain. Goring must have a third of his air force operating here, and it is bombing every nook and cranny, hamlet, village and town in its path . . .

Following the capitulation of the Yugoslav armies, rumours were rife in Greece that surrender was imminent. The King of the Hellenes was determined that his country should fight on, and resolved to stay in Athens until the last possible moment, although others counselled that he and his government should evacuate to Crete forthwith. At 1245 on **18 April**, 16 Hurricanes from 33 and 80 Squadrons flew low over Athens to strengthen morale among the population, but in the city martial law was declared. During the day the air force was reinforced by the arrival of five more Hurricanes from Egypt, together with new pilots for the two squadrons; these were Flg Off George Noel-Johnson, and Sgts Maurice Bennett, Fred Leveridge, Alec Butterick and Ralph Ware.

The Greek president, Alexander Korizis, was against a retirement to Crete, since he considered that pro-German elements would then seize power on the mainland and seek an armistice. Following an emergency cabinet meeting at which no decision was reached, this unhappy man shot himself, having learned that the commander of the Army of the Epirus, Lt Gen George Tsolakaglou, had initiated negotiations with the German 12th Armee for its surrender. Mr Kodzias, the Governor of Athens, took over as temporary premier until relieved by the King two days later; Emmanuel Tsouderos was then appointed. One of his first actions was to replace Lt Gen Tsolakaglou, and order the Army of Pirus to fight on. It was by then too late, the Army's officers deposing the new commander and continuing their negotiations with the Germans; surrender would take place on 21 April. At this point a British withdrawal from the mainland was agreed between Gen Wavell, the Supreme Commander, and the Greek King, one of the main reasons being the strength of the opposing air forces, and the inability to counter them with the resources and airfields available.

The **19th April** was to prove a busy day for the RAF, beginning at 0635 when Sqn Ldr Pattle was reported to have intercepted bombers approaching Athens, the first of an almost continuous chain of raids throughout the day – and apparently claimed two Ju88s shot down and a third probable. At daybreak Luftwaffe reconnaissance aircraft spotted the Australian, New Zealand and Greek troops retreating across the Thessaly Plain when they were near Pmokos. Soon some 40 Ju87s arrived, bombing and strafing, and causing much damage and confusion, and many casualties.

On this occasion seven Hurricanes of 80 Squadron, led by Timber Woods, arrived in the area and promptly claimed four of the Stukas shot down before escorting Bf109s of II/JG27 could intervene. Cheering troops reported seeing at least three of these crash; two were claimed by Bill flying V7134, and one each by Dowding and Rivalant. Apparently two Ju87s were lost, one from Stab/StG2, flown by Oblt Sebastian Ulitz with Obfw Emil Kuklau, which crashed south-west of Elasson with the death of the crew, and one of I/StG3 which crash-landed near Kozani, Ltn Herbert Wingelmayer being killed and his gunner wounded. The escorting Messerschmitts then attacked, two Hurricanes being claimed shot down, one each by Oblt Wilhelm Wiesinger and Uffz Alfred Heidel; in fact, only Casbolt's aircraft was hit, and he was able to return to Eleusis without undue trouble. He claimed to have damaged one of the attackers, and Eldon Trollip to have shot one down, but no Messerschmitts were hit on this occasion.

Further defensive patrols were made by the Hurricanes, one at 0758 seeing nothing, while at 0920 seven 33 Squadron aircraft were led off by Pattle to cover the Lamia area, where the Army was still hard-pressed as it approached the end of its current withdrawal. Here a lone Hs126 from 1.(H)/23 was seen

– 6K+AH flown by Fw Herman Wilhus. Although the slow reconnaissance machine was flying very low, Pattle led his section down onto its tail and fired a brief burst into it. His attack was followed by Woodward, and then by Flt Lt Littler, after which the Henschel caught fire, tipped forward and crashed in flames. The Hurricanes regrouped and continued their patrol for another half an hour when an estimated nine Bf109s (actually six aircraft from 8./JG77) were encountered head-on.

Pattle's quick reactions allowed him to get on the tail of one Messerschmitt, and he reported that following his attack it went down in a glide, flipped over and crashed into the ground inverted. The sky was now full of dogfighting aircraft, but Pattle managed to get on the tail of another Bf109, which he spotted flying low down in a valley towards Lamia. He believed that he had killed the pilot with his first burst, as this aircraft went into a dive and crashed. Meanwhile, Woodward had claimed a further Messerschmitt, as had Plt Off Moir, while Littler and Flt Lt Mitchell both claimed damage to others. In return Moir's aircraft was badly hit and he was forced down at Amphiklia, where the Hurricane was later destroyed as there were no spares available to repair it. Mitchell's aircraft was also hard hit, but he was able to get back and force-land at Eleusis.

Three Hurricanes were claimed shot down by the German pilots, one each by Oblt Kurt Ubben, Ltn Hans Schopper and Obfw Erwin Riehl. However, Ubben's aircraft was badly damaged and he force-landed in Allied lines (from where he was rescued), while the Staffelkapitän of 9./JG77, Oblt Armin Schmidt, was shot down and killed north-east of Lamia. Ubben later related his story to German war correspondent Hans-Joachim Volland:

> We were en route with six Me109s when eight aircraft met us on an opposite course. We couldn't recognise them and took up an offensive position as a precaution. They were Hurricanes. The first one, which I took a shot at, turned tail, but the second one went down. Just as I pulled up, I suddenly saw three Hurricanes behind me, whose tracer was sprayed at me. I wanted to dive down, but just at this critical moment the engine let me down. An emergency landing was my only option. I had to land 20km behind the front.
>
> I took all the important charts and documents with me, destroyed the aircraft and made for home on foot. It was blazing hot. At midday I lay down to rest in the reeds of a small river. Suddenly I saw people coming towards me from two sides, who had obviously found me. I drew my pistol, but then they tied a white handkerchief to a stick, and raised their hands. I made it apparent through hand signals that I didn't have any hostile intent. They were Greek peasants who invited me to come to their village. In the village two heavily armed

policemen awaited me. However the villagers were against my arrest. The argument was still going on in full, when I suddenly heard the familiar engine sound of a Me109. It was my wingman (Kaczmarek) Oberfeldwebel Riehl, who was looking for me and flew over the village at low level. I waved as hard as I could. He flew two more turns, shortly after which a Fieseler Storch landed in the middle of the small village square. Out of it came our Gruppenarzt (Group doctor) who had organised the rescue. The two policemen were disarmed by their fellow villagers and shortly thereafter I was flying home in a Storch with a Me109 fighter escort.[3]

A third Messerschmitt flown by Oblt Werner Patz, was also hit and crash-landed at Larissa during the day, but there is no definite confirmation that he had been involved in the fight with 33 Squadron. Ltn Ekke-Eberhard Reinbrecht of I(J)/LG2 also claimed a Hurricane during the day.

By now Pattle's condition had worsened to a point where Sqn Ldr Tap Jones, acting as Wing Commander, Eleusis, ordered him to reduce his flying and to take off only when the air-raid alarm sounded. Pattle took him at his word, and was in the air again with Casbolt when the alarm went off at 1450. The two flew around for some time without seeing anything, and became separated before Pattle at last saw two aircraft over Khalkis harbour – Casbolt had found the raiders, and as Pattle watched, the Ju88 he was attacking went down trailing black smoke. Pattle then spotted another bomber heading north and diving for its lines. Giving chase, he soon caught up and attacked, reporting that it dived into the sea after its crew had baled out. One Ju88 was indeed reported lost in this area, 9K+EK of I/KG51 failing to return, although the Gruppenkommandeur, Hptm Heinrich Hahn, who was abroad, survived to return to his unit. A second Ju88 from I/LG1 flown by Hptm Siegfried von Eickhorn crash-landed at Salonika – reportedly due to icing-up – the pilot being injured.

Apparently, Pattle was again involved in an interception at 1820, when according to his fitter's diary he engaged a number of Bf109s, claiming one shot down and possibly a second, but no further losses were recorded by the Luftwaffe in such circumstances. Two Do17Zs were lost by I/KG2 during the day, both apparently to small-arms fire from Imperial infantry, one crew being lost and one surviving, while another Dornier from III/KG2 suffered severe AA damage. Over this hectic period Dahl flew a dozen sorties in four days:

> And each one of us knew that every time a sortie was made, somebody was probably going to get killed, either a Hun or the man in the Hurricane. I figured that the betting on every flight was about even money against coming back. Like all the others, I was always sent

up alone. Sometimes I was over Piraeus harbour, chasing some Ju88s that were bombing the shipping there. Sometimes I was around the Lamia area, trying to deter the Luftwaffe from blasting away our retreating army. Once or twice I met bombers over Athens itself. On three occasions my Hurricane was badly shot up, but the riggers in 80 Squadron were magicians at patching up holes in the fuselage or mending a broken spar.

Despite its losses, the RAF continued to operate – although next day (**20 April**) was to be its ultimate nemesis. Faced by the continued successful resistance of the British air units, the Luftwaffe now launched a sustained attack on the Athens area. At dawn two Hurricanes from 80 Squadron were up on patrol, but although hostile aircraft were reported approaching, none were seen. Soon 12 more Hurricanes were airborne from Eleusis, six drawn from each of the squadrons, and these began to patrol to the south of Domokos. Again no Luftwaffe aircraft were seen, but as the formation headed for home a lone Do17Z of 8./KG2 was encountered near Larissa – probably US+ES, flown by Ltn Gert Laurinat. It was at once engaged by several Hurricanes and shot down into the sea, but Frank Holman's aircraft appeared to be hit by return fire and he broke away to make a belly-landing in a field near Megara. Striking an obstruction, the Hurricane flipped over on its back, the pilot's neck being broken in the crash.

Between 0550 and 0650, 36 Bf109s of Stab, II and III/JG77, five of them carrying bombs, attacked shipping targets around Athens, claiming a direct hit on a 3,000-ton steamer and a near miss on a 1,500-ton vessel. A *Schwarm* from III Gruppe broke off to attack Menidi airfield, where they claimed five Blenheims destroyed on the ground. Several were indeed badly hit, and an ancient Valentia biplane transport went up in flames. About an hour later a formation of Bf110s from II/ZG26, led by Oblt Ralph von Rettburg, made a second strafe of the airfield. AC1 Marcel Comeau of 33 Squadron graphically described the action:

> Preceded by a terrified assortment of stray dogs racing across the landing ground, the 110 destroyers hit Menidi. Bellies scraping the grass, they flashed past as if propelled by the rhythmic thumping of their cannons. Suddenly the aerodrome was alight with Bofors and small-arms fire. A Greek Junkers burst into flames on the hangar apron. A Blenheim collapsed suddenly on a broken oleo. The noise was terrific. So low were the Messerschmitts flying that a nearby Bofors sent a burst into another Bofors across the aerodrome, killing the officer in charge. Then they were diving back for a second run in. Out in the open a bunch of eight Aussie soldiers having a late breakfast alternated between taking mouthfuls of tinned sausage and rifle-

potting the passing aircraft. A dozen columns of smoke arose among the Blenheims.

Two hours later at 0945, two 80 Squadron Hurricanes were dispatched to intercept German aircraft reported to be attacking Khalkis harbour, where the Greek *Moscha L. Goulandri* (5,199 tons) was bombed and sunk. As the two Hurricanes approached, they were engaged by three Bf109s from Stab/JG27, Plt Off Ginger Still promptly being shot down and killed near Tanagra by Maj Wolfgang Schellmann, while Sgt Bennett's aircraft was badly damaged, although he managed to return to Eleusis. Still's body was found next day in the burned-out remains of his Hurricane by members of a Repair & Salvage Unit (RSU) on its way to Lamia airfield. LAC Frank Paul recalled:

> Before reaching the airfield at Lamia we were stopped in a Greek village and told of an aircraft that had been shot down the day before. We found the burnt-out remains of the crashed Hurricane [V7748] and the body of one Pilot Officer Still. The only identification to be found was his name on the inside of his oxygen mask. He had many wounds that had not bled. I had picked up and handled dead bodies before and many since but I have never forgotten that day. A Greek farmer was standing nearby; he had brought a spade with which he dug a shallow grave. We left the scene promising to stop on the way back.
>
> We stopped again at the site of the grave of P/O Still on our return journey. It was getting dark and we were hungry and worried. We made a makeshift cross and placed it at the head of the grave. We stood each side of the grave; Sgt Wallis ordered us to attention and said, 'We salute a very gallant gentleman.' Then we walked back to our vehicles. We were told by a local Greek that P/O Still had taken on four Me109s and had shot down one before he himself had died.

By midday formations of Luftwaffe bombers and fighters were roaming over the plains of southern Greece at will, bombing and strafing almost with impunity, although the few Hurricanes at Eleusis were constantly going out on patrol. Bill Winsland of 33 Squadron later wrote:

> Somehow or other during that hectic day though I went up a number of times I never made contact with the enemy. There was a good deal of cloud about amongst which their bombers and fighters sneaked in and out. Every time we spotted any machines they hopped into the clouds so that we were often unable to get any 'duck-shooting' at all. Others however had very different stories to tell. Every time they went up they ran into absolutely hordes of the bastards! Though I never fired my guns that day I honestly think it made me an older man.

I was on edge every second. Every speck on my windscreen was an enemy, every bird behind me was a Hun; my head was all but twisted off my neck with continuously looking round behind my tail. In and around every cloud I expected to come up against one of those hordes. I honestly thought I was bound to 'catch my packet' that day. We all thought the same deep down somewhere.

At about 1400, 29 Bf109s from II and III/JG77 appeared over Eleusis and Tanagra airfields, Sqn Ldr Pattle engaging one formation from III Gruppe and claiming two shot down during a brief combat. One of these is believed to have been the aircraft flown by 9 Staffel's Uffz Fritz Borchert, which failed to return, while the second – Black 10 of 4./JG27 flown by Obfw Fritz Röckel whose shin had been shattered by a bullet – crash-landed at Larissa. Dahl witnessed Röckel's arrival:

> The plane hit the ground on its belly with a fearful scrunch of tearing metal and it slid on for about 30 yards before stopping. I saw several of our people running out to help the pilot and someone had a red fire-extinguisher in his hand and then they were out of sight in the black smoke and trying to get the German out of the plane. When we saw them again they were hauling him by his arms away from the fire and then a pick-up truck drove out and they put him in the back.

Eleusis came under further attack by II/JG27's Messerschmitts, their fire destroying several aircraft including two 33 Squadron Hurricanes and two of the three surviving Greek fighters here. Dahl later wrote of the attack:

> There were many 109s circling the aerodrome, and one by one they straightened out and dived past the hangars, spraying the ground with their guns. But they did something else. They slid back their cockpit hoods and as they came past they threw out small bombs which exploded when they hit the ground and fiercely flung quantities of large lead balls in every direction . . . then I saw the men, the ground crews, standing up in their slit trenches firing at the Messerschmitts with their rifles, reloading and firing as fast as they could, cursing and shouting as they shot, aiming ludicrously, hopelessly, aiming at an aeroplane with just a rifle. At Eleusis there were no other defences. Suddenly the Messerschmitts all turned and headed for home, all except one, which glided down and made a smooth belly-landing on the aerodrome.

Dahl continued:

> Then there was chaos. The Greeks around us raised a shout and jumped on to the fire tender and headed out towards the crashed

German aeroplane. At the same time more Greeks streamed out from every corner of the field, shouting and yelling and crying for the blood of the pilot. It was mob intent upon vengeance and one could not blame them.

Fortunately for Röckel, RAF personnel reached him first and he was lifted from the cockpit and driven to the Medical Officer for emergency treatment. Winsland had a narrow escape during this attack:

> I was enjoying the luxury of a hot bath, when suddenly all hell was let loose on the building; two cannon shells smashed through the window over the bath and exploded against the tiled wall three feet to my right, and just below the level of the top of the good old-fashioned cast iron bath. Bits of concrete and shell hit the outside of the bath without penetrating it, and the window glass spent its force against the inside top edge before falling quite gently onto the water and settling down all over me without actually cutting me or damaging the 'family jewels' at all!

Sqn Ldr Pattle was airborne at the time the attack developed, and came upon a Ju88, which he claimed shot down. He then returned to Eleusis to replenish his ammunition ready for the next attack. Following the assault on the airfield, there had been a pause in activity which allowed a little time for the ground crews to bring the maximum possible number of Hurricanes up to readiness state. Sqn Ldr Jones decided that if no further attack had developed by 1800, all available Hurricanes would undertake an offensive sweep in an effort to raise morale among the civilian population of Athens and the surrounding areas, and as a boost to the defenders of Eleusis as well as to the pilots themselves.

At about 1645 a formation of 100 plus Ju88s and Do17s, escorted by Bf109s and 110s was reported approaching Athens. The Junkers – aircraft of LG1 – peeled off to make low-flying attacks on shipping at Piraeus, while individual Bf110s of II/ZG26 scoured the area, shooting up likely targets. One appeared over Eleusis just as the Hurricanes – 9 of 33 Squadron and 6 of 80 Squadron – were preparing to take off. Fortunately, none were hit, and all took to the air individually, climbing to 20,000ft. They headed for Piraeus, forming sections of two or three en route.

The first trio to arrive over the port, flown by Wickham, Starrett and Flg Off Ping Newton, caught 15 Ju88s dive-bombing ships in the harbour; indeed, the Greek hospital ship *Ellenis* was sunk during the attack. The three Hurricanes followed them down and attacked as they pulled out of their dives; Wickham claimed one shot down, while the Rhodesian Newton claimed two more. Just then Bill arrived on the scene, reporting seeing some 30 Ju88s:

I carried out eight attacks on the Ju88s. One caught fire and started going down. I left him and attacked another. Big chunks broke away from his wings and fuselage, and smoke poured from his engines. He went down vertically. I was then attacked by a 109, but I easily outmanoeuvred him, had a crack at some more, and came home when my ammo was exhausted.

One Ju88 flown by Uffz Helmut Behnke (L1+ZH) was lost near Athens with all the crew (Gfr Emmerich Döhndorfer, Obgfr Fritz Steckel and Obgfr Josef Kalusa); a second, L1+UK, piloted by Ltn Werner Ziegler, was hit by a Hurricane's fire and the navigator, Gfr Heinrich Baumgartner, received three bullets in the head and neck, dying almost at once. The gunners believed that they had shot down the attacking fighter, reporting seeing it fall into the sea near Kalamaki (it was probably the crash of Behnke's Ju88 they had seen, or the explosion of bombs). A second Hurricane then attacked, putting the starboard engine out of action. This was also claimed hit by Gfr Hans Baumann, the radio operator/air gunner, and was seen making for land. However, the Ju88 was rapidly losing height and although the crew threw out all removable equipment to reduce weight, it ditched in shallow water near Karies, at the foot of Mount Athos. The remaining members of the crew survived the crash. A third Ju88 suffered engine trouble/damage, but struggled back to Krumovo, where it crash-landed.

The Hurricane hit by Baumann was probably that flown by Harry Starrett, which caught fire as a result. Starrett decided to fly back to Eleusis to attempt to save his aircraft, and Winsland witnessed his approach, wheels-up:

> A Hurricane came in, in flames from end to end, to try and land at Eleusis. He was holding off, going up and down between 50 and 100 feet, being terribly burnt no doubt, and feeling for the ground, almost certainly being unable to see it, except possibly at right angles sideways. He soon hit the ground very hard.

The Hurricane had almost slid to a halt when the glycol tank blew up and the aircraft was enveloped in flames. Starrett managed to get out, but had been very severely burned; he was rushed to hospital but died two days later.

Four more 80 Squadron Hurricanes now joined the battle, Timber Woods leading Casbolt, and the Frenchman Wintersdorff, to attack a formation identified as Bf110s, but probably composed of Do17Zs from I and III/KG2, escorted by the twin-engined Messerschmitts. Woods carried out two or three separate attacks, believing that he had probably shot down two before breaking off to return to Eleusis to rearm. Wintersdorff claimed one aircraft shot down in flames, which he identified as an Fw187 (*sic*), but he was then attacked by a Bf110 and wounded in one leg; his Hurricane was hard hit and he baled out into the sea from where he was soon rescued. Casbolt claimed two aircraft as Bf110s, but was also then attacked from astern and had his rudder shot away. Breaking away, he encountered a Bf109, which he reported he had shot down in flames. Meanwhile, the fourth pilot, Hewett, found himself above six Bf109s and later reported:

> I dived on the rear one, and he rolled on his back, and crashed to the ground with smoke pouring out. I made a similar attack on a second, and the pilot baled out. Then I had a go at a third, but didn't see what happened this time.

These Messerschmitts were possibly from III/JG77, two aircraft from this unit crash-landing, badly damaged. Three Do17Zs also failed to return: US+AL (Uffz Helmut Rien), U5+HL (Ltn Joachim Brüdern) and U5+AR (Oblt Ludger Holtkampe) were all lost with their crews. Apparently Bf109s from 4/JG27 were also involved in combat at this time, possibly with the 80 Squadron aircraft. Oblt Gustav Rödel claimed three Hurricanes shot down in just over ten minutes, while Obfw Otto Schulz claimed another.

At Eleusis the returning Hurricanes were being refuelled and rearmed as swiftly as possible, before climbing back into the fray. Sqn Ldr Pattle was by now very ill with influenza, his temperature having been recorded as 103 degrees. Nonetheless he took off with Woodward, following Timber Woods, who was now off for the second time. Pattle and Woodward had not taken off before, as their aircraft had not been ready. Woodward recalled:

> I took off late with Sqn Ldr Pattle – we climbed into a swarm of Ju88s protected by masses of Messerschmitt 110s. We were overwhelmed. In sun I recall shooting a 110 off Pattle's tail, in flames, then probably a Ju88. Shortly afterwards Pattle got a confirmed Ju88 (or Bf110). Subsequently I lost contact with him, then damaged three more 110s. Then, being out of ammunition returned tentatively to Eleusis. It was all over – for that day.

Ahead of Woodward, Pattle was seen going to the aid of the Hurricane flown by Woods, which was being attacked by a Bf110. He opened fire at this aircraft and it was seen to burst into flames (presumably the aircraft Woodward had seen him destroy), just as Woods's Hurricane also caught fire and dived into Eleusis Bay. Two more Messerschmitts latched onto the tail of Pattle's aircraft and it quickly began to blaze. There was an explosion, and the wreckage fell into the sea. Kettlewell arrived on the scene just in time to see the demise of his gallant leader and attacked one of the two Messerschmitts responsible, shooting this down into the bay also. He too was then attacked by another, and was forced to bale out. He landed heavily, cracking two vertebrae in his spine. Yet another Hurricane was falling to the 110s at this time. Cottingham had claimed three of the big Zerstörer in flames, but he was hit by a fourth and wounded, baling out of his stricken aircraft.

Probably one of the last pilots in the air was Dahl, who saw numbers of aircraft before attacking a Ju88, which was already going down to ditch in the sea. He was shot at by the aircraft's gunners even as it started to settle in the water! Dahl managed to get his badly damaged Hurricane – the result of earlier tussles with Messerschmitts – back to Eleusis:

> Over Athens on that morning, I can remember seeing our tight little formation of Hurricanes all peeling away and disappearing among the swarms of enemy aircraft, and from then on, wherever I looked I saw an endless blur of enemy fighters whizzing towards me from every side.
>
> They came from above and they came from behind and they made frontal attacks from dead ahead, and I threw my Hurricane around as best I could and whenever a Hun came into my sights, I pressed the button. It was truly the most breathless, and in a way the most exhilarating time I have ever had in my life. I caught glimpses of planes with black smoke pouring from their engines. I saw planes with pieces of metal flying off their fuselages. I saw the bright-red flashes coming from the wings of the Messerschmitts as they fired their guns, and once I saw a man whose Hurricane was in flames climb calmly out on to a wing and jump off.
>
> I stayed with them until I had no ammunition left in my guns. I had done a lot of shooting, but whether I had shot anyone down or had even hit any of them I could not say. I did not dare to pause for even a fraction of a second to observe results. The sky was so full of aircraft that half my time was spent in actually avoiding collisions. I am quite sure that the German planes must have often got in each other's way because there were so many of them, and that, together with the fact that there were so few of us, probably saved quite a number of our skins.
>
> When I finally had to break away and dive for home, I knew my Hurricane had been hit. The controls were very soggy and there was no response at all to the rudder. But you can turn a plane after a fashion with the ailerons alone, and that is how I managed to steer the plane back. Thank heavens the undercarriage came down when I engaged the lever, and I landed more or less safely at Eleusis. I taxied to a parking place, switched off the engine and slid back the hood. I sat there for at least one minute, taking deep gasping breaths. I was quite literally overwhelmed by the

feeling that I had been into the very bowels of the fiery furnace and had managed to claw my way out. All around me now the sun was shining and wild flowers were blossoming in the grass of the airfield, and I thought how fortunate I was to be seeing the good earth again. Two airmen, a fitter and a rigger, came trotting up to my machine. I watched them as they walked slowly all the way round it. Then the rigger, a balding middle-aged man, looked up at me and said, 'Blimey mate, this kite's got so many 'oles in it, it looks like it's made out of chicken-wire!'

I remember walking over to the little wooden Operations Room to report my return and as I made my way slowly across the grass of the landing field I suddenly realised that the whole of my body and all my clothes were dripping with sweat. The weather was warm in Greece at that time of year and we wore only khaki shorts and khaki shirt and stockings even when we flew, but now those shorts and shirt and stockings had all changed colour and were quite black with wetness. So was my hair when I removed my helmet. I had never sweated like that before in my life, even after a game of squash or rugger. The water was pouring off me and dripping to the ground.

At the door of the Ops Room three or four other pilots were standing around and I noticed that each one of them was as wet as I was. I put a cigarette between my lips and struck a match. Then I found that my hand was shaking so much I couldn't put the flame to the end of the cigarette. The doctor, who was standing nearby, came up and lit it for me. I looked at my hands again. It was ridiculous the way they were shaking. It was embarrassing. I looked at the other pilots. They were all holding cigarettes and their hands were all shaking as much as mine were. But I was feeling pretty good. I had stayed up there for thirty minutes and they hadn't got me. They got five of our twelve Hurricanes in that battle.

The Hurricane pilots were credited with 20 shot down, the breakdown of types differing in various reports; this account considers the claims to have been for five Ju88s, eight Bf110s, one Fw187 (*sic*), one Do17 and five Bf109s. Eight were also listed as probables, including seven twin-engined types and a Bf109. Fourteen of the twenty 'confirmed' were claimed during the final battle, as were the eight probables; ground defences claimed two more Bf109s shot down. For the RAF, the greatest loss had to be that of Sqn Ldr Pattle, who in his last battle had accounted for what may well have been his 50th victory, by far the top-scoring RAF pilot of the war:

In terms of heroism in the face of odds, the pilots of these 15 fighters deserve to rank with the heroes of the Battle of Britain. They destroyed

22 enemy aircraft, perhaps eight more, but in the action they lost a third of their number. And that indeed constituted a Pyrrhic victory.[4]

During this day of incessant combat, the Luftwaffe claimed fourteen Hurricanes and one Spitfire (sic) shot down, whereas eight Hurricanes had actually been lost, and a ninth badly damaged; four pilots had been killed (Pattle, Woods, Holman, and Still), one died subsequently (Starrett), two were wounded (Wintersdorff and Cottingham) and one injured (Kettlewell). The victories were credited to II/JG27 (four) and five to 5./ZG26 which, led by Hptm Theodor Rossiwall, claimed five Hurricanes shot down in this engagement, one each by Rossiwall himself, Oblt Sophus Baagoe, Obfw Hermann Schonthier, Uffz Fritz Müller and Obfw Theodor Pietschmann. Two of the Gruppe's aircraft were lost in return, 3U+EN (Oblt Kurt Specka/Uffz Günther Franke) and 3U+FN (Fw Georg Leinfelder), while a third crash-landed with severe damage. Claimants for the remaining five were uncertain, but probably pilots of 4 and 6./ZG26. Total Luftwaffe losses amounted to four Do17Zs, two Ju88s, three Bf110s and five Bf109s (one of which crashed into a hillside in bad visibility).

It was the virtual end of the RAF in Greece. No Blenheims, no Wellingtons and only a handful of war-weary Hurricanes.[5]

The Germans pressed their advantage next morning (**21 April**), starting at Eleusis, which was attacked between 0700 and 0730 by 20 Ju87s and escorting Bf109s, which strafed. It had become apparent from previous attacks that the Luftwaffe hoped to take Eleusis for their own early use, and while strafing attacks had been made, no bombs had been dropped. Although several Hurricanes had been damaged in these attacks, few had been destroyed, and with the realisation that bombers would probably not appear, the damaged aircraft had been moved into one of the hangars where they could be repaired reasonably free from attack. Other units of the Luftwaffe were busy elsewhere. Fw Johann Pichler of 7./JG77 wrote:

> On 21 April, Oblt [Wolfdieter] Huy and myself made a dive attack on Allied troop transports off Athens. We then received the order to move to Tanagra where all elements of our Gruppe gathered to be united after a long time. We were pleased to have food again from our field kitchen, for during our moves we had lived only on what the British troops had left during their retreat; corned beef and biscuits, served warm and cold alternatively, plus some jam. This food was unpalatable and was not sufficient to keep us fit. In May, we also suffered considerably from the great heat and, in the days when we sat at readiness in the cockpits of our Emils in temperatures up to 40°C, we felt like dried plums. Our cook, though, did his best to get us back on our feet again.

Bill (in V7134) flew a defensive patrol over the Larissa area during the early morning, he and his No. 2 meeting a Do17 at 0800, which they jointly claimed shot down. This was a reconnaissance machine from Stab/StG2 – T6+GA flown by Obfw Josef Engler – that crashed nearby with the injured crew (Oblt Gottfried Kupfer and Obfw Fritz Kremer) being taken prisoner. During the evening German air reconnaissance information indicated that the British defence line consisted of light field fortifications, the construction of which did not seem to have progressed beyond the initial stage. Other air reconnaissance reports showed that British troops were being evacuated from Salamis; 20 large and 15 small ships were loading troops in the port of Piraeus, 4 large and 31 small ones at Khalkis. Heavy anti-aircraft fire was encountered over the ports of re-embarkation. A German war correspondent wrote of this period:

Two fighter pilots report back from a sortie. On route they report hundreds of vehicles. All going to the south-east. There was no identification for the air force, so they strafed them with cannon and machine-gunfire. 'You are absolutely sure that they were Tommies?' 'Yes Herr Major.'

The Major has his doubts. The Kommodore turns to his adjutant. 'Fly with the *Kriegsberichter* [war reporter] to clear up this case. Take the Storch, but don't take risks. And fast it has to be if we want to catch anything.'

Junkers land, throwing up sand in unbelievable amounts of dust. They bring bombs and fuel. We have to wait for minutes with the propeller turning till the dust settles. Then we climb over the 1,400 metre-high mountains. The coastal road can be seen. It lies under heavy fire. If it is artillery or bombs can't be seen yet. From the direction of the Thermopylae, across the valley, comes a Do17.

Straight ahead the city of Lamia. On the road to Thermopylae – vehicles. They're German. They drive toward the fire that lies at the entrance of the valley. On the roadside two planes are parked. A Henschel Hs126 is just landing. Also a scout plane. We can find out what we want to know right here. We land and roll to the end of the hayfield. Oddly enough not a soul in sight. Only a herd of cattle is near by. A fountain of mud and dirt goes upwards between the animals and a detonation rings. Two of the cows stay down, the others continue to graze. Enviable stupidity.

Now I see the men who belong to the plane. In a shallow trench they have taken cover. The place is under artillery fire, which is unusual for an airfield. Between two impacts we jump into the shallow trench. When one lies flat it gives some shelter. A Feldwebel gives us the story.

The tank spearheads broke though Thermopylae but on both sides off the pass the Tommies still have the high ground and fire with multiple batteries on the road and . . . well . . . on us. For the last hour our own artillery has taken position and shells the retreating Brits.

'Is the position of the British batteries already spotted?' 'Yes Herr Leutnant, I was just there. May I note it on your map? A few Stukas and if they . . .' 'Enough, shouts my pilot. Within a half hour they will be there! Two Staffeln should be enough. But now we have to go.'

I need two men to start up the Storch. 'Who will lend a hand?' A few heads are raised and look at each other. Four men get up. With no rush they walk towards us. For decency's sake we have to get up too. Again the sky screams. We take two men and walk towards the machine. We have to take cover twice. The strikes are in rapid succession of the firing, that between the horrible screams there is ample time to take cover. Hopefully the engine will start immediately. While the men start the Storch I can take two pictures of hits. The next one is as close as 40 metres. The engine is smart and starts right away. We hightail out of there.

30 minutes later, the Ju87s, two Staffeln as the adjutant promised, rain down their deadly cargo on the British batteries. They will be silent forever.

Bill and Tap Jones were still at Larissa, as was a detachment of 33 Squadron Hurricanes. Tap apparently enquired what Bill was going to do about Janina. He replied that he would take her with him to Crete, and if all other means failed, he would fly her there in a Gladiator. This proved an unnecessary risky venture, and passage was secured for her aboard one of the last departing ships. War correspondent John Hetherington later wrote:

The freighter *Elsie* probably grossed about 2,000 tons. She was in the Aegean trade in peacetime. She was in no way an imposing ship, but that night she looked to me more lovely than the *Queen Mary*. She meant escape; at least, the chance of escape. She lay beside a wooden wharf at Piraeus. Men and women were streaming on board. The port was in darkness – a pathetic precaution against raids by the Luftwaffe which it had pinpointed to the inch – but electric bulbs burned dimly at intervals in the *Elsie*'s 'tween-decks. Their light splashed on to the wharf through the open ports by which the refugees were boarding the ship. It lit the faces of men and women, and on those faces was written every shade of emotion. Fear, sorrow, despair, hysterical gaiety, steady courage were there.

There was a good sprinkling of British civilians, children as well as men and women. Some were from Athens. Others had moved south as

Germans had occupied country after country in the Balkans, and now they were on the run again. There were a few Greek women, smuggled on board by sympathetic or romantic soldiers. One of them was married a week or so later in a little church in Crete to the Australian driver who had helped her escape. There were soldiers, British and Australian. Most of them wore tin hats and carried their arms.

It seems likely that Janina was among the passengers aboard the *Elsie*; if not, she would have had a similar experience in her escape from Greece. Almost every vessel that could make the journey from the mainland to Crete had already done so, or would be following if able. John Hetherington continued:

> German bombers had been battering Piraeus at intervals of a day or so for a fortnight. The port had already been raided once that day, and we knew that the bombers would come again. The nerves of every man and woman on board the *Elsie* were drawn fine. Only one thing helped us. Physical tiredness had dulled the nerves of most of us so that we were incapable of grasping the full measure of the peril.

In *Elsie's* hold were upwards of 100 German prisoners, mainly Luftwaffe aircrew who had been shot down and captured during the past few days. They lay or lounged against the bulkheads in a generally jovial mood, confident that they would soon be released when their countrymen overwhelmed Crete. On the other hand, should the Luftwaffe target *Elsie* as she made her escape, their fate would be sealed. A mile out to sea, German bombers arrived over the port and proceeded to blast the few remaining ships. But *Elsie* was unharmed. The mountains of Crete were in sight by about mid-morning but shortly thereafter two Do17s appeared, and all on board feared the worst. They turned out to be survivors of the Yugoslav Air Force, also heading towards the island. By mid-afternoon, with the old freighter heading into Suda Bay, a flight of SM79s appeared overhead and released their bombs among the many vessels in port, sinking a Greek freighter. Again *Elsie's* luck held, as it did when German bombers arrived as the passengers were disembarking. They may have reached Crete, but they had not reached safety.

Meanwhile, Frank Paul and his RSU detachment had reached the abandoned airfield at Lamia:

> We pressed on to Lamia airfield to find it deserted. Whatever British squadron had been there had left days before. A few Greek aircraft stood about and we found the Hurricane we had come to repair or collect. It stood alone near some olive trees. It had severe flak damage to the fuselage but could be repaired at Hassani and rendered airworthy again. That was the decision made by Sgt Wallis. We set

about removing the main plane's propeller to load on the flat-topped articulator; we did this as quickly as possible to be off back to Hassani. The air stank of trouble and many Me109s buzzed about.

As we worked two 109s arrived. They circled and 'scrutinised' from the air. We tried to look as if we were not there by getting under the olive trees and staying still. They circled once then made several strafing runs at the other side of the airfield. We waited for our turn but they buzzed off. There's nothing like hostile 109s to speed up a job on an airfield. We worked like mad to get away. Before we had finished loading the fuselage of the Hurricane we had another visit by the Luftwaffe. This time four Me109s. It seemed as though they had come especially to shoot us up. They did. Calmly circling the airfield they then came back line astern, out of the sun.

A Greek Blenheim, an old Dornier and what looked like an old Avro Tutor were strafed and set alight. We cringed under the olive trees waiting our turn. One hears the bullets smacking the ground or the target about a second or two before one hears the cannon. 'Don't move' was the rule. The olive tree trunk is about nine-inches thick so one breathes out to feel thinner. The Luftwaffe knew very well that we hid in the olive trees. They strafed at random. One wishes to look and see where the aircraft are, usually the attacking aircraft will come out of the sun. Even if one can see it coming it's impossible to tell what he's aiming to strafe. All one can do is cringe and hope. They made several attacks with very short bursts to preserve ammunition. Everything except our Hurricane was on fire or ruined by machine gun bullets.

Two Greeks in a gun pit kept banging away with a heavy cannon; it was something like an early anti-tank cannon. Unfortunately they had been seen and received the attention of one of the 109s. We could not believe that we had not been seen. Although we must have been visible those four pilots did not strafe our position. Perhaps they had not learnt by that time that our hiding place was under the few olive trees nearby. Eventually they ran out of ammunition. Needless to say we finished loading our vehicles and got moving as fast as possible. The airfield was littered with wrecked and still burning aircraft. Nothing could be done about it.

From Eleusis, soon after dawn on **22 April**, six Hurricanes were flown down to Megara – including Bill in V7134. The landing ground, 10 miles south, was no more than a field on the coast, surrounded by olive groves. Here as soon as it was light, several hundred local villagers – old men, women and children – appeared and scattered armfuls of heather and bracken over the flattened grass in an attempt to camouflage the new strip. The fighters were hidden among the gnarled olive trees, not being called upon for action throughout the day. That evening they were ordered to move on to Argos where a further dozen flyable Hurricanes from Eleusis had arrived a few hours earlier in various states of repair. Nervy Greek gunners had opened fire as the first of the Hurricanes arrived, and one had been badly damaged. Argos was another smallish field among the olive groves, the pilots finding that the closeness of the trees gave them some problems when landing. A Greek training field, Argos was to be shared with large numbers of elderly aircraft; all machines were dispersed among the groves. Ground defence was provided by local Greek troops with two Bofors guns and two Hotchkiss machine guns; in the confusion the British AA unit allocated to defend the airfield had gone to the wrong location.

At Argos on the morning of **23 April**, ground crews were working hard in very primitive conditions to get as many Hurricanes as possible serviceable, but many tools and spare parts had been lost during the retreat, and only sufficient aircraft would be readied for limited patrols and reconnaissance sorties. During one reconnaissance during the late morning Bill (in V7134) encountered a Do17 near the airfield and chased it away, claiming damage; it is possible that this was 5K+DS of 8./KG3, reported shot down by AA near Corinth, in which Uffz Hans Wiesmüller and his crew (Gfr Willi Wruck, Gfr Otto Joachim and Gfr Otto Herding) were lost.

Two more Hurricanes had been dispatched on a defensive patrol to the north, these encountering three Ju88s of I/LG1 in the process of bombing the road between Athens and Corinth. The bomber crews had been out on armed reconnaissance looking for ships between the mainland and Crete, but failing to find any had decided to attack a secondary target rather than carry their bombs back to base. Ping Newton attacked L1+LK, causing considerable damage and wounding both the navigator and radio operator/gunner. With the starboard engine knocked out, Uffz Alt crash-landed the bomber among olive groves near Almyros. The trio of Junkers had previously attacked a lone Bf109 of Stab/JG77 in error; Obfw Erwin Sawallisch had returned fire and hit one of the bombers, one member of the crew being killed. The pilot managed to regain his base at Krumovo before force-landing.

A further section of Hurricanes was sent to give some protection to hard-pressed Piraeus, where the pilots saw many Ju87s dive-bombing shipping. Chico Genders made a spirited attack on these, claiming three shot down. Two Ju87s of I/StG2 – T6+JH crewed by Uffz Wartmann/Gfr Zapletal – and T6+LK flown by Gfr Hermann and Gfr Lange – were lost in the Athens area, and a third Stuka, S7+LL of I/StG3 (Ltn Edmund Reichardt/Uffz Riegel) failed to return from Khalkis. These may have been Genders' victims. Meanwhile, five replacement Hurricanes had arrived at Argos from Maleme, flown by

80 Squadron pilots. No sooner were these down, however, when hordes of Luftwaffe aircraft appeared overhead, the Germans having discovered the whereabouts of the RAF fighters. An estimated 20–25 Do17s made a level bombing attack from altitude, followed by a similar number of Ju88s which dive-bombed, escorting Bf109s from II and III/JG77 then sweeping down to strafe. Again, Marcel Comeau recorded:

> Spitting fire, the 109s hit the strip at 400mph – cutting down the Bofors crew almost before they had a chance to fire. A Hurricane, hit by a cannon shell, roared across the landing field, caught in a ditch and flipped over on its back. Four more Hurricanes, quickly airborne, disappeared from view, but most of the remaining fighters were destroyed on the ground before pilots could reach them. Nearby a handful of Greek Avro trainers folded up in flames.

The Hurricane which had been hit attempting to take off was piloted by Sgt George Barker, who was slightly wounded and burned. Other pilots hauled him out of the cockpit and helped him to a nearby slit trench. Eyewitness Comeau continued:

> There was a Lysander airborne, skimming the trees with its wheel barely 50 yards away with a diving 109 on its tail. Hugging the ground the 'Lizzie' flew past us, its parasol wing and squat body already ripped by the strings of tracers hacking into the aircraft like golden chisels. Neither fire from our machine guns nor the desperate bursts of .303 from the rear gunner could alter the course of events. As the pilot threw his machine towards the protection of a tree-lined gully, a burst at point-blank range from the fighter sent it crashing into the hillside.

During an earlier attack on airfields around Athens by Bf109s of II and III/JG77 and I(J)/LG2, Hptm Franz-Heinz Lange, Kommandeur of II/JG77, had reportedly been shot down and killed near Karopi, south of Athens, by a direct AA hit, but it is possible that he was shot down by Genders, who claimed one Bf109 during the morning (in addition to the three Ju87s), either while returning from the sortie to Piraeus, or when scrambled from Argos. Numbers of German aircraft continued to attack the airfield during the afternoon, but it was not until shortly before sunset that a further major attack developed. Three Hurricanes were up on patrol, one of them flown by Winsland, who recalled:

> Three of us were up together on a dusk patrol over our retreating army when suddenly one fire after another blazed up below us, particularly along the road and round our own landing field. We were as nervous

as hell already, and the sight of the fires did not improve matters, as it meant enemy fighters were strafing our troops from treetop height and we could not see them. The fading light together with their excellent camouflage made it virtually impossible to distinguish anything below from the shadows of fields and woods and innumerable fires. It was obvious that there were swarms of enemy machines somewhere below us, but I am damned if I could see them. During that patrol I was on edge from start to finish. My head never stopped turning up and down, round and round for fear of being surprised by the enemy's covering fighters somewhere high above us.

The failing light, the fires, the dense columns of black smoke, all those enemy machines, the knowledge that sometime shortly through lack of fuel we would have to go down to land with the enemy ruling the air – all those thoughts did not put me at my ease. Eventually we could keep in the air no longer and went down to land. The wood in which we had hidden all our grounded machines was in flames. Thirty twin-engined German fighters had raked it with cannon-shell and machine-gun fire a few minutes before we landed – and once again we never saw them. When I say 'we' I only refer to two of us who were following our leader, for, strangely enough, our leader had seen them as he afterwards admitted. His action therefore of not attacking them may seem bad in the eyes of many. His defence however for not doing so was quite reasonable, and I admit I would have done the same had I been leader. Supposing we had attacked and shot down four each (almost impossible and extremely unlikely anyway) the enemy would never have noticed the difference, and we would certainly have suffered very heavily in the process. He maintained that in this case it would not have been clever or anything else to have attacked – it would have been sheer stupidity, especially as the remaining two of us were comparatively inexperienced pilots at the time. Thank God, anyway, for what he eventually did!

On the airfield all available Hurricanes had been preparing to take off at 1800 to carry out an urgently ordered shipping protection patrol, but when an estimated 40 Bf110s of I/ZG26 – led by Maj Wilhelm Makrocki – arrived, only two (Coke and Dahl) had departed. All the remaining Hurricanes were hit, but the pilots managed to scramble clear and reach the safety of nearby slit trenches, although Ted Hewett received a shrapnel wound in the back while sheltering. The Zerstörer remained over the airfield for some 40 minutes, blasting every wreck again and again. Airmen on the ground, hiding among the olive groves and in trenches, fired at the low-flying aircraft with machine guns and rifles, while Air Commodore Grigson, Deputy AOC Greece, stood in the centre of the field with a rifle, calmly pot-shooting at the many targets while an airman acted as his loader.

By the end of the attack some 13 Hurricanes had been wrecked. Almost all the Greek aircraft had been destroyed, the Luftwaffe claiming 53 destroyed at Argos during the day. Only two Hurricanes were found still to be flyable following this latest strike, plus the five aircraft that had been airborne. Two of these, those flown by Coke and Dahl, returned to the scene of devastation shortly after the Messerschmitts had departed, the pilots having been unaware of the attack. Following the day's disastrous attacks, Air Commodore Grigson ordered that the seven remaining Hurricanes should fly out to Maleme at dawn; the nine pilots left without aircraft to fly were to be evacuated in the Rapide, which had arrived safely. After dark three Lodestar transports flew in to collect key personnel.

On **24 April** the full evacuation of troops from Greece commenced under the codename Operation *Demon* and 80 Squadron was transferred to Crete. Bill was allocated Hurricane V7795 with orders to fly to Maleme. He took off from Argos at 0605. Meanwhile, LAC Frank Paul and his RSU detachment had by now reached Argos:

> There was on Argos airfield one or two Hurricanes. One had a damaged radiator and it stood in the open near a wide drain. W/O Casey of 80 Squadron was calling out for engine tradesmen to work on it. With only myself to please I went with one or two other airmen whom I did not know. As we arrived to look at the job with a view to 'patching it up', the real trouble started. There was no air raid warning system as there had been in England. Enemy aircraft would arrive without any warning, and open fire straight away. The Hurricane we hoped to get airborne had a shell splinter in the radiator and was beyond repair in those conditions.
>
> Our decision to run for it was made by the sudden arrival of three or four '110s mitt der yeller nose'. I was told that the 110s with yellow spinners were from the 'Herman Göring' Squadron of the Luftwaffe. That night three Hudson [*sic* – Lodestar] aircraft landed and I remember hearing them take off very early in the morning. I didn't know then, but I later learnt that those pilots and senior officers for whom it was necessary to get over to Crete, had left in those Hudsons. It didn't affect me; with no aircraft available, pilots were to go where they could be of use. I did learn one lesson. I realised that without technical airmen, of whom I was one, the greatest air ace on earth is stymied, especially when the enemy is operating from just over the hill.
>
> The next day I was caught in the open during a strafing raid. For some reason, now forgotten, Pay and myself, with one or two other

Sqn Ldr Bill Vale DFC*, AFC.
This was probably the last photo taken of Bill
before he retired from the RAF, c.1946.

Bill's father 'Nips' in his Royal Marine Reserve uniform.

RAF Shooting VIII, 1934. Bill, back row, second from right.

33 (LB) Squadron, Mersa Matruh, Egypt, 1935.

33 (LB) Squadron, Mersa Matruh, Egypt, 1935. Bill, far right. Rather a scruffy lot of individuals!

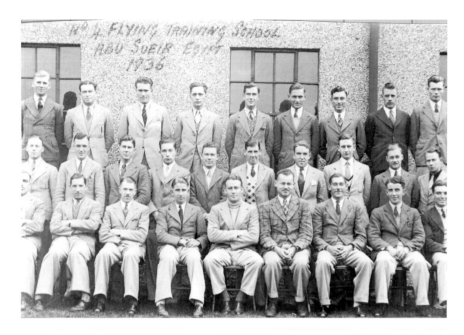

No. 4 Flying Training School, Abu Sueir, Egypt, 1936. Bill, front row, third from right. Note first signs of moustache.

Photograph from Bill's album showing a demised RAF aircraft, *c*.1937.

Shell Hockey Cup Winners. Bill extreme left, back row.

RAF Shooting VIII, Middle East, 1936. Bill, standing, second from left.

Portrait of Bill on being commissioned, 1940.

Sqn Ldr Bill Hickey.

Bill's Hurricane NW-L
(N5784), showing the
Framlingham College coat
of arms behind the cockpit
access hatch.

Woody Woodward in
NW-L, which Bill later
inherited.

Flt Lt Pat Pattle in his
'personalised' Gladiator.

A group of 80 Squadron pilots in early 1941.
Left to right: Ted Hewett, Bill, Keg Dowding, F.W. Hosken,
Flg Off Trevor-Roper (84 Squadron), Pat Pattle,
Hugh Wanklyn Flower, John Lancaster.

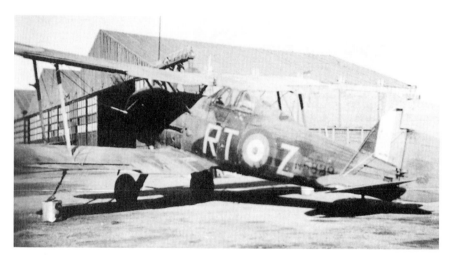

RT-Z of 112 Squadron was flown by Bill on 28 February 1941 when he accounted
for a G.50 and an SM.79 over Himari.

Bill indulging in a little pistol-shooting practice, watched by other 80 Squadron pilots and Greek soldiers.

Bill (right) and Flt Lt Jimmy Kettlewell at Paramythia after a patrol.

Bill, centre, with (left to right) Cas Casbolt, George Barker, Don Gregory, Pat Pattle and Ape Cullen.

33 Squadron at Larissa. Left to right: Dixie Dean, Pete Wickham, Woody Woodward, David Moir and Charles Cheetham.

80 Squadron at Eleusis. Left to right: Keg Dowding, Ginger Still, Cas Casbolt, Ted Hewett, Mick Richens, Hugh Wanklyn Flower.

Bf109 Black 10 of 4./JG77 crash-landed at Larissa on 20 April 1941, believed victim of Sqn Ldr Pat Pattle. Obfw Fritz Röckel was wounded.

Bf109 White 5 of II/JG77 after it crash-landed at Larissa on
15 April 1941. Ltn Jakob Arnoldy was killed.

German groundcrew inspect an abandoned Hurricane, Argos.

Derelict Hurricanes of 33 and 80 Squadrons were destroyed or abandoned at Argos
and possibly elsewhere in Greece. One photograph shows the temporary grave of
a pilot (below), which may have been taken near Lamia where Plt Off Ginger Still
was killed and buried.

Wrecked Hurricane at Argos, with Stukas in the background.

British POWs passing a destroyed Hurricane at Maleme. Note the Ju52s in the
background. The Hurricane may have been Bill's V7795.

Central Gunnery School, Sutton Bridge, 1943. Bill, third from left, seated, was Chief Flying Instructor.

RAF Milfield 'English' Football XI, 1943.
Bill was captain and centre forward.

Bill, Chief Flying Instructor, 59 OTU, RAF Milfield, sixth from left, seated, 1942–3.

Senior Commanders' Admin Course, RAF College, Cranwell, 1944.
Bill, middle row, fourth from right.

engine/airframe fitters were walking over the open ground between the olive groves and the long drain ditch at Argos airfield. Messerschmitt 110s – there must have been six or more – suddenly appeared from over the hills to the north. The first thing I realised was that they were here to put an end to Argos as an airfield. The very first 110 came in, smoke trailing behind as his cannons fired. They were using incendiary/explosive ammunition to start fires wherever possible. We took cover in the ditch until we realised that down the end of the ditch was a store of petrol barrels, 40-gallon steel drums visible from the air without doubt.

Strafing does not ruin a landing strip but it will ruin everything else. The stack of petrol barrels would be a target – and it was. We got out of the ditch and ran as fast as possible. One of my most clear memories is of airmen's legs and how fast they can move. Looking towards the other side of the 'strip' I saw a few more airmen running for shelter. In the distance their little legs were moving so fast that it was a funny sight. Amid all that excitement I remember being amused! Thank god for comic sights. Argos was not a good place to be in. There was no point in staying. Anything that would fly had gone. I failed to find anyone of my unit so I was virtually alone.

On **27 April**, German motorcycle troops entered Athens, followed by armoured cars, tanks, and infantry. The people of Athens had been expecting the Germans to enter the city for several days and kept themselves confined to their homes with their windows shut. The previous night Athens Radio had made the following announcement:

> You are listening to the voice of Greece. Greeks, stand firm, proud, and dignified. You must prove yourselves worthy of your history. The valour and victory of our army has already been recognised. The righteousness of our cause will also be recognised. We did our duty honestly. Friends! Have Greece in your hearts, live inspired with the fire of her latest triumph and the glory of our army. Greece will live again and will be great, because she fought honestly for a just cause and for freedom. Brothers! Have courage and patience. Be stouthearted. We will overcome these hardships. Greeks! With Greece in your minds you must be proud and dignified. We have been an honest nation and brave soldiers.

The German motorcycle troops drove straight to the Acropolis and raised the Nazi flag. In the days that followed, the people of Athens, and newspapers around the world, told different stories of the raising of the German flag. According to the most popular account, the Evzone soldier on guard duty,

Konstantinos Koukidis, took down the Greek flag, wrapped himself in it, and jumped off the Acropolis. Whether the story was true or not, many Greeks believed the story and looked at the soldier as a martyr.

With the RAF gone, remaining British and Commonwealth troops heading southwards came under unrelenting assault from the air:

> What came next was the Luftwaffe. The battalion was just leaving Markopoulon, with a swarm of children still running alongside, when four Messerschmitts suddenly swooped out of the blue and dived on the road. The men ran desperately for open country, but the trucks and guns couldn't do that. They were caught with no cover handy, and didn't have a chance. The planes (now joined by about fifteen more) strafed along the road, concentrating on each vehicle in turn till it went up in flames. Then they machine-gunned at random over the surrounding country, where the men were lying huddled in furrows or under trees as inconspicuously as possible. Some men stood their ground and fired back, but without success. Incendiary bullets set alight a dry field of grain in which Headquarters Company had taken refuge, and the men had to move out in a hurry.
>
> It seemed hours that the planes were overhead, but actually it was only ten minutes. They left a shambles behind them, burning trucks all along the road, an ammunition truck going up in countless small explosions. In 18 Battalion [NZ] six men had been killed and twelve wounded. The battalion was so scattered that it took some time to reassemble; then it moved on again, across a flat tree-studded plain that ended four miles ahead in low hills hiding the Promised Land of Porto Rafti. Abandoned weapons and gear littered the countryside, and at one spot the men saw dozens of trucks sitting smashed and desolate among the trees, just like the ones they themselves had left.[6]

With German units pushing steadily forward, abandoned airfields were soon occupied by the Luftwaffe, including Argos, as noted by a German war reporter:

> That the British had 'dug in' in Greece early on, long before the German troops crossed the border, did have its good points. At least for the Luftwaffe. With the building of airfields the Tommy did take a lot of labour out of our hands. And one has to say, they did a good job. Only thing missing is that they didn't leave an officer who could surrender the place. This little formal error has been forgiven generously by the German fliers, as was the considerable mess that they left behind.
>
> But what do you know, the first sifting of this mess was very enjoyable. At the airfield that we are observing, were hundreds of

200-litre drums full of nice RAF fuel. To appreciate the value of this booty one has to know that our flying troops went in at the same time that our ground forces occupied the territory without their ground support. Admittedly the next day the transport Junkers brought bombs and fuel but that was the next day. The kindly left-behind British fuel was enough for another sortie by our forces at the day they arrived.

The next place in the appreciation of our fliers took the Australians with their nice tents, then came the left-behind provisions was the nice beer from Sidney [sic] and Shanghai. Anything else left behind was just in the way. Lots of yellow painted British bombs in all sizes and prices, mountains of ammunitions belts and left-behind planes that were not serviceable.

The Stukas were soon in action against the departing evacuation ships:

It's 8 in the morning. The sun is already high up and it is so hot that one hardly sees fully dressed soldiers. Memories of Spain were revived at the site of these savage warriors in their camo pants and their knobbly knees. The Kommodore returns from an early sortie that he has flown with his adjutant. While he is sitting on a cable reel and enjoying breakfast a Staffelkapitän reports in.

'Mission accomplished with six aircraft I attacked enemy forces in the bay of Eleusis. Three transporters of together 12,000 tons and a cruiser were sunk.'

'What??' The Kommodore exclaims, 'and that in the early morning and an empty stomach? Ordonnanz! Coffee for the gentleman!! Now tell me about it.'

'With Leutnant S, I was flying the first rotte. At the cruising height the outlines of the bay were well distinguishable, one could also see ships beneath but details were obscured by morning mist. As we dived, Leutnant S next to me, the visibility improved rapidly. And then I recognised the warship. Quite clearly at the shape and the two gun towers in the front. It must have come in the bay at night time because yesterday it wasn't there. We were high enough to take on the cruiser. I notified Leutnant S let the bombs go. In a left hand turn I pulled up and saw the smoke pouring upwards from the fore ship. At the same time the bombs of Leutnant S hit target. Direct hit midship. Immediately sky-high flames, sulphur-yellow and sulphur-red. That couldn't have come from the bomb alone. S must have hit the munitions chamber. Pieces of scrap as large as 30 metres flew through the air. The cruiser listed heavily to port.'

The Kommodore stood up. 'Congratulations', he said. 'I didn't have so much hunting luck. I wanted to kill the two steamers in the bay I attacked in a dive but noticed at the very last moment the Red Cross. It is probably used for cargo but they won't be saying a bad thing about us. So we pulled away and attacked the little one of 3,000-tons. It got the 250 [bomb] in the side. Smoke bulging out. A hole in the waterline as big as a barnyard door.'

Chapter 9

HURRICANE FLIGHT CRETE

By the beginning of May, the Greek forces consisted of approximately 9,000 troops: three battalions of the 5th (Crete) Division of the Hellenic Army, which had been left behind when the rest of the unit had been transferred to the mainland to oppose the German invasion; the Cretan Gendarmerie (a battalion-sized force); the Heraklion Garrison Battalion, a defence battalion – made up mostly of transport and logistics personnel; and remnants of the 12th and 20th Hellenic Army divisions, which had escaped to Crete and were organised under British command. There were also cadets from the Gendarmerie academy and recruits from the Greek training centres in the Peloponnese who had been transferred to Crete to replace the trained soldiers sent to fight on the mainland, supplementing them with experienced men arriving from the mainland.

The British Commonwealth contingent consisted of the original 14,000-man British garrison and another 25,000 Commonwealth troops evacuated from the mainland. The evacuees were the typical mix found in any contested evacuation – substantially intact units under their own command, composite units hurriedly brought together by leaders on the spot, stragglers without leaders from every type of unit possessed by an army. Most of these men lacked heavy equipment. The key formed units were the New Zealand 2nd Division, less the 6th Brigade and division headquarters; the Australian 19th Brigade Group; and the British 14th Infantry Brigade. In total, there were roughly 15,000 combat-ready British Commonwealth infantry, augmented by about 5,000 non-infantry personnel equipped as infantry, and one composite (Australian) artillery battery.

The defending air force under the command of Grp Capt George Beamish comprised just 14 Gladiators at Heraklion, of which only 6 were operational. The FAA's 805 Squadron at Maleme could offer 7 Sea Gladiators, 5 Fulmars and 2 non-operational Buffalos. And the 7 evacuated Hurricanes were also at Maleme.

Maleme aerodrome was wedged between sea and road, little more than a reclaimed stretch of sandy beach. To the south the ground, bare of cover except for a small vineyard, rose to the base of Kavkazia Hill, 340 feet high. To the west lay the River Tavronitis.[1]

* * *

Soon after Bill's arrival at Maleme he set out to find Janina, accompanied by Tap Jones, who had followed Bill and the others to Crete. She was located at a makeshift campsite near Suda Bay. Many British and Greek women and children had been evacuated from the mainland, particularly the latter with British connections, who would have been in great danger of being interrogated about their associations. Apart from girls like Janina, involved in romantic liaisons with servicemen, others such as Marianne, the dancing girl at *Maxim's*, were able to get away – firstly to Crete and later to Egypt. It is possible that Janina and Marianne met each other.

Although, under normal circumstances, Bill would have flown to the safety of Egypt with others from 80 Squadron in an evacuating Lodestar, he volunteered to remain at Maleme to be with Janina, together with Wanklyn Flower, and two NCOs, Rivalant and Bennett. At Maleme they joined others of 33 Squadron to form a composite unit with seven Hurricanes. One of these had an irreparable hole some 10in in diameter through the main spar of one wing, but was still to be used due to small numbers available; the pilots agreed to take turns in flying it, although it was feared that any tight turning would probably result in the wing breaking off! Among the 33 Squadron pilots selected to remain was Plt Off Ray Dunscombe. In a letter to his parents in Croydon dated 30 April, he commented about the evacuation from Greece:

> The most annoying part of it all was we had to leave most of our kit behind. There are pants and socks labelled either '741772' or 'Dunscombe' scattered all over Greece from Mount Olympus to Athens. It was rather tragic throughout. Women carrying bundles of stuff and babies. I think they must have taken rather a poor view of us rushing by in our cars and lorries. The war does not seem very near to an end. The chief point is to keep the Nazis out of England.

On Crete preparations for the continued air defence of the island were being pressed, but a new airfield at Pediada Kastelli, west of Maleme, was rendered completely unserviceable as it was by now clear that it could not be ready in time. It was decided to send one flight back to Egypt, one flight of 112 Squadron due to lack of aircraft, and, on the toss of a coin the eight pilots of A Flight flew out in a Bombay, the flight's ground crew following by sea next day. Ten pilots remained under Flt Lt Charlie Fry, hoping to receive early reinforcements of Hurricanes; their strength was rapidly augmented by the arrival of six new pilots from 1430 Flight (but no aircraft), recently arrived from East Africa, under Flt Lt James Dennant.

805 Squadron at Maleme also dispatched some of its less-essential ground personnel to Egypt at this time, 23 Naval ratings and borrowed RAF other ranks leaving by ship. Four non-combatworthy Fulmars had already flown back to Aboukir, leaving only five Fulmars and the seven Sea Gladiators operational, although in need of proper servicing. At the same airfield 30 Squadron could boast seven operational Blenheim IFs, but all were suffering constant wear and tear from the long convoy patrols and sea reconnaissance. Reinforcements generally were urgently needed.

Sqn Ldr Tap Jones, Wanklyn Flower and the Frenchman Rivalant now departed Crete, leaving the small Maleme detachment under Bill's command. His sole squadron companion was Sgt Bennett. It can be assumed that Bill again volunteered in order to be with Janina.

Bill flew patrols over Suda Bay on four consecutive days – 25 to 28 April – covering the evacuation. On the first of these three days, Bill was among an assortment of Hurricanes, Fulmars and Sea Gladiators from Maleme that provided cover as evacuation vessels approached Suda Bay, which had twice been attacked by Ju88s from I/LG1. One of those involved in hunting for evacuating ships was Ltn Gerd Stamp flying L1+NK:

> A sunny day, and we were sent to look for ships embarking British troops in the Athens, Corinth and Nauplion areas. As there seemed to be almost no more fighter planes in those areas, each of us flew on his own. I took off in the early afternoon and I went to Cape Sunion first. No ships around there. So I flew to the Corinth area. No ships either. I turned south to investigate the Nauplion area, and on my way I tried to identify Mykene. I told my crew that we were passing over a territory, which had seen at least 3,000 years of Greek history. Wasn't this King Agamemnon's home down there?
>
> My navigator, sitting right next to me, was more concerned about Argos airfield straight ahead of us. He expected Hurricane fighters to take off from there, if they weren't in the air already, and were waiting in the sun in order to put themselves into an advantageous position for a surprise attack. For a few moments we forgot the antique scenery around us, but after a while we found that there were obviously no fighters in the air. So, at least my eyes were looking again to the ground. The villages and the little towns looked like a playground of white dots, as the houses were mostly plain white. The sun was pouring her mild afternoon light over the scenery of yellow-brown soil, blue sea and blue sky, and the 'white dots' accumulated to a town along the border of the sea. From a small harbour the houses

climbed up to a rocky hill, the entrance to the port was protected by a small island covered by the stonewalls of a small medieval fort. The map showed that this could only be Nauplion. We were not fired at by AA salvoes, at least I saw none. Everything looked peaceful and untouched. But there was something which made my heart beat faster.

Right in the middle between the jetty and the small island fort, there was a big ship. Two funnels, a high superstructure, a passenger liner. This was the first ship of this kind I had ever seen. It was a fascinating sight. There it was, motionless, no wake, and we were moving towards this unique target: 'Switch the fuse box on, all bombs at once!' The navigator acted accordingly. I turned my Ju88 a little in order to approach the target slightly diagonal. Cooler flaps shut, propellers back into the half-past-eight-position. Their rotation became slower and the noise became lower. The target down there slipped through the red stripe across the window below my feet. We now were in the 60° grade angle for diving. I pushed a little knob, the air brakes came out of the wings – and down we went with increasing speed. The ship, now in front of my nose, seemed to become bigger and bigger. I hardly felt my navigator's fist hammering on my knee. 'Thousand!' he cried. I lifted the aircraft's nose a little and pushed the red button. The bombs went their way and the Ju88 hers, flattening out her dive. This had been a textbook attack, and I brought the aircraft back to normal. I could not see whether the bombs had hit, but my radio-operator and my air-gunner, both looking to the rear, suddenly shouted simultaneously: 'We've hit her! Two full hits, two bombs near misses. Water cascades and high flames.' I risked a quick look back, and I saw what they had described. What did I feel? Relief after maximal tension. Being proud, that a junior crew had been successful. Sorrow, that a beautiful ship was gone. Satisfaction, that she would no longer transport British Forces, and that was all that counted on this day.[2]

Bill was up again next day, but not when Ju88s were present, although a Hurricane pilot from 33 Squadron, Flg Off Sir James Kirkpatrick, managed to shoot down a reconnaissance Ju88 of 4.(F)/121, Ltn Hans Michaelis and his crew of 7A+AM perishing in the sea. Another Ju88 was intercepted by two 805 Squadron Fulmar pilots, Lt(A) Peter Scott and Sub-Lt(A) Reg Bryant. There was revenge on 28 April when a Ju88 shot down a Seagull amphibian (HMAS *Perth's* aircraft) that had taken off from Suda Bay. The crew survived. Meanwhile, Flg Off Kirkpatrick reported engaging an enemy aircraft he tentatively identified as a Luftwaffe reconnaissance Hs126 or an Italian Ro44, claiming to have shot this down.

No enemy aircraft had been encountered by Bill during these flights, but at 1015 on **29 April**, he was scrambled with others from Maleme when the island suffered its first air-raid alarm of the day:

> Raid Alarm. Took off in Hurricane and intercepted Do17 heading out to sea. Got within 400 yards of enemy aircraft and fired all my ammunition. Enemy aircraft last seen losing height with black smoke pouring from port engine. Own aircraft slightly damaged.

The alarm sounded again at 1615, as some 20 Ju88s approached Suda Bay. This time all available Hurricanes were scrambled, as well as 805 Squadron's Fulmars and a Sea Gladiator in the hands of 805 Squadron's CO Lt-Cdr Alan Black. Again it was Bill (V7795) who made contact:

> Intercepted nine Ju88s. Attacked formation of two at 6,000 feet and, after firing short burst at starboard engine, enemy aircraft went down in flames to crash in sea just north of Maleme aerodrome. I then chased two more, which were escaping out to sea, and after about five minutes got near enough to open fire. After long burst the enemy aircraft nosed into the sea. I observed two survivors, which I reported on R/T. While returning to base I carried out a head-on attack on a single machine, but after one short burst I ran out of ammunition.

The bombers had attacked shipping in the bay, the Greek freighter *Konistra* (3,537 tons) being badly hit and beached. Two Bofors guns sited to protect the anchorage were also knocked out, but without any casualties to the gun crews.

Just after 1700 next day (**30 April**), six Ju88s were seen low over Suda Bay, and were intercepted by Bill, who chased them northwards. He reported:

> I attacked one after a very long chase, firing nearly all my ammunition into it from very close range and it hit the sea. I was then fired upon by another Ju88, which came up in line abreast, so I carried out a quarter attack which finished off my ammo. No apparent damage. While returning to base I saw four aircraft in line astern, very low down. I went very close and recognised them as Blenheims with what appeared to be English markings . . . I reported this and was informed that no Blenheims were airborne.

Obviously the Operations Room at Maleme was unaware of what was going on at Heraklion, for the four Blenheims were 203 Squadron aircraft, the vanguard of the detachment now ordered back to Egypt. Each carrying three ground crew, the aircraft had just taken off from Heraklion, and were heading off for Egypt.

The start of May found a tense air of expectant calm pervading the skies around Crete following the conclusion of the evacuation. That Crete would soon be invaded was already known. What could be done to stiffen the island's defences in the lull while the Germans pressed forward their preparations for the next round was a greater problem. The Bf109s of II and III/JG77 had moved into Molaoi by the end of April. 7 Staffel's, Fw Johann Pichler, recalled:

> It was extraordinarily hot on Molaoi, the airfield at the southern end of the Peloponnese, and the ground crews especially were under great stress. The fine dust deposited on the engines and airframes resulted in supercharger damage and the fuel booster pumps became clogged. The consumption of lubricating oil was unusually high and, since the oil temperature was 95° to 100°C, oil changes were frequently required. With temperatures of up to 40°C, the ground crews naturally preferred to work naked to the waist but the *Fliegerführer,* von Richthofen, demanded that the men wear their black working clothes. In the Gruppe's opinion, this was a foolish order, so we posted an additional lookout who was to watch for any approaching Storch staff aircraft. When one was spotted approaching the airfield, the lookout raised an alarm and the ground crews quickly got dressed again in their black working clothes.

Strong winds which whipped up dust storms over Crete reduced flying on **2 May**, only a few uneventful patrols being undertaken. The plan for the employment of the Hurricanes was to maintain aircraft at readiness. On early warning of enemy aircraft being plotted one aircraft would come to stand by; if enemy aircraft approached the island, and were positively identified as hostile, the stand-by aircraft would take off. During periods of congestion at Suda Bay, when unloading ships, standing patrols were maintained. The periods of readiness were a great strain on the pilots, and it was deemed desirable to pool pilots of the units at Maleme to relieve the burden. Lt Cdr Black offered 33 Squadron the services of a number of his more experienced pilots, and over the next few days half a dozen of the Navy pilots familiarised themselves with the Hurricane. The stormy conditions this day allowed urgently needed servicing to be carried out, while from Maleme one unserviceable Fulmar was flown back to Egypt, leaving just six of these fighters on the island, none of them in the best of condition.

Next morning (**3 May**), Luftwaffe intrusions over Crete resumed, sporadic attacks being made on Suda Bay throughout the day. Most of these intrusions were by small groups of aircraft, but at 1440 an estimated two-dozen bombers – Ju88s of I/KG51 and I/LG1 – arrived overhead to bomb and damage a supply vessel. Four Hurricanes and a Sea Gladiator were scrambled, Capt Skeet Harris RM in the latter aircraft intercepting three of the bombers but finding to his chagrin that only one of his guns would fire. The Hurricane pilots enjoyed more success; Chico Genders claimed two Junkers shot down and two others damaged, Chico Woods claimed one and one damaged, Moir a probable and Newton one more damaged. AA gun teams around Suda Bay submitted two further claims for bombers destroyed but the aircraft seen falling were probably those downed by the Hurricanes. In the event, two aircraft from 1 Staffel of KG51 were lost, Fw Georg Fanderl's 9K+LH crash-landing at Krumovo on return (written-off), while Ltn Rudolf Ortner's 9K+GH went into the sea off Suda Bay, the pilot at least being rescued. Interrogation of prisoners established that I/KG51 had only arrived at Krumovo on 18 April with eight aircraft, just three of which had survived to participate in this raid.

With weather more sultry than had been the case over recent days, the intrusions over Suda Bay continued on **4 May**, 16 Ju88s appearing at about 1800 hours. The supply ship damaged during the previous day's raid was now sunk, while one of the AA gun positions was also hit and two members of the gun crew were wounded. Four Hurricanes and a Fulmar were scrambled, Lt Rupert Brabner RN in the Fulmar claiming one bomber shot down over the Bay, while the Hurricanes chased the others off to the north. Newton claimed one probable, Chico Woods and Noel-Johnson each claiming two damaged, only breaking off and returning when the southern extremities of the Greek mainland appeared below. Two more bombers were claimed damaged by the guns. During this attack one Ju88 from I/KG51 was badly damaged – possibly by Brabner – and crashed at Krumovo on return and was destroyed. One more bomber from I/LG1 was also hit, landing at Eleusis with a dead engine.

On **5 May**, Ju88s again appeared over Suda Bay in small numbers, but now also approached the Heraklion area. Hurricanes were up from Maleme, Noel-Johnson making contact with a lone aircraft but unable to get within firing range. Among the patrols flown, one Hurricane was piloted by Capt Harris RM of 805 Squadron but no enemy aircraft were seen. It was not until the early evening that an effective interception was made, Bill (V7181) catching a Ju88 over the bay and claiming it shot down; he also claimed a second as damaged.

Over the Heraklion sector Ju88s were intercepted by two 112 Squadron Gladiators flown by Canadian Plt Off Len Bartley and Plt Off Jerry Westenra, a New Zealander, each pilot claiming a bomber damaged. Later, on a solo Hurricane patrol, Sgt Ralph Ware intercepted a reconnaissance SM79 high over the airfield and claimed it probably shot down, this action apparently being confirmed by Army witnesses. Patrols continued over the approaches to the island next day, but without any engagements occurring. Of this period John Hetherington, the war correspondent, wrote:

The Germans had lost no time in organising themselves for the invasion of Crete. Their drive to the south had halted at Cape Matapan, 70 miles from Crete. As May began, the Luftwaffe, operating from the southern Peloponnese, the Athens area, the Dodecanese, and the islands of Melos, was pounding Crete with rising savagery. Its chief objective was Suda Bay. Heraklion, the only other port of any value as a supply channel, and the aerodromes at Heraklion and Maleme were also heavily attacked. The RAF and the Fleet Air Arm were no match for the great formations of German bombers escorted by fighters which came over four or five times a day. At neither place was British air strength the equivalent of a squadron. And yet day after day the pilots went up to face odds of rarely less than ten or twelve to one.

The miracle is that any British pilot fighting over Crete should come out alive, any British aircraft survived. The aircraft were a mixed lot – a few Hurricanes, Blenheims, Fulmars and obsolete Gladiators. Their fight to blunt the edge of the air blitz was hopeless, pitiable, magnificently heroic. More than once watchers on the ground saw a couple of fighters climb into the sky to tackle a big enemy formation, shoot down an aircraft, then itself be shot down.

Operations around Crete continued in a desultory fashion, daily patrols netting no engagements between 7 and 10 May. During this period five unserviceable Blenheims were flown out to Egypt for complete overhaul, while 805 Squadron was further depleted in like manner, three Fulmars and two Sea Gladiators leaving on 8 May, one more Fulmar and another Sea Gladiator within the next couple of days. This left the unit with just two Fulmars and four Sea Gladiators; of the three Buffalos two were unserviceable, the other badly damaged.

Finally, during the evening of **11 May**, five Bf110s of II/ZG76, which had arrived at Argos from North Germany four days earlier, swept in over Heraklion airfield to strafe. Insufficient warning allowed only a single 112 Squadron Gladiator to get into the air, but Bofors and Lewis gunners opened fire as the Zerstörer swept round the airfield. As they completed their circuit, Plt Off Neville Bowker attacked one and a low-level dogfight commenced, during which the lone Gladiator pilot attempted to lead his opponents over the gun positions. After a few minutes the Bf110s made off to the north-west, Bowker landing to claim one probably shot down.

At Maleme the composition of the fighter defence now underwent a complete change when Wg Cdr Geoffrey Francis landed his 230 Squadron Sunderland in Suda Bay, bringing with him Sqn Ldr Edward Howell to take over command of the remnants of 33 Squadron, together with three relatively inexperienced pilots, Flg Off Jack Butcher, a former 112 Squadron pilot, and

Sgts Butterick and Leveridge, who had originally joined the unit in Greece but had been evacuated back to Egypt. The majority of the unit's pilots were now about to leave, as it was intended that more replacements would soon fly in with new Hurricanes. Of the originals, only Woodward (now Flt Lt) and Dunscombe would remain, together with Flt Lts Mitchell and Dennant and Flg Off Stan Reeves. The new CO, Sqn Ldr Howell, was a highly experienced fighter pilot and former instructor, who had not, however, flown on operations, nor even flown a Hurricane. He later wrote:

I had come over from Egypt with some rested pilots to relieve the hard-pressed garrison who returned in the flying boat which brought us for some well-earned leave. I found that we were lodgers at Maleme – the little airstrip belonged to the Fleet Air Arm and was commanded by a naval officer – Commander George Beale. The remains of a Fleet fighter squadron were also there commanded by Alan Black. They had two or three old Gladiators and a couple of Fulmars. We also had the remains of 30 Squadron with us for a few days – two or three clapped-out old Blenheims which could only just get off the short strip.

With this motley array, we had to defend the west of Crete including the great natural harbour of Suda Bay. With improvised radar warning and fighter control equipment, we had little hope of seriously reducing the scale of enemy attack. We could only nibble at them. The Blenheims and Gladiators were useless against more modern aircraft and the Fulmars would not stand a chance against a Me109. So the defence of Crete fell to the few Hurricanes of 33 Squadron at Maleme with a few more belonging to 112 Squadron at Heraklion, some seventy miles to the east.

I was specially anxious to conceal my inexperience from the squadron – it was bad enough being new to the job and I had the further disadvantage of taking over from Pat Pattle. Succeeding Pat would have been difficult for anyone, even under normal circumstances, and my task was even harder. I had come to take over the remnants of a famous fighter squadron, which had been cut to pieces in Greece. 33 Squadron had been decimated. Even with the remains of 80 Squadron – our great rivals – we could now only muster some five Hurricanes of which we were lucky to have three serviceable. We had lost all our equipment and spares during the evacuation of Greece a few weeks earlier.

A few days later the squadron had moved to Crete – what was left of it – still fighting. Half the personnel had gone straight back to Egypt where I had the task of re-organising them. The other half had to carry on in Crete. They had done wonders too – eighteen enemy bombers shot down in two short weeks without loss, but it could not go on indefinitely. Pilots and ground crews were exhausted, going from day to day without even a change of clothes, constantly harried by enemy air raids and operating from dawn to dusk without relief.

Next day (**12 May**), Wg Cdr Francis embarked as many passengers as it was possible to cram into the Sunderland, every space being occupied until 74 persons were aboard as well as the ten-man crew; this even included six standing in the lavatory. Most of these evacuees were aircrew, among them the seven departing 33 Squadron pilots, a number of Blenheim crews – and Capt James Roosevelt USAAF, son of the US President, who had been in Greece and Crete as a 'Military observer and adviser.' It is interesting to note that due to the shortage of trained and experienced aircrew in Egypt, orders had been issued regarding priorities for evacuation, indicating orders of preference beginning with Blenheim pilots, then Wellington pilots, followed by Hurricane pilots, while among the crewmembers, radio operators were to be given priority over air gunners, then observers. After aircrew, engineer officers were the next most important category, followed by cypher and signals officers and airmen. Accounts officers, carpenters and metal workers were bottom of the list. Thus laden, Wg Cdr Francis had trouble getting the Sunderland into the air, the big flying boat having the largest number of persons ever to be carried in such an aircraft, requiring some three miles' run before it finally lifted from the water.

At Maleme patrols continued, but high-flying reconnaissance aircraft were not to be intercepted on **13 May**. At 1100 on this date Plt Off Ray Dunscombe overshot the runway while coming in to land from a practice flight, crash-landing a Hurricane and damaging it. This serious loss was somewhat offset by the arrival of two replacement aircraft in the hands of Sgt Charlie Ripsher, a Scot, and Southern Rhodesian Sgt Glawil Reynish (of obvious Welsh descent), who were led to the island by a 30 Squadron Blenheim; both men remained to strengthen 33 Squadron. A number of aircraft pens had by now been built from sandbags and earth-filled petrol drums, while to provide some defence for the grounded Hurricanes, one airman had constructed a small gun pit and installed a Lewis gun. A number of Bofors were sited on either side of the runway.

While 33 Squadron was being rebuilt, Bill was operating virtually as a 'one-man air force' so far as 80 Squadron was concerned, with his personal Hurricane, V7795. The only other member of the unit still present was Sgt Bennett, while Hurricane V7181 was on the unit's strength, although shared with the naval pilots of 805 Squadron. That same evening, at 2000, Bill scrambled in the latter aircraft after an unidentified plot was reported off the coast. Within 30 minutes he had been vectored onto a Ju52 and had landed again, claiming to have shot this down into the sea.

At Heraklion a number of aircraft – identified as Bf110s but probably Do17s of I/KG2 – attacked the airfield in a desultory fashion, which caused little damage and a few minor casualties to Army personnel. Five Gladiators got off, two flown by 1430 Flight pilots, but only Plt Off Westenra was able to attack, fighting with six of the intruders and getting in several good bursts, though his own fighter was badly shot about, landing with four mainspars shot through, large areas of fabric missing and numerous bullet holes. This action, witnessed by many of the defenders on the ground, had proved quite a tonic to morale. Airfield defence Bofors and Lewis guns kept up an intense fire, as did a convoy offshore. Claims were made and U5+DK (Ltn Katers) of I/KG2 failed to return from an attack on Heraklion, while three more of the unit's aircraft returned to Menidi suffering AA damage.

Crete had not been left free from night raids either, frequent small-scale forays by He111s being made from time to time. A new airstrip came into use by the Luftwaffe, constructed on the recently occupied island of Melos.

The first really serious attacks on the RAF in Crete were launched on **14 May**, beginning at first light when a number of Ju88s bombed Suda Bay and Maleme airfield, six bombs falling on the latter target, damaging one of 30 Squadron's unserviceable Blenheims; the unit's operational aircraft had already been dispatched to Heraklion to undertake convoy escort sorties. Sqn Ldr Howell at Maleme had put himself on readiness. He prepared for his first flight in a Hurricane:

> It was cold in the early morning as the first glimmer of light announced another day. The world seemed to be wondering whether it was worth waking up at all; the birds and the trees and even the mountains seemed to be holding their breath, listening. Only the whisper of the ripples on the nearby beach broke the stillness.
>
> But if you held your breath and listened too, you could hear other sounds. Men were moving about in the distance, their footsteps and voices muffled as if by the darkness. I moved away from my tent in the olive grove, down the hillside and on to the road that flanked the landing strip. At the end of the strip three Hurricanes were lined up, ready to take off at a moment's notice; one of them (W9298/X) was mine.
>
> I clambered awkwardly into the unfamiliar cockpit. I had never flown a Hurricane before, but I did not want anyone to know that. I had managed to conceal the fact from the Commander-in-Chief when he had given me the squadron. The truth was that I had flown Spitfires in England and nearly every other type of aircraft then in use, but somehow a Hurricane had never come my way.

I called over one of my newly joined Sgt-pilots and he went over the cockpit with me showing me the position of the various controls. I could not make the radio work, and we spent some time turning the different knobs in vain. In the grey dawn, I noticed that the other two pilots were in their places, sitting quietly in the aircraft, waiting. We were at stand-by – ready to take off at a moment's notice.

At 0600, some 60 Bf109s of II and III/JG77 swept over the airfield and beach. Fw Georg Schirmböck recalled a bizarre incident, but was obviously mistaken:

> During one of the first missions to Crete, with our whole Gruppe in the air, we experienced a great surprise, as we realised that a Greek Hurricane – with big Greek roundels on its sides – had squeezed in between us; how it managed to do so, I can't imagine. Anyway, we all pitied this poor little fellow so much that the R/T rang with calls: Let him fly, let him go home!

This time two Hurricanes piloted by Sgts Ripsher and Reynish were scrambled at once, turning and twisting to gain altitude as they came under attack. They were quickly followed by Sqn Ldr Howell, who was attacked head-on by a group of five Messerschmitts just as he became airborne:

> Suddenly there was the roar of engines starting up. I saw the other two Hurricanes take off in a cloud of dust. I waved the Sergeant away and prepared to start the engine. As soon as it kicked, I noticed the fitter pull the starter battery to one side and run; I thought this is efficiency – they run about their business. Then I looked up. Through the subsiding dust, I saw the others twisting and turning among a cloud of Messerschmitt 109s. Even as I watched, an enemy aircraft dived into the ground in flames.
>
> I opened the throttle and saw a string of five Messerschmitts coming in over the hill firing at me. It seemed an age before my wheels came off the strip. I went straight into a turn towards the approaching 109s, my wing tip within inches of the ground. The faithful old Hurrybus took it without a murmur; the enemy flashed past and I went over instinctively into a steep turn the other way.
>
> My mind was set on practical things. How to get my undercarriage up, the hood closed, the gunsight switched on, the prop into coarse pitch, the firing button on, the engine temperature down. All the time I kept the nose up, straining to gain height to manoeuvre. I found many difficulties. My rear view mirror was not adjusted so that I could see over my tail. This meant that I had to do continuous steep turns with my head back to see what was coming after me. Every time I put my

head back, my helmet, which I had borrowed and was much too big for me, slipped over my eyes. Then I could not find the switch to turn on my gunsight. I had to look about inside the cockpit for it. Eventually I found it and saw that familiar red graticule glow ready to aim.

Enemy aircraft kept diving in on me in threes or fives. They were travelling fast and did not stay to fight. They just had a squirt at me and climbed away out of range again. It kept me fully occupied with evasive action. Out of the corner of my eye I saw two aircraft diving earthwards in flames. One was a Hurricane. There was no sign of the other. I was alone in a skyful of Germans.

All of a sudden, the sky seemed to empty of aircraft. There was nobody in my immediate vicinity. I found myself at 4,000 feet over the sea. Five miles to the south was the airfield. Streams of tracers and red Bofors shells were coming up focused on small black specks which were enemy fighters still strafing it fiercely. Four pillars of black smoke indicated the position of burning wrecks on the ground.

The Messerschmitt Howell had seen falling in flames had been shot down by Sgt Reynish and was that flown by Gfr Hans Gabler of 6./JG77, which fell inverted into the hills, but Reynish was then shot down by another – probably by Hptm Helmut Henz of 4 Staffel, who claimed a Hurricane at 0605 – the Hurricane falling blazing into the sea. Reynish, on his first operational sortie, was able to bale out, but was presumed lost. In fact he managed to swim towards the shore and after two hours was picked up by a Cretan fishing boat. He finally got back to Maleme to find that he had been given up for dead. Meanwhile, Sqn Ldr Howell, having evaded his attackers, spotted two more Bf109s flying low over the sea:

> Just level with me and about a mile away two 109s were turning in wide line astern formation. I headed in their direction. I cut across inside their turning circle and was soon closing in on them from astern at full throttle. They made no alteration but continued to turn, evidently unaware of my approach. I drew in closer and closer with an eye on my own tail to make sure that I was not jumped. I restrained myself with difficulty. It is only the novice who opens at long range. My own teaching!
>
> I went right in on the tail of the second 109 till I was in close formation on him. I was slightly below him and his slipstream was just above me. I could have lifted my nose and touched his tail with my prop. I dropped a little and pulled up with my sight on his radiator. I pressed the firing switch and the Hurricane shook and shuddered as rounds poured from the guns into him. Bits broke away and a white trail burst from his radiator as the coolant came pouring out.

He turned slowly to the right in a gentle dive. I was determined to see my first victory confirmed and made the mistake of following him down. I had no difficulty as he was past taking evasive action and I continued pouring ammunition into him [this was probably Uffz Willi Hagel of 4 Staffel, who failed to return] till I noticed tracer coming past me. The other 109 was on my tail. I realised my mistake and pulled quickly up into a turn to port, then flick rolled over into a steep turn the other way and found myself coming in on the enemy's quarter and gave him a burst. . . . We screamed down together to water level . . . I kept him dodging in a cloud of bullets and spray till I ran out of ammo . . . he was certainly full of holes.

The third Hurricane, flown by Sgt Charlie Ripsher, was seen by those at Maleme to attack Bf109s flying out to sea and was believed to have shot one down, which hit the sea with a mighty splash (this was probably in fact Howell's victim, Uffz Hagel's aircraft). Two Messerschmitts then latched onto Ripsher's Hurricane, which took desperate evasive action before heading for Maleme as the aircraft was repeatedly hit, it is believed, by Fw Wilhelm Baumgartner of 9 Staffel. Ripsher had lowered his undercarriage and flaps in an attempt to land, but tragically the Hurricane was hit by Bofors' fire and crashed on the edge of the airfield, killing the pilot. Out of fuel and ammunition, Howell landed W9298 at Retimo landing ground, his non-arrival at Maleme being assumed to indicate his loss also:

As I approached Maleme the Bofors guns started firing and strings of red balls floated gently up towards me. I turned and reduced height keeping a watchful eye on the tracers. It was still unhealthy around there. I headed east along the coast. In Suda Bay a tanker was ablaze. The bombers had been in again. A huge pall of black smoke drifted away to the west. I skirted the bay to keep clear of our own batteries. Down the coast I knew there was a landing ground at Retimo. I began to wonder whether I could put the Hurricane down safely in a small field. But I was at home in it. I felt part of it after what we had been through. Below, on a level stretch by the beach, I saw the landing strip. I flew once across it, low down to look for ditches, and came straight in to land. Undercarriage lights gleamed green, flaps checked firmly and I touched lightly down to a nice short landing. A maintenance party refuelled and rearmed the aircraft, and I took off again soon afterwards for an uneventful trip back to Maleme.

A crowd gathered round me as I taxied in to the refuelling pens. Everyone had assumed that I had been shot down. They had seen my

109 come down and they were delighted that I had opened my score. We had accounted for six [sic] Me109s and had lost the other two Hurricanes, shot down in flames. Sgt Ripsher had been shot down near the airfield and was credited with two enemy aircraft destroyed [sic]. We buried him the next day in a little cemetery by Galatos a few miles down the road. Sgt Reynish had also accounted for a couple [sic] and had baled out of his flaming Hurricane over the sea. We had given him up when he walked in late that evening. He had been two hours in the water and had been picked up by a small Greek fishing-boat. We had also lost one Hurricane on the ground. It had been unserviceable, but could have been flying again within a few hours. Now it was a mass of charred wreckage. We had only one aircraft left. The Fleet Air Arm squadron had lost their Fulmars, burnt out on the ground, as well as a couple of Gladiators. The prelude to invasion had entered upon its last phase.

Three Hurricanes were claimed shot down, one by 4./JG77 (Henz) and two by III Gruppe (Ltn Diethelm von Eichel-Streiber and Fw Baumgartner), this unit claiming five more destroyed on the ground. Those Messerschmitts not engaged with the trio of defenders strafed Maleme airfield, one unserviceable Hurricane and the unserviceable Fulmar going up in flames, while down on the beach the three Buffalos were all hit. In Suda Bay a tanker – the 10,694-ton Danish *Eleonora Maersk* – was hit and set on fire, while further up the coast the island's principal town of Canea was bombed. Later in the morning a further small formation of Bf109s repeated the attack, but caused little damage – there were not many targets left.

It was then the turn of Heraklion, where about a dozen II/ZG26 Bf110s and Bf109s of III/JG77 appeared overhead. Two Gladiators were scrambled, Reeves of 1430 Flight and Westenra getting airborne. The New Zealander bounced one of the low-flying Zerstörer, that flown by Oblt Sophus Baagoe, a 14-victory ace from 5 Staffel, the aircraft falling into the sea just offshore, the pilot and his gunner, Obfw Daniel Becker, being killed; this aircraft was also claimed by the Bofors gunners whose accurate fire brought down a second Messerschmitt, 3U+EM of 4 Staffel. The latter crash-landed half a mile from the airfield with the port airscrew, fin and rudder all shot away. Gfr Adolf Ketterer and his gunner, Gfr Hans Bromba, were both captured. Returning Bf110 pilots claimed four victories, but Reeves's Gladiator was the only casualty, which force-landed badly damaged. Two more Gladiators were damaged on the ground. Several of the Bf110s had carried bombs, while others were seen to jettison long-range tanks over the coastline. Little serious damage resulted from this attack. Accompanying Bf109s claimed two Gladiators shot down, one by Maj Alex von Winterfeldt of Stab and the other by Fw Herbert Perrey of 8 Staffel, although the latter's was not confirmed. One of the Zerstörer pilots Ltn Johannes Kiel later commented:

> Crete was a huge rats' nest of British AA positions. We, the Zerstörer, started the action against Crete. During mission after mission, day after day we flew over and rearranged the AA positions, first with our bombs and after that at low level with our heavy machine guns and cannon. We flew all over the island mowing down anything that moved: AA guns, artillery positions, tent camps, armoured vehicles, machine-gun emplacements . . .

Grp Capt Beamish visited the survivors at Maleme before lunch and said a few kind words about the morning's work and offered condolences for the losses, as recalled by Sqn Ldr Howell:

> George Beamish gives people the impression he is pleased to see them; he looks them straight in the eye, and he is a born leader of men. I felt that I should be happy to do anything in the world for him, but found it difficult to say. He said: 'You've a man's job ahead of you', and it certainly seemed so. The appearance of the Me109s meant that the airfield in the Peloponnese was in operation. The enemy could always send over a screen of fighters to occupy us while his bombers came in unopposed. There seemed to be no way around it. Our landing strips were too small for the operation of large numbers of aircraft even if we could have them, which we could not. We thought it might be possible to use the airfields only for refuelling and rearming and operate from Egyptian bases. But having to fly all that distance meant that we could still be outnumbered over Crete with ease by a fighter force based close by in the Peloponnese.
>
> I suggested that we should try to intercept the bombers out over the islands before they reached Crete and picked up their fighter escort. Beamish agreed that this might succeed for a time and we intended to try it out when and if we received a few replacements. In the meantime he would arrange for some long-range Beaufighters to come over and attack the enemy fighter base. But it was clear that we had not sufficient resources in the Middle East to make any significant reduction to the enemy air effort over Crete. In effect we were a token force, token of the unbreakable resistance of Britain, token of the future, when the position would be reversed. In the meantime our course was clear. We should fight to the end.

Just before dusk Maleme was again alerted when aircraft were heard approaching, and on this occasion one of the Bofors gun crews obtained a direct hit on a Messerschmitt, which reportedly blew up and fell into the sea. This was probably Ltn von Eichel-Streiber's Bf109 from III/JG77, which returned heavily damaged from an evening attack, during which three more aircraft were claimed destroyed on the ground. Of von Eichel-Streiber's plight, Fw Herbert Kaiser of 8 Staffel wrote:

On the return flight Ltn von Eichel-Streiber had considerable difficulties keeping his aircraft in the air because of heavy flak damage. He repeatedly used the R/T to call the Kommandeur – who was also his uncle. Not using the regular callsigns, but completely in the clear with more or less the following words: 'Uncle, what am I supposed to do?' After this call had been repeated several times, Hptm von Winderfeldt gave the following reply: 'My dear Diethelm, if you really don't know what to do and you can't go on any longer, repeat after me very slowly: Our father. Who art in Heaven . . . !

Von Eichel-Steiber eventually crashed at Molaoi on return, his aircraft being written-off. Three Heinkels attempted to raid Maleme after dark. Sqn Ldr Howell wrote:

I went down to the far end of the strip to see how the guards were. As I walked down the road in the darkness I heard an aircraft flying low towards us from the east. It was being fired at and was returning the fire from its nose and tail guns. It was coming straight along the road towards me. I looked hurriedly for a ditch. There was none. So I lay flat on the ground in a slight dip just off the road. Just before it reached the edge of the airfield, the enemy aircraft started dropping a stick of 50-kilo bombs. The thumps of the successive explosions came rapidly nearer. The last bomb went off less than one hundred yards from where I lay, and the splinters screamed across just above my head. The enemy gunners were by then firing at where they thought our aircraft should be so their bursts went wide of the road. They hit nothing, but they caused a good many of us to be thoughtful.

I walked on to where the men were standing in a deep slit trench. I assumed a calm, which I did not feel, and asked if they were all right. Just then another aircraft approached so I got down in the trench with them, thankful for cover. It came straight at us, low down, firing and dropping bombs. This time I had a rifle, borrowed from one of the guards. We aimed at the shadowy shape as it flashed past over us – like shooting geese in the gloaming on an East Anglian estuary. We fired together and had the great satisfaction of knocking a large piece of cowling off.

It clattered to the ground where we later collected it, a battered sheet of metal about three feet square, probably off one of the engines. The aircraft was a Heinkel. The next one came along the road again and we fired at it too. It returned our fire with a vicious burst from the tail gunner. But the shots went wide. Later, when all was quiet, I walked back along the road and met some of the men on their way to inspect the aircraft for damage. We could see nothing in the darkness so we left them till the morning. I was very tired and crept thankfully into bed.

The assault resumed at 0500 on **15 May,** when a single bomber approached unobserved and dropped a stick of bombs on Maleme, damaging a Blenheim and wounding three airmen in a lorry. The airfield was now becoming too dangerous for these aircraft and, an hour later, the last three serviceable Blenheims departed for Egypt, one of them accompanied by an 805 Squadron Sea Gladiator. Halfway to Mersa Matruh the Gladiator's engine failed and Lt(A) Peter Scott was obliged to ditch. The Blenheim circled the position, but could see no sign of the pilot, who was not found by a 228 Squadron Sunderland sent out to pick him up.

No sooner had the Blenheims gone than an estimated nine Bf109s swooped on the airfield, shooting up dispersed aircraft and gun positions, while a second Staffel circled above at 3–4,000ft, and another at 10,000ft as top cover. Woodward, whose DFC had just been announced, was at readiness, and recalled:

I started my aircraft and seconds later whilst commencing to taxi the engine stopped and burst into flames. I jumped out and dashed to a stand-by aircraft (partially u/s, I recall). No time to fasten parachute or harness – again attempted to get airborne, but as I gained ground speed there were two 109s firing at me from 600–800 yards – I almost made it, but flames again, so up undercarriage and skid to a stop and exit very smartly to cover in a ditch off the edge of the airstrip. Frankly I'd had enough for one day – it had to be the most uncomfortable few minutes of my life – if there is such a thing as a 'guardian angel' he was working overtime that day on my behalf!

A Sea Gladiator also attempted to take off, but tipped over, trapping the pilot. At once a New Zealand soldier rushed to his aid and freed him, but the Messerschmitts then promptly shot up this aircraft and a second Sea Gladiator nearby; the wrecked Buffalos also received a further strafing.

During a lull in the attacks four further replacement Hurricanes arrived from Mersa Matruh, flown by 30 Squadron pilots, guided and escorted to the island by a 24 SAAF Squadron Maryland. Two of the fighters landed at Maleme for 33 Squadron, while the other two went to Heraklion for 112 Squadron. The ferry pilots would not remain and would return to Egypt on a departing Sunderland. A further raid on Maleme and Suda Bay at midday by Do17s of III/KG2 brought a scramble for several Hurricanes, but no contact was made, although one Dornier was hit by AA shrapnel.

Again dawn on **16 May** brought a resumption of attacks on Maleme. At 0615, Hurricanes were scrambled from Maleme and encountered a number of Bf109s, one of which Bill (V7795) claimed to have shot. His victim may have been Ltn Adolf Dickfeld of 7./JG52 (attached to II/JG77), who later wrote:

> Following a half-roll and dive we were right over the entire flotilla, which was apparently on its way to Egypt. Almost all the boats were firing now. There were a good dozen fishing boats and in their midst several English motor torpedo boats, all loaded with soldiers, munitions, and equipment.
>
> 'Low-level attack!' I called over to Rickmer.
>
> I flipped up the safety catch and opened fire. The Tommies weren't old men and they put up a veritable wall of fire to meet us. I heard several thumps, it sounded like I had been hit aft in the fuselage. Rickmer had a tulip in his right wing, a shell had passed clean through. One of the torpedo boats began to glow bright red like a street light and seconds later blew apart. It was time to get away, fuel was running low, we had to get home and lick our wounds. I climbed toward the mountains. Soon Heraklion was below us. It was still in English hands and heavy anti-aircraft guns began firing. Then we were over Suda Bay, in which lay numerous English warships, sunk by our people. I turned north over Maleme and was already looking forward to lunch. Then, suddenly, tracer flashed past my cockpit and at the same time Rickmer screamed:
>
> 'Hurricanes, four of them behind you!'
>
> I was able to pull up to the right just in time and then I spotted the Tommies. How had they moved in so close without us seeing them? But there was no time for further consideration. Rickmer had dived away. Below us was Antikythera, in front of me the Tommies. They turned toward me. I was alone, where the devil was Rickmer? The battle drifted northward. I turned tighter than my opponents and in fractions of a second I had the first one square in my Revi. A press on the triggers and tracer poured into the Hurricane. It began to smoke and peeled away. I was still at 1,000 metres. Suddenly bullets struck my cockpit. The instrument panel caught the full force of the burst and was riddled like Swiss cheese. What was worse, glycol vapour was

streaming into my face, that meant that the radiators had been hit.
I dived away steeply. The other Hurricanes had disappeared, thank
God! I searched for a place to land. At 300 metres I spotted a machine
lying on its belly on the beach, its British roundels stood out clearly. I
lowered the flaps, left the landing gear up, and set my machine down
on the sand next to the Tommy. The underwing radiators were ripped
off, the ailerons flew away. I opened the canopy, jumped out, and ran
away from my smoking Messerschmitt. Taking cover behind a large
rock, I waited for the aircraft to explode. But nothing happened and
the smoke slowly died out.

I left cover and began thinking about the Tommy I had brought
down, who must be hiding on the botany somewhere nearby. As a
precaution I pulled my 7.65mm pistol from my fur-lined boot and
looked all around me. But there was no sign of life, no one for me
to take prisoner. Where could the fellow be hiding? Not ten minutes
had passed since his forced-landing. I looked inside his machine; the
parachute was still in the cockpit. His instrument panel had been
shot up just like mine, and there were several holes in the fuselage as
well. But there was no sign of blood. It appeared that he had escaped
unhurt; I didn't grudge him that.

In view of the difficult terrain there didn't seem to be much sense
in searching further. So I took my parachute out of my Messerschmitt,
which was riddled with bullet holes, threw it over my shoulder and
began walking in the direction of the interior. After several hours of
walking I came to a small fishing village, whose name I have forgotten.
In an instant I was surrounded. They all spoke to me but my schoolboy
Greek seemed not to be understood there. Then, finally, an old man
came up to me and spoke to me in English. I explained that I needed
a car to get back to my airfield, which lay not ten kilometres from
there, and soon a donkey-drawn cart appeared. The old man drove me
through the area at a leisurely pace and we began to talk. He told me
quite openly that we Germans weren't welcome there, after all we had
invaded his country. When I asked him if he knew the whereabouts
of the shot-down Tommy he smiled to himself and asked me: 'Would
you turn in a friend?'

Right then I knew that Greek patriots had hidden 'my' Englishman
in a safe place. Finally, late in the afternoon, I arrived back at my
airfield, dirty and disappointed, but otherwise none the worse for
wear. I reported my return to the 'old man'.

'My dear fellow,' he began, 'where did you come from, we gave you
up for lost a long time ago. Rickmer has been back for some time. He
got away with a few bullet holes. Make your report after you've eaten.'

I was unable to have my kill confirmed. No witness, no confirmation, that was it! That's how it was in that part of the world.

Ltn Dickfeld[3] had force-landed on the southern coast of Greece, not far from Molaoi. It would seem that the Hurricane he inspected on the beach was not his victim, but one that crash-landed previously.

A midday scramble brought no further combat but, at about 1600, Sqn Ldr Howell set off to carry out a reconnaissance over the island of Melos at Grp Capt Beamish's request.

My interest in the island was not that of the artist so much as to see whether there was any evidence of enemy shipping there and whether an airfield was being constructed. Milo (Melos) was about twenty minutes' flying away from Maleme. It was a hot hazy day and I was afraid that I might miss the island. But it appeared out of the haze all right and I circled the lovely natural harbour there in search of shipping. The bay was empty, except for a wreck stranded on the beach, a little coaster, which was a relic of the evacuation from the mainland. I flew low across the island and could see no trace of an airfield being prepared. People waved to me as I skimmed low across the fields and vineyards.

I headed back out to sea towards Crete again. Suddenly, silhouetted against the dazzling sea, up-sun from me, I saw a single aircraft heading in the opposite direction. It was a three-engined Junkers 52, a German transport aircraft probably returning to Greece from Rhodes. I swung across towards it and came straight in on a quarter attack. Tracers flashed past me from the rear gunner. I fired a long burst as I came in. I was travelling very fast and shot past him under the starboard wing within a few feet of the propeller. I pulled up and round as for a peacetime practice exercise. This time I aimed at his starboard motor. The pilot was by now right down close to the water taking violent evasive action. He was so low that his wheels touched the water at one point throwing up a cloud of spray. My bullets seemed to have no effect, except that the rear gun was now silent. I overshot again and came in for the third time from well astern and more slowly. This time I took the port engine and gave it a steady burst. Flames started to come from the wing-root near the fuselage. I pulled away to port and watched.

The flames grew in size and licked back along the fuselage to the tail. Suddenly the whole aircraft pulled up into a steep climb and turned over on to its back, a mass of flames. It fell back into the water tail first and disappeared straight away. A plume of black smoke drifted away, detached from any source. The water resumed its calm and peaceful appearance. There was no sign of survivors. Like the smoke, I felt strangely detached from the whole episode. I was glad the end had come quickly for them. I always hoped it would be so for me.

There were no survivors from the Ju52 – IZ+GX of IV/KGzb.V1 flown by Fw Walter Steinbach. Continuing on towards Crete, Howell then saw more aircraft below, again flying in the opposite direction. These were Ju87s of I/StG2, escorted by Bf110s of II/ZG26 and Bf109s, which had just attacked Maleme and Suda Bay.

I opened up to full throttle and closed in fast on the Stukas. They shot at me with their rear guns as I drew in on the tail of the nearest. I concentrated on my sight and on the target now growing rapidly larger within the glowing red ring. As its span seemed to touch the outside ring I pressed the firing button and held the quivering aircraft straight and steady. The rounds poured out from the eight guns, the muzzle flames leaping round the leading edges of the wings. The tracers converged into the target. It seemed an age before anything happened. Then the Stuka flicked rapidly over onto its back and went straight down at the water in a vertical dive.

Tracers were passing me in both directions now and unpleasantly close. I pulled up and away into the sun preparing to fight it out with the Me109s behind me. But they must have had enough and they were probably getting short of petrol for the return journey. They did not follow me. The air was suddenly empty of aircraft again. I went on homewards. I found I was covered in sweat and a little breathless. My legs felt weak. It was as if I were coming off the field after a hard game of rugger.

Sqn Ldr Howell called the controller for advice:

He replied to my call and instructed me to land at Retimo and not at Maleme. His voice was deep and guttural and it was not the man who had been on duty when I left. It suddenly crossed my mind that the airborne invasion might have started and that the radio might have been taken over by the enemy. I was determined not to be enticed down at an enemy-controlled airfield. So I replied that I had insufficient petrol and would land at Maleme. This produced an urgent message saying on no account to land at Maleme. Over the airfield I called the fighter ops control and was told to look out for enemy fighters. I looked everywhere for signs of Me109s but there was nothing I could see. So I came in on a very quick turn to land. I nearly touched down with my undercarriage still retracted as the machine was an old one and had a slightly different undercarriage mechanism. I went round again just in time, an easy target for enemy fighters if they had been there.

I taxied in to the pens quickly in case the airfield should be attacked. There, I was reassured. There had been no invasion. My imagination had run riot. There had been a very heavy bombing attack, however, and the usual horde of Me109s had engaged all three of our available Hurricanes. The Fleet Air Arm boys had been on stand-by and they had fought magnificently and gallantly with ten times their number of Me109s. They had knocked down at least six [*sic*] but none of them had come back. I was apparently the sole survivor, but one other came limping in much later, full of holes, having had to land at Retimo.

The three FAA pilots had soon ran into Bf109s, from both I(J)/LG2 and III/JG77, Lt(A) Tony Ash being shot down into the sea almost at once and killed. Lt(A) Herbert Richardson's Hurricane was also seen to be under attack, and he baled out not far from the airfield, his parachute apparently failing to open. His body was found by local peasants, who laid him in their village church. The third pilot, Lt(A) Alec Ramsay, encountered Bf109s of 8./JG77 and shot down two of them, Fw Herbert Perrey's Black 4 force-landing on its belly near a village, while Ltn Harald Mann baled out, wounded, but managed to evade capture. Ramsay's Hurricane was badly damaged in the fight, and he put down at Retimo, causing those at Maleme to believe that all three 805 Squadron pilots had been lost.

Fw Johann Pichler of 7./JG77 and Fw Herbert Kaiser of 8 Staffel each claimed a Hurricane shot down, while Hptm Herbert Ihlefeld and Ltn Fritz Greisshardt of StabI/LG2 claimed two more. Ofhr Günther Hannak of I(J)/LG2 claimed a fifth. Of this period of intense operations, Pichler wrote:

> The operational missions to Crete put a great strain on our nerves and before taking off we could only pray that our engines would not give trouble. The outward trip over the sea was 160km, and then we had to make the return flight, sometimes with damaged engines, and our greatest thought was, 'I only hope I don't get engine trouble.' Over the sea we had to endure the terrible heat in our cockpits and I never saw any ships which might have saved our lives had we been forced to come down in the sea.

Sentiments echoed by Fw Kaiser:

> Flying against Crete puts the nerves under heavy strain. A few days before the German airborne attack, we were already flying multiple low level missions to the island, 160km across the sea on the way in and we to go back as well. Our prayers before take off were foremost dedicated to the engine, hopefully it would hold on. In the end no

one wanted to make better acquaintance with the wet element; ships which perhaps could have served as safety net were not seen during the daily sorties. And then the terrible heat in the cockpit – as we had to fly low level, in order to avoid British radar detection, there wasn't any cooling to be expected from higher altitudes – was a strain, that not all pilots could take and which caused considerable health problems to some of us.

Bill was also in action over Suda Bay. He reported attacking the Ju87s, which were bombing shipping in the bay, and claimed one shot down before being attacked by Bf109s, which he successfully evaded. This action may have been that recorded by a Greek teenager aboard one of the vessels:

Thinking that the Stukas would bomb us sooner or later, I got off the ship and fell onto some rocks, which resembled trenches. I lay on the rocks, while the British soldier stood near the ship's mast. I gestured to him to come on shore and hide, but he did not stir at all. Barely moments later, the Stukas seemed to be returning in full force. I buried my head in the rocks and listened as the bombs whistled by. I was covered in stones and water. I froze. I thought the bombs had fallen directly on top of me. The bombs fell on the harbour, one on the beach, the other in the middle of the port. There were about fifteen ships of various sizes in the harbour. They had all been hit and were no longer seaworthy. The *Evrotas* was lucky and suffered no damage, neither did the British soldier who had not moved from his post.

The British soldiers who were hidden in the bushes dared not move. While all this was going on the Stukas continued to drop bombs and circled the harbour possibly in order to drop more, or to survey the results or even to leave.

Suddenly we caught sight of a third aeroplane, which began to fire and head off the Stukas, who in turn returned fire. Consequently a small-scale air battle erupted above our heads. The Stukas withdrew straight away. The third aeroplane was a Hurricane, which had come for us. The general who was the highest ranking officer among us, had already contacted the British base at Suda, and a plane had arrived with instructions. After the Stukas had left, the Hurricane returned to the harbour. It flew low. On catching sight of the plane, the British jumped out from behind the bushes and began shouting, as if they wanted to touch it with their own hands. All of a sudden the pilot threw out a small package, waved goodbye and left. The soldiers took the package to the general who opened it and read the message. We were to be ready by ten o'clock that night.[4]

The dive-bombers had caused considerable damage during their attack. Two tankers were hit, the 10,694-ton Danish *Eleanora Maersk* again being hit and being set alight before she could discharge her cargo, and with several of her crew killed; she was beached near Kalami Point, where she burned for five days. The British chartered *Logician* (5,993 tons) and *Araybank* (7,258 tons) were both set on fire, the former being a total loss, while three Greek ships were sunk – *Nicolaou Ourania* (6,397 tons), *Thermoni* (5,719 tons) and *Kythera* (1,070 tons). Since the start of May 15 supply ships had reached Suda Bay, but 8 of these had been sunk or damaged in harbour, and only 15,000 tons of stores had actually been offloaded, including just 3,000 tons of munitions from the anticipated total of 27,000 tons.

At Heraklion, meanwhile, 112 Squadron was preparing to put its two new Hurricanes into use, but only three pilots had previously flown the type, and only Flt Lt Fry had any real experience. Crete was hardly the ideal place to undertake operational training, but most pilots managed to get at least one flight between raids. When yet another strafing attack by Bf110s approached – this time undertaken by 30 aircraft of I and II/ZG26 – both Hurricanes and three Gladiators were ordered off. Fry in a Hurricane managed to bounce one of eight Messerschmitts at 6,000ft and got some telling hits on Uffz Erhard Witzke's 3U+SM of 4 Staffel. Unfortunately for him, as he broke away Witzke's gunner, Fw Karl Reinhardt, got an accurate burst of fire into the Hurricane's engine and as it streamed glycol, Fry was forced to bale out. Struck a glancing blow by the tailplane as he did so, he landed three miles from the airfield with a badly bruised chest.

Meanwhile, Witzke's Messerschmitt was forced to ditch as he struggled to get back to Argos, when the damaged port engine failed. Rescued from the sea by a Cretan fishing boat, the crew were brought back to Crete where they were hospitalised. The second Hurricane had come under attack by other Bf110s, and force-landed after sustaining damage, but Bofors gunners of 7th Australian Light AA Battery hit U8+MK of 2 Staffel, this aircraft crashing into the sea with the loss of Uffz Erwin Bauer and Gfr Karl-Heinz Heldmann.

At Retimo during the day a low-flying Hs126, probably from 4.(H)/22, appeared, obviously on reconnaissance. Australian troops were entrenched in the hills on either side of the airfield, and two Greek battalions around Adhele village, their joint small-arms fire bringing down this aircraft. On board were found photographs of the area which indicated that their positions were so well concealed that only one trench could be seen from the air. During the evening nine Beaufighters arrived at Heraklion from where they carried out strikes against German-occupied Greek aerodromes the following morning. Much success was achieved, though too little to prevent further attacks on Crete. At Heraklion, during a lull in attacks, three more Hurricanes flew in from Egypt, led by a SAAF Maryland. The ferry pilots, from 30 Squadron, were to return to collect further aircraft ready for another reinforcement flight.

Maleme was submitted to further intense gound strafing, the last Fulmar and last Sea Gladiator being destroyed. During the many such attacks being endured, personnel not required immediately on the airfield retreated to slit trenches prepared in the surrounding hills; hence casualties were kept to a minimum. Early in the afternoon the three remaining serviceable Hurricanes were scrambled – V7795 flown by Bill, V7761 (Lt Cdr Black) and N2610 (flown by a pilot of 33 Squadron) – as Ju88s approached. Bill claimed damage to one aircraft on this occasion, but later in the day he and Black were unable to make an interception when ordered off again.

At Maleme the morning of **18 May** was spent by 805 Squadron burying Lt(A) Richardson in Canea cemetery following his death two days previously. As the truck carrying the funeral party returned to Maleme, it was attacked by a Bf109, although all aboard escaped injury. Almost continuous strafing attacks were made during the morning by Bf109s and 110s, without interception. At midday, however, a Royal Marine Bren-gun crew shot down a low-flying Bf110, believed to have been an aircraft of 6./ZG26 flown by Ltn Heinz Knecht and Fw Georg Schultz, which came down in the sea south-east of Spetsai Island while trying to get back to Argos after suffering damage; the crew was rescued from the water.

Ju87s of I/StG2 dive-bombed Maleme and Suda Bay, where the RFA oiler *Olna* was seriously damaged and beached, while Bf109s also strafed Maleme in support of the Stukas. In the midst of this attack a lone replacement Hurricane arrived from Egypt, piloted by 21-year-old Welshman, Sgt Vernon Hill, on his first operational flight. Probably short of fuel and unaware that the attack was in progress, since he was not in radio contact, Hill lowered his undercarriage and prepared to land just as eight Messerschmitts swept in behind him. Obviously suddenly aware of his predicament, he was seen to pull away out to sea as the 109s vied to get on his tail. As one overshot, watchers believed that he may have shot this down, but by then Fw Otto Niemeyer of 4./JG77 had got in a telling burst of fire and the Hurricane crashed into the sea with a mighty splash, Hill being killed.

At 1700, Bill flew his last – and 32nd – op from Crete in V7795. In barely three weeks he had claimed three Ju88s, a Ju52, a Bf109 and a Ju87, plus two Ju88s damaged, to raise his score to 27 plus four shared.

The only German loss recorded during this raid was for a Ju87 (T6+JH) flown by Uffz Ernst Tauscher, which was hit by AA fire and crash-landed; the pilot was killed, but the gunner (Uffz Düring) survived and evaded capture. Meanwhile, at Maleme, a number of He111s appeared overhead, one bomb scoring a direct hit on the pen sheltering Sqn Ldr Howell's Hurricane, N2610, which went up in flames. On the other side of the airfield Bill's faithful V7795, and V7761, were both put out of action.

Following this latest attack only one Hurricane remained serviceable at Maleme, W9298, which was flown off by Lt Cdr Black on a reconnaissance of Kalamata and the surrounding area. On his return Grp Capt Beamish ordered that the minimum operational formation was to be a pair, and no one, including Black and Howell, were to fly the Hurricane again unaccompanied. Bill recalled, on expecting the invasion to occur at any moment: 'One massive Australian stuck a Tommy-gun into my hands and said I had to get on with it.'

Heraklion was also attacked repeatedly, and the airfield was rendered unserviceable. Two Hurricanes and two Gladiators were airborne at the time, and were ordered to land instead at Retimo. The remaining Hurricane and Gladiators at Heraklion were no longer flyable. On arrival at Retimo the four pilots were ordered to evacuate to Egypt, and after refuelling, all took off. Flg Off Alf Costello and Sgt Bill Bain flew the two Hurricanes, Flt Lt Dennant and Plt Off Jerry Westenra the Gladiators; all arrived safely.

That evening at 1800 Flt Lt Lywood brought Sunderland N9020 down on the waters of Suda Bay to deliver a few passengers and some freight, but primarily to take back to Egypt a full load of personnel, including Bill, who had been ordered to leave. Presumably he was able to say goodbye to Janina. They were never to meet again.

Lt Cdr Black was also ordered to leave by Cdr George Beale RN, OC Maleme, to make representations to Rear Adm Boyd that more fighter aircraft should be sent. 805 Squadron was now represented by just Lt(A) Alec Ramsay and Sub-Lt(A) Roy Hinton, two TAGs, L/Air Tom Jarvis and L/Air Bill Jary, about 55 ground personnel, and no aircraft. This party was to return by sea should no further aircraft become available. Additionally, Lt(A) Lloyd Keith of this unit was in hospital on the island, suffering from dysentery.

33 Squadron still expected the arrival of further Hurricanes, and new aircraft pens were in the course of construction. Early on **19 May** some 40 bomb-carrying Bf109s of II and III/JG77 attacked Maleme without prior warning having been received. After scattering 50kg fragmentation bombs over the area, they flew out to sea before returning to strafe. Fw Johann Pichler of 7 Staffel flew on this sortie:

> Oblt Huy led a *Schwarm* from 7 Staffel for a strike against positions on Maleme airfield. I was one of the pilots. We took off early in the morning while it was still dark and foggy. It was an impressive flight, high over layers of haze and mist, which prevented us from seeing the water. Our orders were to carry out low-level attacks against the British anti-aircraft positions at Maleme.

As we dived down from 4,000 metres, the British anti-aircraft guns opened up, their red tracers coming up at us in a withering wall of fire. At the same time, the white tracers from our cannon and machine guns flew downwards until our shells disappeared into the British positions. We were lucky to return without being seriously hit, but despite the large number of operations carried out, we were unable to destroy the AA defences with cannon or bombs because the positions were perfectly built and difficult to recognise.

Despite Pichler's pessimism regarding success, when this attack ended all the airfield's Bofors guns had been silenced and a number of casualties suffered by the gun crews. During the afternoon the Messerschmitts returned and resumed shooting-up the airfield and surrounding area. Subsequently the surrounding area was heavily bombed by Heinkels. In between these attacks Grp Capt Beamish ordered Sqn Ldr Howell to dispatch all airworthy Hurricanes at Maleme to Egypt, but by now only W9298 remained flyable. From the many hopefuls eager to make this flight, Howell selected the sole remaining 80 Squadron pilot, the seemingly forgotten Sgt Bennett, who took off forthwith. At Heraklion three more Gladiators had been made airworthy, and these too left for Egypt. There were no more operational aircraft left on Crete – the first phase of the island's defence was at an end.

The invasion of Crete commenced at dawn next morning with the arrival of the first German paratroops. One of the many thousands of German paratroopers preparing for the invasion, Uffz Martin Pöppel, later recalled:

On 19 May we received our orders for the next day – a parachute drop on the island of Crete. We reckoned that such a small island wouldn't be a problem for us. How wrong we were – it was to be an enormous and bloody task. That evening we gathered under a huge olive tree, drank beer and sang our songs accompanied by Oberleutnant Büttner's band. Was it premonition that we didn't just sing cheerful soldiers' songs as usual, but also included nostalgic songs of home? For most of the men it would be the first parachute jump and only a few – such as myself – knew what death in action was really like. Maybe many realised, even had a premonition, that they might be killed. No one commented on it. But many of these lads, so fresh and young and so full of optimism, were to fall in battle during the next few days.[5]

(See Appendices VIII and IX for further information regarding the Battle of Crete.)

Chapter 10

AN ARGUMENT WITH THE FRENCH

The Vichy French and Allied forces confronting each other in Syria and Lebanon were evenly matched in general. The Armée de l'Air de Vichy in the Levant was relatively strong at the outbreak of hostilities. The Armée de l'Air had 25 D.520 fighters based at Rayak (GCIII/6) plus a detachment of three M-167Fs (Glenn Martins) of GBI/39, and a dozen Potez 63s at Damascus-Mezze (GBII/39), with an assortment of other fighters, bombers and reconnaissance aircraft located at various other airfields in Syria. The meagre RAF units were up against it until the arrival of reinforcements to the region.

Starting with over 90 aircraft, three additional groups were flown in from France and from North Africa. This brought the strength of the air force in Lebanon and Syria up to 289 aircraft. But the initial advantage they enjoyed did not last long. The Vichy lost most of their aircraft during the campaign. The majority of the lost aircraft were destroyed on the ground, where the flat terrain, absence of infrastructure and absence of modern anti-aircraft artillery made them vulnerable to air attacks.

* * *

By the end of May, 80 Squadron was being re-formed and was based at Haifa in Palestine. Few of the originals remained and new blood had been posted in. Two-dozen new Hurricanes were made available, although initially eight of these were loaned to 3 (RAAF) Squadron until their promised Tomahawks arrived, and a further six to 112 Squadron, which was also re-forming. Sqn Ldr Tap Jones oversaw the re-formed unit and Bill now became a flight commander. Apparently, he was still raring for a fight and rather than be rested, opted instead to continue operational flying. The fact that he had no knowledge of the whereabouts or safety of Janina would have been paramount in his refusal to be posted away. Roald Dahl was still with the squadron, and of this period wrote:

> 80 Squadron were to assemble at Haifa in northern Palestine in the last week of May. Each pilot was told to collect his new Hurricane at Abu Sueir and fly it to Haifa. I asked if someone else could fly my

plane to Haifa for me because I wanted to drive myself up there in my own motorcar. I had become the very proud possessor of a 1932 Morris Oxford saloon, a machine whose body had been sprayed with a noxious brown paint the colour of canine faeces, and whose maximum speed on a straight and level track was 35mph.

Surprisingly, the authorities agreed to let Dahl drive to Haifa, a journey that he thoroughly enjoyed.

We had nine Hurricanes at Haifa and the same number of pilots, and in the days that followed we were kept very busy. Our main job was to protect the Navy. Our Navy had two large cruisers and several destroyers stationed in Haifa harbour and every day they would sail up the coast past Tyre and Sidon to bombard the Vichy French forces in the mountains around the Damour river. And whenever our ships came out, the Germans came over to bomb them. They came from Rhodes, where they had built up a strong force of Ju88s, and just about every day we met those Ju88s over the fleet. They came over at 8,000 feet and we were usually waiting for them. We would dive in amongst them, shooting at their engines and getting shot at by their gunners – and the sky was filled with bursting shells from the ships below. Sometimes the Vichy French joined up with the Germans. They had Glenn Martins, Dewoitines [D.520s] and Potez 63s, and we shot some of them down and they killed four of our nine pilots.

Four Hurricanes were sent to Cyprus on **3 June**, leaving 80 Squadron with just eight, and these were dispatched to Aqir to provide cover for British warships operating off the coast. 80 Squadron received some reinforcements in the guise of a number of pilots from 213 Squadron, who had arrived in Palestine from the aircraft carrier *Furious*, via Malta. Though mainly inexperienced, they provided welcomed fresh blood.

At 0900 on **6 June**, a Vichy French Glenn Martin flew over Aqir and dropped leaflets written in French. It was believed to have been the aircraft flown by Lt Labas, who had defected to the Vichy a few days earlier. Two of the squadron's new pilots, Flt Lt John Lockhart and Plt Off George Westlake took off and claimed the Glenn Martin shot down between Haifa and Beirut – the victory apparently confirmed by the Royal Navy.

Following the temporary loss of the carrier HMS *Illustrious* (bomb-damaged at Malta earlier in the year), the carrier's Fulmar-equipped 803 Squadron had in the meantime been dispatched to Lydda (Palestine). The Fulmars were also tasked to provide protection for the British warships operating off the coast and, at 1300 on **8 June**, a Fulmar patrol was attacked off Sidon by two D.520s of GCIII/6. The French pilots, Lt Robert Martin and Sous-Lt Brondel, believed their opponents were Hurricanes. In the ensuing combat, Martin's aircraft (No. 331) was shot down but he managed to bale out over land and was captured by Australian troops. His wingman returned to report that his leader had been shot down by a fighter. At 1532, six more D.520s took off to patrol the same area, meeting six Fulmars (again identified as Hurricanes) and took revenge. Lt John Christian, 803 Squadron's CO, was shot down and killed, together with his observer Sub Lt Norman Cullen. A second Fulmar also fell to the French fighters with the loss of PO(A) Jimmy Gardner and L/Air Harry Pickering. It seems that two more Fulmars were hit, one ditching from which the crew was rescued. Two 'Hurricanes' were claimed by Cne Leon Richard and Lt Marcel Steunou.

80 Squadron was called upon to carry out the next patrol, Roald Dahl reporting an encounter with a Potez 63, claiming to have set one engine on fire and being credited with a probable. Another 80 Squadron section (three Hurricanes) carried out a strafing attack on Rayak, Canadian Sgt Fred Wilson reporting strikes on two Potez 63s. At least two aircraft were claimed to be on fire as the Hurricanes withdrew. Dahl was also on this raid:

> As we swept in surprise low over the field at midday, we saw to our astonishment a bunch of girls in brightly coloured cotton dresses standing out by the planes with glasses in their hands, having drinks with the French pilots, and I remember seeing bottles of wine standing on the wing of one of the planes as we went swooshing over. It was a Sunday morning and the Frenchmen were evidently entertaining their girlfriends and showing off their aircraft to them, which was a very French thing to do in the middle of a war at a front-line aerodrome.
>
> Every one of us held our fire on the first pass over the flying field and it was wonderfully comical to see the girls all dropping their wine glasses and galloping in their high heels for the door of the nearest building. We went round again, but this time we were no longer a surprise and they were ready for us with their ground defences, and I am afraid that our chivalry resulted in damage to several of our machines, including my own. But we destroyed five of their planes on the ground.

Next day, **9 June**, Plt Off Westlake reported a similar engagement and was also credited with a probable during a morning patrol, before a major confrontation between three Hurricanes and a raiding force occurred at 1525. Flt Lt Lockhart, Plt Off Tom Lynch and Plt Off Peter Crowther comprised the 80 Squadron section that encountered six M-167s of GBI/39, four Bloch 200s of EB3/39 escorted by six D.520s. Lockhart immediately led his section against the bombers, shooting down two of the Blochs before the escort shot down Lynch and Crowther, the former being killed, victims of Sous-Lt Pierre Le Gloan.

Three more Hurricanes had taken off to relieve Lockhart's patrol, and these arrived as the fight was in progress. At more or less the same time, three more D.520s also arrived, having been summoned to assist. The relief Hurricanes waded in and Plt Off George Westgate and Sgt Bob 'Wally' Wallace claimed two of the Vichy fighters, while Sgt Maurice Bennett collided head-on with another – No. 366 flown by Sous-Lt Georges Rivory. Both pilots baled out and were recovered by the Navy, Bennett (Bill's sole 80 Squadron companion at Crete) having suffered severe burns. It is possible that an attack by Westgate and Wallace had damaged Rivory's aircraft, causing him to collide with Bennett. A second Dewoitine returned badly damaged and crashed on landing.

On **11 June**, six Hurricanes were tasked to escort a Blenheim raid on Rayak airfield. Bill (V6939) and his No. 2 broke away to investigate a Potez 63 seen approaching British warships. Bill carried out an attack and believed he had shot it down before it disappeared into haze. This was in fact No. 676 of GRII/39 flown by Cne Forget, who managed to evade and escape and return to base. Only two bullet strikes were found following an inspection and no crew members were injured.

Next day (**12 June**), the Hurricanes were dispatched individually to fly protective patrols over the fleet. Bill encountered a section of D.520 fighters and claimed two shot down, one of which crashed with the death of the pilot on the coast near Haifa. French sources, however, credit these losses to Australian AA fire. Cne Roger Jacobi was killed when his aircraft crashed about four miles south of Sidon. The aircraft of two other pilots of his section were also hit, Sgt Louis Coisneau being wounded in the face, while Sgt-chef Pierre Monribot crash-landed. Bill later told a friend that one of his victims had crash-landed (Monribot?) and that he had landed his Hurricane nearby to check on the pilot's condition.[1] Finding the French pilot was unhurt, he took off and headed for base, but was obliged to force-land at Tyre following engine failure. The Hurricane (Z4200) was totally wrecked, but Bill was unhurt. However, one source suggests a very different version of events:

> At 1609, a patrouille double from GCIII/6 led by 5eEscadrille commander Cne Jacobi, took-off on a reconnaissance mission over Deraa and Hasbaya, looking for British troops and vehicles. Fire from a column of vehicles hit three of the fighters and Jacobi crashed to his death in No. 229 six kilometres south of Sidon, on the coast. Sgt Coisneau was wounded in the face but managed to return, and Sgt-chef Monribot lost control of his damaged aircraft whilst trying to land at Rayak, crashing No. 294, but suffering no injury.[2]

Cne Jacobi's wingman, Sous-Lt Brondel reported:

> Now we are in trouble to find targets. The English have used every inch of the uneven ground to disperse their vehicles and they await us firmly. I dive behind the Capitaine and the trap closes on us. From everywhere automatic weapons open the fire. In front of me, the Capitaine flies straight ahead, disregarding the bullets concentrating on his aircraft. He is hit several times. His Dewoitine enters a shallow dive, then skids on its right. The Capitaine has probably been hit as he makes no attempt to recover and his aircraft crashes into the ground at full speed before blowing up.[3]

A later 80 Squadron patrol encountered two Potez 63s from GAO 583 over the sea, Sgt Wally Wallace engaging Sous-Lt Tatraux's aircraft, which was last seen with a smoking starboard engine. However, it returned safely to base, as did Wallace, whose aircraft had been hit by return fire. The squadron also provided escort for 84 Squadron Blenheims, Sgt Fred Wilson meeting a Potez 63 which he claimed damaged. Another Potez 63 was claimed probably destroyed at 0627 next day (**14 June**) by Sgt John Hancock, who was then engaged by three escorting MS406s. He managed to evade and return, having suffered slight damage. His victim was not, in fact, a Potez 63 but a LeO451 from GBI/12, which also returned to base with slight damage.

Fleet patrols during the afternoon resulted in two clashes with Vichy fighters. At 1725 Flg Off David Coke, who had been undertaking a recce flight, was called to provide aid for the warships when MS406s appeared, one of which he claimed damaged. Shortly thereafter, at 1810, the next patrol of Hurricanes was engaged by a patrol of D.520s from GCIII/6, two of which were claimed shot down by Keg Dowding and Sgt John Hancock, with the latter also claiming a probable. The Royal Navy confirmed two aircraft crashing into the sea, but it seems that Sous-Lt Brondel was the only casualty, crash-landing and overturning on return to Rayak.

During an afternoon patrol over the fleet on **15 June**, Dahl engaged one of nine Ju88s from II/LG1 operating from Crete and attacking the warships off the coast. He promptly engaged one, which was reported to have pancaked on the sea some 12 miles north of the fleet; it was claimed that another force-landed in Syria and a third in Turkey. Only one failed to return, the machine that landed in Turkey, where the crew was interned. Dahl was increasingly suffering severe headaches, a legacy of his earlier crash, and was now taken off operations. Bill, also, was feeling the effects of almost 12 months of continuous operational flying.

On **16 June**, a section of Hurricanes led by Bill in V6969 carried out a strafe in a Vichy gun site, all three returning safely. This turned out to be Bill's final operational flight. A couple of days later, a dozen new pilots (260 Squadron from the UK, that had travelled with 213 Squadron aboard the carrier via Malta) arrived at Haifa and were attached to 80 Squadron for operations, thereby releasing the battle-fatigued handful of original squadron pilots, including Bill and Roald Dahl. Bill then spent a couple of weeks to-ing and fro-ing between Aqir and Haifa, managing to get flights in one of 3(RAAF) Squadron's Tomahawks and an ancient Hawker Hart, before being posted to Sector Headquarters as Senior Operations Officer at Haifa with the rank of Acting Flight Lieutenant. He was awarded a Bar to his DFC at the end of the month, this being gazetted on 11 July. He was also notified of the award of the Greek DFC.

The KING has been graciously pleased to approve the following awards in recognition of gallantry displayed in flying operations against the enemy: – Bar to the Distinguished Flying Cross.

Pilot Officer William VALE, DFC (44068), No. 80 Squadron.

After the evacuation operations from Greece, this officer remained at Maleme aerodrome with some members of his unit. In the course of enemy air attacks on Crete, Pilot Officer Vale proved himself to be a staunch pilot. Frequently against odds, he continued his attacks against the enemy and destroyed four of their aircraft during an attack on the anchorage at Suda Bay. He displayed great courage and determination.

What of Janina? It is understood that she was sent back to Athens but died during the German occupation of Greece.[4] It has been suggested that she was executed as a 'collaborator' when her relationship with Bill became known, though this is not an established fact. She may have died from malnutrition. It is believed that Bill had by now received notification of Janina's death. Whatever the truth, sadly Janina did not survive the war. This was to be the fate of many Greek men and women (*see Appendix III*).

Chapter 11

RETURN TO ENGLAND

Bill remained at SHQ Haifa until April 1942, during which time he managed to keep his hand by flying whatever aircraft became available, including Harts, Hurricanes, Magisters, Lysanders – even a Blenheim and a Fulmar. The latter (N7642) he flew target-towing for the local AA guns to gain some practice. The latest assessment graded his flying ability as 'Exceptional'. When finally posted back to the UK, he had been away for six years. Here he learned that his brother George, a sub-lieutenant in the RNVR, had been killed in an accident.

Following his return to England and a period of rest and recuperation, during which he had requested a non-operational posting, Bill was posted to the Central Gunnery School at RAF Sutton Bridge, before being appointed as Chief Flying Instructor at No. 59 Operational Training Unit at RAF Crosby-on-Eden and later RAF Millfield in the same capacity. Between May and December 1943 he logged almost 230 flights, mainly in the OTU's Master trainers although he did manage the occasional flight in Spitfire Vs, a Hurricane and even in a RAF P-47 Thunderbolt.

While employed at 59 OTU he was also appointed as Station Gunnery Officer at RAF Wittering between June and September 1943. The original official press release covering his appointment, prepared by the PRO at HQ 12 Group RAF Watnall, contained some errors but basically triumphantly lauded his arrival in jingoistic terms:

> A fighter pilot who fought in Crete with a Tommy-gun against Nazi paratroop troops [sic] has now been appointed 'Guns' at a Fighter Command Station in the Midlands (Wittering).
>
> To give that pilot, S/Ldr W. Vale DFC and Bar his proper title, he is Station Armament Officer, looking after the guns that will knock the Hun out of the skies. He himself has shot down 32 aircraft and damaged seven.
>
> S/Ldr Vale, who comes from Framlingham, Suffolk, joined the RAF as a boy apprentice. His first serious introduction to war

was in the early Libyan campaign as a sergeant pilot, and he was commissioned in 1940, shortly before his squadron of Gladiators flew over to Greece to try to stem the onrushing Germans. The enemy proved too strong until, after eight months of fighting, the remnants had to make for the island of Crete.

'Those last days in Greece were pretty hectic,' S/Ldr Vale now recalls. 'When we went to Argos, as defenders of Athens, we were seldom on the ground. When we were, we had terrific ground strafing. One night we hid our aircraft in a copse, but still the weight of bombing over the area near our makeshift aerodrome resulted in only six planes being serviceable out of 15, next morning. A few days later we flew to Crete. This was in early May. As we had only two aircraft serviceable, after the grim ground strafing, our patrols over the people evacuating were practically nil. Flying boats and ships came to take off as many as they could, but we had to take on fighting against the Germans. Eventually we evacuated the island ourselves, the Sunderland taking off in the light of a badly bombed and burning ship.'

* * *

On 19 October 1943, Bill attended an Investiture at Buckingham Palace where he received the DFC and Bar from the hands of the King. The year 1944 saw him record almost 300 training flights as CFI at 59 OTU with the odd jaunt in a Spitfire IX and a Typhoon, although he also held the post of OC No. 11 Armament Practice Camp (RAF Fairwood Common) as from 1 January 1944. He was awarded the Air Force Cross for his performance.

> *VALE*, William, A/S/L, DFC (44068, Royal Air Force) – No. 11 Armament Practice Camp – Air Force Cross – awarded as per London Gazette dated 1 September 1944.
>
> *Since returning from a long tour in the Middle East, where he distinguished himself as an outstanding operational pilot, this officer has, during the last nine months, been in command of No. 11 Armament Practice Camp. The excellent results produced by the unit have been entirely due to the outstanding work carried out by this officer. Squadron Leader Vale has produced and developed many schemes for the betterment of armament training, many of which have been adopted throughout the command. His total operational flying hours amount to 870.*

A further 44 training flights were accomplished in 1945 before his final flight, in a Master with Sgt Tewkes, on 6 April. His logbook records a total of

3,703.35 flying hours (of which 870 were operational) and, apart from combat damage, without apparent mishap. None are recorded while performing his duty as CFI, quite some achievement.

With the war over, Bill attended the Fighter Leaders' Course at Tangmere in 1945, preceded by an Administration Course at RAF Cranwell. Subsequently he was appointed OC Gunnery and Armament Testing at RAF West Raynham, but left the service in October of that year. During an idle moment Bill penned the following, summing up his progress in the RAF in poetic verse. Possibly he had plans to apply for a post with the Aviation Inspection Directorate, which the piece was entitled:

> Through the academic training at a public school,
> Gained a Cambridge Certificate, I was no fool.
> And the choice of a first class career.
> A pass into the RAF as a boy engineer.
>
> Three years of swatting the 'Theory of Flight',
> The H.E.T. was then in sight.[1]
> The practical was fitting with the highest precision
> 'Above the Average' being the final decision.
>
> An apprentice no longer, a man with a trade.
> With promotion to pilot, my career was made.
> The Bulldog and Fury, both biplanes of yore,
> The Hurricane and Spitfire flown in the war.
>
> And then on to jets, test flying's no game
> But the theory of flight was still the same.
> A spin, bale out, am I to die?
> It's only birds and bloody fools that fly.
>
> From the wreck of the aircraft was plain to see
> A fractured rod found by the AID.
> And that is the reason for such rigid inspection
> If the compound isn't right, it must have a rejection.

* * * * *

While based at RAF Crosby-on-Eden in 1943, Bill had started a liaison with Betty Wilson (neé Matthews), known as Bette, the young wife of a missing serviceman. Since missing servicemen were not officially classified as deceased until three years after presumed death, Bill and Bette were not able to marry until mid-1946, but in the meantime an intimate relationship developed and Bill moved into the family house in Framlingham (Mount Pleasant), about half-a-mile from the college. February 1944 saw the arrival of a baby daughter,

Gaynor, who was born at her grandmother's house in Nottingham. Due to the legal situation covering the relationship, she was given her mother's married name of Wilson, although with the ultimate marriage of Bill and Bette, she became the 'adopted' daughter of Bill.

By the early 1950s the family had moved to picturesque Bridge Street, also in Framlingham. A son, named William after his father, followed and finally Amanda (middle name Janina!) was born in August 1953. One wonders if Bill had discussed Amanda's middle name with Bette, or if she was even aware of the connotations. While living at Framlingham, Bill and Bette entered into business and managed a small company selling wool and manufacturing woollen garments, trading as 'Bette Vale's' in Bridge Street.

Nips had remained at Framlingham College during the war and for a few years thereafter. Old Framlinghamian Jim Blythe recalls:

> During the war he masterminded the College Dig for Victory effort, and was well known for discussing his cabbages with the stress on the latter four letters. I recall him still being in charge of the armoury. Revd Rupert Kneese was in charge of the shooting.

Another post-war old boy, Trevor Trevethick, recalled:

> I remember Sergeant-Major Nips Vale well. He waxed the ends of his moustache. In my scrapbook I have two photographs of him, one in the uniform of a Captain RM and the other with the College shooting team at Bisley in 1952. I have labelled the former as 'Permanent Instructor, Corps, swimming and boxing'. I think this must have been his official title.
>
> He did not live in the college and I can remember him arriving on a bicycle. Socially he would have been on par with 'Doody' Day the woodwork instructor for the junior house – they were not allowed access to the Masters' common room! I remember the potty incident but I think it was on the centre college spire. The then head was furious so its mysterious removal would not have been seen by the boys – seems logical for it to have been shot down. Later when I was in the Sandhurst shooting team I remembered shooting 'Tips from Nips' that other members lacked the benefit of. One of these was 'lights up, sights up' and another was in heavy rain let all your rounds of ammunition get wet (if some were dry and some wet). This affected the pressure in the chamber and the velocity of the bullet.

Nips the widower had found solace with the landlady of the Queen's Head public house in Framlingham, where he lived until his death in 1957, aged 74. While living in Framlingham, Gaynor recalls that the family were never short of decent food, since fresh vegetables came from Granddad Nips's allotment and cooked dinners were often brought down from the pub.

Sadly, Bill's marriage was failing. Bette finally left the family home, gained a divorce and eventually remarried. Bill was left literally holding the baby, taking on the responsibility of bringing up Amanda with the help of her older sister. Gaynor left home at an early age, however, met and married Stephen Roberts and gave birth to Andrew – Bill's first grandson.

With the break-up of the marriage and the failure of the business venture, Bill moved to Nottingham, where he joined Hawker-Siddeley as an engineering inspector. During this time at Hawker-Siddeley's he became friendly with Tommy Sopwith Jr, the son of the aviation pioneer, who was a 'gentleman' racing driver of high standing. Bill, again a 'single' man and apparently suffering a mid-life crisis, joined the in-crowd of the Swinging Sixties and Seventies and bought himself a series of fast cars. He was seldom seen without a pretty young girl on his arm or at his side. His passion for fast driving must have peaked when he became the proud owner of a 4.5 litre Bristol.

By the late 1970s Bill was working for Hermitage Engineering of Mansfield, an engineering company specialising in the manufacture of aerospace components. He became chief inspector for the company that had links with Rolls-Royce. He bought himself a bungalow just 300yd from his place of work. Fellow inspector and friend Reg Kingman recalled that Bill's favourite saying when annoyed was 'I've shot better than you!' But he was a reticent man, recalled Reg, and rarely spoke of his wartime achievements, although during one lunchtime, he recalls that Bill did show him and other inspectors his medals and logbook.

Following his retirement, Bill moved to Mapperley Park, Nottingham, where he married 65-year-old divorcee Kathleen Carson (known as Kay) on Valentine's Day 1981 – ever the romantic. They settled in West Bridgford, Nottingham (Kay's house), not far from the famous Trent Bridge cricket ground. As a Member of the MCC, Bill undoubtedly enjoyed his all-too-brief retirement during the summer watching County Cricket matches and probably the First Test against the Australians, played at Trent Bridge. He also enjoyed an occasional beer with his friend, retired Sqn Ldr John Hopper. He would have been delighted that his grandson, Andrew, followed the family tradition and attended Framlingham College.

Tragedy was to shorten Bill and Kay's time together, Bill losing his life in a road accident just nine months later. Kay was driving when their car was hit by another coming out of a side road on the A43, approximately a quarter of a mile east of the Abbey Road junction in the village of Syresham, near Brackley in Northamptonshire, on 29 November 1981. He died instantly from multiple injuries, including bilateral rib fractures and pneumothoraces.

He was 67 years old. Having survived so many actions in the air, it was sad and ironic that he was to lose his life in such a way. Kay survived the accident. The funeral service for Bill was held at Wilford Hill Crematorium on 7 December. A bleak Christmas for not only Kay but also for Bill's family.

EPILOGUE

Brian and Val met Kay Vale in 1992 at her home in Scarborough, to where she had moved following Bill's death. She kindly made available a copy of Bill's logbook and had a number of photographs copied, which she generously donated, several of which are included in this tribute to Bill, the forgotten ace. Sadly, Kay died in 1997. But, in 2008, after many months of searching, Bill's daughter Gaynor was located (in a neighbouring county), and thereafter a meeting took place with her and her son Andy, Bill's grandson. At the time of writing (mid-2009) Gaynor is convalescing following breast cancer.

Appendix I

BILL'S COMBAT CLAIMS

1940

1 July	CR32	Gladiator N5769	33 Squadron	Fort Capuzzo
15 July	SM79*	Gladiator N5766	33 Squadron	Mersa Matruh
20 Nov	CR42	Gladiator N5784	80 Squadron	Koritza area
	CR42*	Gladiator N5784	80 Squadron	Koritza area
29 Nov	Z1007*†	Gladiator N5784	80 Squadron	Tepelene area
4 Dec	CR42	Gladiator N5784	80 Squadron	Argyrokastron
20 Dec	SM81	Gladiator N5784	80 Squadron	Kelcyre area
21 Dec	3 CR42s	Gladiator N5784	80 Squadron	Argyrokastron

1941

27 Jan	Z1007*	Gladiator N5784	80 Squadron	Kelcyre-Premet
9 Feb	CR42	Gladiator N5825	80 Squadron	Tepelene–
	SM79†	Gladiator N5825	80 Squadron	Argyrokastron
28 Feb	G.50	Gladiator N5829	80 Squadron	Himari
	SM79	Gladiator N5829	80 Squadron	Himari
3 March	SM81	Hurricane V7288	80 Squadron	west of Larissa
4 March	G.50	Hurricane V7589	80 Squadron	Himari–Valona
14 April	Ju87	Hurricane V7795	80 Squadron	Servia
15 April	2 Ju88s	Hurricane V7795	80 Squadron	Athens
16 April	Ju88	Hurricane V7134	80 Squadron	Eleusis
19 April	2 Ju87s	Hurricane V7134	80 Squadron	Larissa
20 April	2 Ju88s	Hurricane V7134	80 Squadron	Piraeus
21 April	Do17*	Hurricane V7134	80 Squadron	Larissa
23 April	Do17†	Hurricane V7134	80 Squadron	Argos
29 April	Do17†	Hurricane V7781	80 Squadron	Maleme area
	2 Ju88s	Hurricane V7795	80 Squadron	Maleme area
30 April	Ju88	Hurricane V7795	80 Squadron	Maleme area
	Ju88†	Hurricane V7795	80 Squadron	Maleme area
5 May	Ju88	Hurricane V7781	80 Squadron	Suda Bay
	Ju88†	Hurricane V7781	80 Squadron	Suda Bay
13 May	Ju52/3m	Hurricane V7781	80 Squadron	off Crete

16 May	Bf109	Hurricane V7795	80 Squadron	off Crete
	Ju87	Hurricane V7795	80 Squadron	Suda Bay
17 May	Ju88[†]	Hurricane V7795	80 Squadron	Suda Bay
11 June	Potez 63	Hurricane V6939	80 Squadron	off Syrian coast
12 June	2 D.520s	Hurricane Z4200	80 Squadron	Syrian coast

† = damaged

* = shared

Total claims: 30 plus 4 shared; 6 damaged plus 1 shared damaged.

AIRCRAFT FLOWN ON OPERATIONS BY BILL, 1938–41

Gladiator
Palestine 1938 (33 Squadron)
L7614

Western Desert 1940 (33 Squadron)
N5769, N5763, N5756, N5785, N5750 (June)
N5769, N5750, L9044, K6138, N5786, N5766, N5755 (July)

Western Desert 1940 (80 Squadron)
K7913, K8036, K7902, K7978 (August)
K8036, K8022, K7912, K8009, K7892, K8013, K7978, K8036 (September)
K8015, K8018, K8017, N5814, N5825 (October)
K8017, N5784 (November)

Greece 1940–41 (80 Squadron)
N5784, N5788, N5814 (November)
N5784, N5817, N5832 (December)
N5761, N5897, N5784 (January)
N5784, N5825, N5813, N5770, N5829/112 Sqn (February)
K8021, K8096 (March)

Hurricane
Greece/Crete 1941 (80 Squadron)
V7589 (February)
V7288, V6749, V7589, V7138, V7122 (March)
V7138, V6629, V7122, V7795, V7748, V7134, V7737, V7767, V7781 (April)
V7795, V7781, V7800 (May)

Syria 1941 (80 Squadron)
V6939, Z4200, V7437, V7643 (June)

Appendix III

JANINA'S FATE?

M any Greek women fought and died with their menfolk during the invasion and afterwards:

> You should have seen the womenfolk carrying the cartridge belts folded round their waists. The women emerged in Chersonissos carrying sickles, sticks and virtually anything they could lay their hands on. The Germans suffered extensive losses at the hands of these women. When we heard that the parachutists had fallen on flat ground here at Lassithi, my wife said to me calmly: 'Take your gun and run.' A teacher from our village with a three metre long stick also ran to go with me. People were suffering tremendously here. The parachutists fell from both Chersonissos and Heraklion and massacred many people. God, however, destroyed them too.[1]

Many women played a dramatic role in the Battle of Crete:

> The story of Georgina Anyfantis has already become a Cretan legend. Georgina, 22 years old, fled from the mainland after all her family had been killed in the Nazi blitzkrieg, and asked for an opportunity to fight with the army defending Crete. She was given a uniform and assigned a machine-gun post on the edge of a landing field. The post was attacked by bombers, and only Georgina survived. Later in the day German troop carriers approached, flying low. She manned the gun, waited until the aircraft were close then fired point blank. Two planes, each carrying twenty men, crashed. Georgina escaped from the field before it was captured by the Nazis, and evacuated with the main British forces to Egypt. She is now serving as a volunteer in the South African Women's Air Force.[2]

Others served with the Greek Army:

> The courage of the Cretan women, some of whom fought side by side with their men folk in defence of their homes, makes a glorious chapter in itself. Ten of them, wearing Greek uniforms and fully armed, were taken prisoner by the Germans. They were shipped to Athens, and

then on Hitler's orders sent to Berlin, the Fuehrer having expressed
a wish to see them. A more ominous note was struck by the report
that the Nazis had been given orders to examine the shoulders of the
Cretan women and girls to see if there were any tell-tale marks of
rifle-butts.[3]

At the Inter-Allied Conference held at St James's Palace, London, on 13
January 1942, Greek Prime Minister Tsouderos produced a Memorandum
regarding the conditions in Greece for those present, part of which revealed:

> The food conditions under Axis rule are appalling beyond words. Four
> hundred and fifty people are perishing daily of hunger in the Athens–
> Piraeus area. Five hundred thousand inhabitants in this area have to
> rely on public assistance for the very barest meal. The Italians view this
> situation with satisfaction as the resistance of a starving population is
> greatly reduced. Whenever an Axis ship happens to be sunk in the
> proximity of Greek waters, the occupation authorities deliberately
> suspend the distribution of the bread ration for three days, falsely
> alleging that the ship sunk was bringing food to Greece from the Axis
> Powers.
>
> The technique of pressure by means of hostages is ruthlessly
> applied: Throughout Greece innocent people are arrested as hostages
> either as a preventive measure or as a sanction. Thus on May 17th
> six hostages were executed at Malaoi. In the first two weeks, which
> followed the German attack on Russia, 750 so-called Communists were
> arrested in Athens by the Italians. These are kept in a concentration
> camp near Larissa, and they are not allowed to have any contact with
> their families. In Salonika on June 2nd, a day after their attack upon
> Russia, the Germans arrested some two hundred lawyers, journalists,
> and professors; and on July 11th they made a raid on the factories of
> the Salonika district and rounded up about seven thousand workmen.
> The fate of these unhappy people is not known.
>
> In the province of Thesprotia, in Epirus, Albanian begs, nominated
> by the Italians as village headmen, carry on a systematic campaign
> of fanatical persecution against the Greek Orthodox population;
> the same policy has been followed in Northern Epirus, and it aims
> at exterminating the Greeks and any other inhabitants of the towns
> and districts of Argyrocastro [Argyrokastron], Premeti, Chimara, and
> Korytsa [Koritza], who are suspected of sympathizing with the Greek
> cause.
>
> In the district of Macedonia occupied by the Germans the situation
> is even worse. Proclamations have been posted up which warn the
> population that for every offence against the army of occupation

punishment will be inflicted collectively on the inhabitants, and the whole district in which the offence occurs. The German military authorities have been instructed to arrest leading citizens and hold them as hostages in any district in which the slightest suspicion arises that disorders may break out. Should a clash occur the hostages are shot. Towards the middle of October a slight disturbance occurred in the village of Mesovouni in the district of Ptolemais, and German troops were sent there to 'restore order'. They set aside the women and the children under sixteen years of age, and then proceeded to execute the whole male population, about 200 in number, after which they burnt the village to the ground. Early in November the village of Stavros, in the province of Chalcidice, was subjected to the same fate. This village also was destroyed and 150 of its inhabitants were murdered. The pretext given in both cases was that of 'harbouring terrorists'. On October 31st thirteen hostages were hanged in the village of Lahana, near Salonika, after two German transport drivers had been found dead near the town.

Following the conquest of Crete, further atrocities were carried out against the civilians, as revealed in a cable sent to the Greek government in London on 7 October 1941 by the Greek Minister of War in Cairo:

After the capture of Crete the German army burned to the ground the villages of Skine, Prasse, and Kandanos. Their sites are now marked by posters bearing the inscription, 'Here once stood Skine, Prasse, and Kandanos'. The Germans looted every single house and store in towns and in villages, leaving them empty of every single object. They proceeded to innumerable murders of people flying for safety in the open country, of children and old people asleep in their homes, and to collective executions after summary parodies of trials. The condemned people were forced to dig their common grave before the executions.

At Kystomadon three men, wounded during the execution, were buried while still alive. Their families were forced to offer a dinner to the murderers of their own husbands, fathers, and brothers, and to suffer the mocking jests of the feasting Germans. The Revd. Koukourakis, curate of the church at Roumaton, as well as the Abbot and Monks of the Monastery of Aghia Gonia, were put to death. The fate of the Bishop of Kissamos and Selines, Mgr. Evdokimos Singelakis, is not known. The altar of the church of Manolio was turned into a public lavatory by the Germans.

The surviving inhabitants of Skine were driven away to Argyroupolis and Margarites. Eight hundred women and children from Lower Cydonia were seen being marched through Cartea after being expelled from their homes. In the village of Vrises, in the Rethymno district, Police Sergeant Ipaitozakis was tortured to death, his limbs being wrenched off one by one with the object of forcing him to denounce the holders of German rifles.

At Perivolia and Sellia, in the Rethymno district, people were executed one by one in the presence of others also condemned to death and of their relatives, after having been forced to dig their own graves. At Heraklion the prefect was executed, and Colonel Tsatsaronakis met the same fate because he tried to help the persecuted to escape. In the same place five more Greeks were executed because they failed to declare that they knew German. According to the first available information, the number of executions in Canea amounts to 506, in Rethymno 130, and Heraklion 50. The male population of the island, especially in western Crete, has taken to the mountains in arms.

It has to be presumed that Janina was one of the sad statistics. *The Times* carried a story of one couple who did escape from Crete.

A British naval officer has now reached hospital. He set out to cross open sea to safety, with a Greek girl in a rowing boat. The boat was partly stove in and flooded by machine-gun attack from the air. Part of the officer's side was blown away. To stop the bleeding and gangrene the girl forced him to lie with his wounded side in the bilge water at the bottom of the boat and herself rowed him more than 50 miles to an Allied island.

Appendix IV

BILL'S WARS

THE PALESTINE UPRISING, 1935–39: AN OVERVIEW

At least 85 Jews were killed during the first days of the 1936 strike. The revolt was a protest against, and put an end to, Jewish immigration to Palestine and was driven primarily by Arab hostility to Britain's permission of restricted Jewish immigration and land purchases, which Palestinian Arabs believed was leading them to becoming a minority in the territory. They demanded immediate elections, which they hoped would result in an Arab 'General Representative' government. The strike was eventually called off in October 1936 and the violence abated for about a year while the Peel Commission deliberated and eventually recommended partition of Palestine.

With the rejection of this proposal, the revolt resumed during the autumn of 1937, marked by the assassination in Nazareth of the District Commissioner together with his bodyguard. The British responded by greatly expanding their military forces and clamping down on Arab dissent. Administrative detention (imprisonment without charges or trial), curfews, and house demolitions were among British practices during this period. More than 120 Arabs were sentenced to death and about 40 hanged. The main Arab leaders were arrested or expelled.

A Jewish organisation, the Haganah, actively supported British efforts to quell the largely peasant insurgency, which reached 10,000 Arab fighters at its peak during the latter part of 1938. Although the British administration did not officially recognise the Haganah, the British security forces co-operated with it by forming the Jewish Settlement Police, Jewish Auxiliary Forces and Special Night Squads. A smaller Haganah splinter group, the Irgun organisation, adopted a policy of retaliation and revenge (including terrorist attacks against civilians).

Between 1940 and 1943 Irgun declared a truce against the British, and supported Allied efforts against Nazi forces and their allies in the area by enlisting its members in British forces and the Jewish Brigade.

BILL'S WARS

WAR IN THE DESERT, 1940: AN OVERVIEW

The Mediterranean is an area of very great strategic importance to the countries of the Western world, a fact which the events of more recent times have so far done little to disprove. Situated between the continents of Europe and Africa, it offers not only seaboards to the countries surrounding it, but also easy access to Asia, via the Black Sea, and to the Far East, via the Suez Canal. To add to this is the vital factor of oil; although today Libya is an important producer of oil, this was not the case until recently, but Syria provides port facilities to pipelines from deep in Iraq, and the Suez Canal offers access to the oil-rich territories of Iran and the Arabian Gulf.

The only natural entry to the Mediterranean is through the Straits of Gibraltar from the Atlantic in the west, and a number of islands, notably Malta, Crete and Cyprus, provide bases from which control over large areas of the sea can be exercised. In 1939, when France and the United Kingdom became embroiled in war with Hitler's Germany, the only real threat to their security in this area was from Italy, where Mussolini, the Fascist dictator, waited to see what course events would indicate as offering the greatest advantage to his country before he made a move. At this stage Spain, although in sympathy with the totalitarian regimes, lay exhausted from her long and bloody civil war, which had ended only a few months earlier; besides this, in order to reach her frontiers, the Germans or Italians must first pass through France – still nominally the great bastion of Free Europe at that time.

Thus from the west, the entry to the Mediterranean was controlled by the British fortress base of Gibraltar; the south of France and the French North African colonies gave easy control of most of the Western Mediterranean, aided by the French island of Corsica. Then in the centre came the Italian domain, Italy on the north coast extending far southwards to divide the Mediterranean virtually into two basins. Opposite lay her colony of Libya, a land of barren deserts stretching deep into the Sahara. Between these two, however, lay the island of

182

Malta, long a British naval base. Beyond Italy lay Albania, which she had recently occupied, and then the neutral Balkans – Yugoslavia, Greece and Turkey. The rest of the coast, from the Turkish border at the eastern end, to the Libyan border, was all in Allied hands; Syria, controlled by the French, Palestine and Egypt, together with the vital Suez Canal, controlled by the British.

Conditions in the desert were very different to those appertaining to the European area. The main trouble was sand – the fine desert dust being driven in clouds of stinging particles by every breath of wind. Great sandstorms would descend at any time, obliterating the landscape in a swirling fog that found its way into everything. This sand, if ingested into aero engines through the normal air intakes, could wear out the moving parts in a matter of hours, turning the lubricating oil into an abrasive paste. For this reason all aircraft had to be fitted with special air filters, which caused drag and resulted in reduced performance. Guns became jammed, Perspex cockpit canopies scored and scratched, and food was ruined by the invasion of this menace, which also filled eyes, ears, noses and fingernails, making life at times a gritty nightmare.

Due to the length of the lines of communication, and lack of natural supply, water was strictly rationed, and that used for washing or shaving was carefully kept to fill the radiators of motor vehicles. Fresh food was virtually unobtainable, and tinned rations with hard biscuits were the staple diet. The violent heat of the day made most movement impossible during the hours around noon, and the metal parts of aircraft, tanks, etc., became so hot that to touch them was to risk a blistered hand. At night the temperature dropped rapidly, making the use of warm clothing essential. To add to these hardships, the troops were plagued by millions of persistent flies, which settled on faces and on food continually. These conditions frequently caused 'Desert sores' which, aggravated by heat and sand, festered on for months. Being so lacking in landmarks, the great wastes of undulating sand, rock and scrub were difficult to navigate over; to be forced down in such circumstances was to risk a lingering death from starvation and dehydration.

To set against these deprivations, the desert was a place of great comradeship, and, due to the extreme of temperature, germs could not flourish so that there was no infectious disease. Further to this the desert was virtually uninhabited, so that the pitiful plight of refugees did not manifest itself, the opposing armies being able to get on with the fighting untroubled by the destruction of homes or the killing of women and children and, so far as it was possible, to have a 'clean' war – it was in the desert that it was fought.

Against such a background, the Mediterranean seemed relatively secure, and with defences at home under strength and an expeditionary force in France to maintain, the British forces in this area enjoyed a relatively low priority. By the spring of 1940 a small but efficient air force, Royal Air Force Middle East, was based mainly in the south-east corner of the area. In Egypt, for the defence of the Suez Canal zone and the port of Alexandria, an important naval base, was 202 Group, commanded by Air Commodore Raymond Collishaw. This Group comprised three squadrons of Gladiators, 33, 80 and 112; a single Hurricane was also available, serving with 80 Squadron; four squadrons of Blenheim Is – 30, 45, 55 and 211 – and one of Blenheim IVs, 113 Squadron; one Army co-operation squadron with Lysanders (208 Squadron); there were also two squadrons of bomber-transports, 216 with Bombays and 70 with Valentias.

To the east were more units; 6 Squadron with Lysanders and Gladiators was in Palestine for army co-operation, while in Iraq were 84 Squadron with Blenheim Is and 244 Squadron with Vincent general-purpose biplanes. On Malta were no squadrons as such, but 12 Royal Navy Sea Gladiators were available in crates, having been brought to the island as replacements for the aircraft carriers operating in the area. Now by special arrangement, some of these were released to the RAF, and four were erected during April to form a Fighter Flight at Hal Far airfield to provide a makeshift defence for the island. Finally, based at Gibraltar, and operating over both the Mediterranean and the Atlantic, was 202 Squadron with Saro London biplane flying boats.

Throughout the campaigns over-claiming in air combat became a feature, particularly by the Regia Aeronautica, whose admission of losses was correspondingly very low. It is suspected that many of these figures were the result of wartime propaganda, and that they have never been modified. The RAF, particularly in Greece, also tended to over-claim on occasion, especially in swirling, whirling combats between agile Gladiators and CR42s. Generally, pilots' 'claims' were valid, but confirmation of claims left much to be desired, and the need for propaganda was essential at this evenly balanced stage of the war.

Extracted from Christopher Shores, Fighters over the Desert
(Neville Spearman, 1969).

Appendix VI

BILL'S WARS

AIR OPERATIONS GREECE, 1940–41: AN OFFICIAL OVERVIEW

Extracts from Air Vice-Marshal J.H. D'Albiac's Official Report

3. At 3 o'clock in the morning of 28th October 1940, the Italian Minister in Athens handed to the Prime Minister of Greece a note from his Government complaining in strong terms of alleged Greek assistance to the Allies and demanding for the Italians the right to occupy certain strategic bases in Greece. General Metaxas regarded this note as an ultimatum, which he promptly refused and a few hours later Greece was at war with Italy.

Unlike the Italians, the Greek forces were little prepared for war. Their regular army units were at their peacetime stations throughout the country and general mobilisation had not been ordered. On being attacked, the Greek units holding the frontier posts on the mountainous borders of Albania, although fighting with the greatest gallantry, were overwhelmed in some cases by sheer weight of numbers and compelled to give ground. This was particularly the case in regions where conditions were suitable for the employment of Italian mechanised forces. The progress of the Italian army was, however, slow, although Italy had concentrated large forces on the Greek frontier, the firm attitude adopted by the Greek government came as somewhat of a surprise as it had been thought that all Italian demands would be met without resort to arms. It was confirmed also from the reports of prisoners taken in the first few days that the opening of hostilities was quite unexpected by the Italian soldiers themselves, who had been led to expect a diplomatic victory and a peaceful advance into Greek territory.

4. It was clear that the problem confronting the Greeks was largely one of time. Could her frontier units hold the Italian forces sufficiently long to enable her armies to be mobilised and concentrated? As is well known, Greece is badly served by communications. Roads and railways on the mainland are few in number and the former are in most cases bad. A number of her reservists had to come from the Greek islands and it was estimated that it would take at least three weeks for the Greek mobilisation to be completed and for sufficient forces to be concentrated in the battle area before she could really consider

herself reasonably safe. In the meantime, the Italian air force could, if handled properly, play havoc with their mobilisation and concentration arrangements. This, for some unaccountable reason, the Italians failed completely to do and wasted their comparatively strong force in abortive attacks on undefended islands and hospitals in Salonika.

5. The Greek Air Force, although small and outnumbered by the Italian, fought most gallantly during this initial stage. Their pilots, many of whom had attended courses in England at the CFS and elsewhere, were keen and what they lacked in modern war technique they made up for in personal bravery. Their aircraft, like those of most small independent nations not possessing an aircraft industry of their own, consisted of a number of different foreign types, French and Polish predominating, with a limited range of spares.

6. Operationally, the Greek Air Force was controlled by the General Staff and was used almost entirely in direct support of their army. They were quite unable to obtain any degree of air superiority and in consequence they suffered severe casualties. In addition, owing to the difficulty of obtaining spares, an abnormally high proportion of unserviceability soon existed and in a comparatively short time, their effort was reduced to negligible proportions.

7. In response to an urgent appeal for help, the British Government decided to send a contingent of the Royal Air Force to Greece from the Middle East. The force decided upon was to consist of two medium bomber squadrons, one mixed medium bomber and two-seater fighter squadron – all armed with Blenheim aircraft, and two single-seater fighter squadrons armed with Gladiator aircraft. On my arrival in Athens on 6th November 1940, the advance elements of this force had already arrived and were ready for action.

8. That evening I attended a conference with the Prime Minister and Commander-in-Chief to discuss the war situation generally. Every pressure was brought to bear on me to employ my force in the same manner as the Greek Air Force, in close support of the land forces. I appreciated, however, that the best help I could give to the Greek armies was to concentrate my small bomber force on the enemy's disembarkation ports in Albania and the important centres in his lines of communication. I argued that such a plan would do far more to delay his advance than if I attacked his forward elements. If, however, the situation deteriorated considerably and a breakthrough occurred, I would of course devote the whole of my force to the immediate task of stemming the enemy's advance. I finally obtained agreement on this policy and attacks were directed forthwith on the enemy's back areas. These attacks were maintained at maximum intensity with the few day-bomber aircraft at my disposal and the detachments of Wellington aircraft sent over from Egypt to operate during the periods of moonlight. By the end of

November, the Italian advance had been stemmed and the Greek forces who had by then completed their concentration were able to take the offensive. The Greek General Staff were most appreciative of the prompt and valuable help we had been able to provide for their gallant soldiers who, with ferocious intensity, had disputed every foot of the Greek soil, and they expressed the view that it was largely due to our assistance that the situation had now become satisfactory.

9. One of the main difficulties I experienced in establishing my force and one which was a constant handicap throughout the whole campaign, was the extreme scarcity of aerodromes suitable for the employment of modern aircraft. There were no all-weather aerodromes, and on the mainland of Greece there are few areas in which aerodromes of any size can be made. In the Salonika area, the country is flat and a number of dry weather aerodromes already exists. For political reasons, however, I was not even allowed to reconnoitre these grounds, let alone use them. In the Larissa plain, there were many sites possible but, by November, the rains had already commenced and, although I did station a fighter squadron in that area on its arrival, it was soon flooded out and aircraft were grounded for a period of ten days before they could be moved. There are few other sites in Greece except an occasional flat stretch on the coast and a certain number of level areas in the valleys, but the heavy rainfall and the prevalence of low clouds and mist make the latter quite unsuitable for operational purposes during the winter months, at any rate for modern bombers. I was forced, therefore, to concentrate my bomber force on the two aerodromes in the vicinity of Athens, and station my fighter squadrons on whatever grounds I could find near the front line, where they had to operate under conditions of the greatest discomfort and difficulty.

10. The main disadvantage of the aerodromes near Athens was that they were a long way from the front and it meant long hours of flying to and from the targets. They were, however, better drained and were only out of action for a few days after heavy rain. Furthermore, being near the sea, they were not so liable to get completely covered in by low clouds. Criticism has been made that the initial force which was sent to Greece was inadequate and many more squadrons should have been provided. I should like to point out, however, that even if these squadrons had been available, which they were not at the time, the lack of suitable aerodrome accommodation would, in my opinion, have prevented us from accepting them. During my first week in Greece, I made a tour of all possible sites and on my return pressed the Prime Minister to undertake immediately the construction of all-weather runways at Araxos and Agrinion. I pointed out to him the operational disadvantages of the situation and that, unless suitable runways were provided near the front, the support that we could give to the Greek nation during the winter months

would be severely limited. He fully agreed with my recommendations and for the construction of runways to proceed immediately.

13. The new year opened with deterioration in the weather conditions. Heavy falls of snow and much low cloud made flying conditions difficult and dangerous. A further handicap now appeared in the form of severe icing conditions which were experienced by our aircraft over the mountainous country between their bases and the targets in Albania. To avoid this serious state of affairs, we were forced to route our bomber aircraft by way of the coast. Over the sea the flying conditions were considerably better, but this longer route limited the operational radius of action of our aircraft and militated against effecting surprise. Furthermore, enemy aircraft opposition was now becoming increasingly stronger, and large numbers of modern enemy fighters were being encountered constantly over the targets. These reinforcements were undoubtedly being brought over in an effort to reduce the scale of our attacks on the enemy's rearward communication system, which were obviously causing him growing embarrassment. Whilst it was comforting to think that our bomber offensive was presumably having the desired effect, this addition to the enemy's fighter strength increased considerably our operational difficulties. It was now necessary to make full use of cloud cover and to adopt a system of fighter escorts for our day bomber raids if heavy casualties were to be avoided. Our lack of modern fighter aircraft and the difficulties encountered in arranging for bombers and their escorts to meet, owing to the distance between our bomber and fighter bases, badly connected by communications, with weather conditions constantly changing, all tended to reduce the operational effort of my bomber force and it became increasingly obvious that, until the fine weather came and more aerodromes were made available, there would be little opportunity for any decisive action on our part.

14. I would here like to pay a tribute to the magnificent spirit in which the pilots and aircrews carried out their work during an exceedingly difficult period of operations. Based as they were in the Athens area, every raid carried out by the bomber squadrons involved a preliminary flight of at least 200 miles to the theatre of operations in weather conditions, which were at times quite indescribable. Throughout the journey, the pilots and aircrews were fully aware that they would meet strong fighter opposition over the targets, and would have to engage the enemy before they were able to deliver their attacks.

21. During the latter part of this period, an event of considerable importance concerning our fighter strength occurred. The first six Hurricane aircraft appeared in Greece. Up till now, the pilots in our two fighter squadrons had

been doing grand work with their Gladiators, but with the gradual appearance of faster and better types of Italian aircraft, they were finding themselves at a disadvantage, and their re-equipment with a more modern type was most welcome. The first appearance of these well known fighter aircraft over Athens was greeted with the greatest enthusiasm by the local population and it was not long before they justified fully their reputation of being first class fighting aircraft. On their first sortie over the lines on 20th February, they shot down four enemy aircraft, and on 28th February, in company with a formation of Gladiators, destroyed 27 enemy aircraft without a single loss to themselves. This fight, which was the biggest ever fought in the air in Albania, was staged over the Greek lines in full view of both armies. All the enemy aircraft destroyed were confirmed from the ground and caused the greatest jubilation.

25. The arrival of the British expeditionary force and the establishment of a new front meant a further reorganisation of any force and a readjustment of my slender resources. Although very few reinforcements had arrived as yet, and my pilots and aircrews were beginning to feel the strain of heavy and continuous operations throughout the winter months, an additional burden was now thrust upon us. I still had to provide air support for the Greeks who were being ferociously attacked in Albania by the Italians, spurred on by the presence of Mussolini himself. I had to provide air escorts for incoming convoys, also some form of air defence for the ports of disembarkation of British troops, which were becoming alarmingly congested.

I had to deliver occasional attacks on the Dodecanese Islands to reduce the scale of enemy attacks on convoys, which were becoming embarrassingly frequent, and finally, I had to allocate a portion of my force to support the position in process of occupation by British troops. Apart from the fact that all my squadrons were much below strength in serviceable aircraft, due to the heavy casualties we had suffered and the unavoidable inability to keep us supplied with replacements, the re-equipping of my fighter squadrons with Hurricanes was not proceeding as rapidly as I had hoped. Furthermore, the arrival of reinforcing squadrons was not keeping pace with the programme decided upon and those that did arrive were much below establishment in aircraft and equipment. In spite of these difficulties and disappointments, however, I still hoped that time would be on our side and that, when the German attack developed, we would be in a reasonable state of preparedness to meet it.

30. At the time when Germany commenced the invasion, my force was organised as follows:
A Western Wing consisting of one bomber and one fighter squadron (Gladiator) supporting the Greeks in Albania.

An Eastern Wing consisting of two bomber and one Hurricane fighter squadrons supporting the Anglo-Greek forces facing the German advance. The squadrons of this wing occupied landing grounds on the Larissa plain which, although still soft after the winter rains, was now drying rapidly.

In the Athens area I had one bomber squadron and one fighter squadron in process of re-arming with Hurricanes.

Expressed in terms of aircraft, my total serviceable strength in the country was some 80 aircraft, to which were opposed, according to all reports, approximately 800 German aircraft on the Eastern front (Bulgaria and Romania) and 160 Italian aircraft based in Albania plus 150 based in Italy but operating over Albania and Greece, mainly from advanced landing grounds in Albania.

31. The first problem with which I was faced in forming the Eastern Wing was that of disposing the air forces I could make available. My intention was to provide each squadron with a base aerodrome, and at least one and if possible two satellite landing grounds. The location of the fighter squadron was influenced by its role. This was threefold:

(a) to protect the base area, which included the army lines of communication, the port of Volos and our aerodromes in the Larissa plain;

(b) to provide fighter escort to our bombers; and

(c) to deal with enemy fighter aircraft in the battle area.

Larissa aerodrome was the most suitable from the geographical and communications point of view, and was one of the few aerodromes, which was serviceable for all but a comparatively short period during the winter. Accordingly, the fighter squadron was based there with a satellite on a piece of suitable ground seven miles to the west. At Larissa, the camp was well dispersed at the opposite end of the aerodrome to the hangars, which would be likely to attract bombing attack. Aircraft pens of sandbags capable of taking Hurricanes, though open at the top, were constructed in dispersed positions.

34. It should be realised that the German invasion of Greece started at a time when very few landing grounds were fit for use on account of rain. They were just beginning to dry, and had the attack been delayed for even a week, we would at least have had several more satellite landing grounds at our disposal. As it was, the change in the weather favoured the Germans.

36. Communication from Larissa to Niamata only twelve miles away was reliable, out to Almyros it was most unsatisfactory, largely due to the fact that the Air Defence Centre used the Almyros line for reporting enemy aircraft. As the campaign proceeded, so the demands both of the Wing and of the Air Defence Centre augmented until finally it took as much as five to six hours to pass a priority telephone message from Larissa to Almyros.

Thus it was decided to use the squadron at Niamata for any fleeting targets which presented themselves, while the squadron at Almyros carried out direct support operations, the need for which could be foreseen some hours previously.

37. The Greek observer system consisting of posts with sub-posts radiating from each and linked to air defence centres by telephone, operated with a certain degree of success, and various interceptions of Italian aircraft had been made over the Larissa area. A fighter operations room was established at Larissa and was run by the squadron stationed there. Depending on alternative duties, aircraft were standing by throughout the hours of daylight. It was, however, inevitable to leave lines of communication and base area unprotected when the fighters were required for escort duty or protective duties over the forward troops. The system worked well, although there was little enemy air activity during the first few days of the campaign. When, however, the withdrawal of our troops began, the personnel manning the posts of the observer system had to withdraw and consequently the system broke down.

39. On the morning of the 6th April, the German forces were on the march. The bulk of the enemy moved west from the Struma valley, filtering by all available roads into each valley and gorge, inundating every plain with their swiftly moving forces. The first air reports indicated that an attack was being made upon Mt. Beles and the Rupel Pass. Simultaneously, our reconnaissance aircraft reported movement of MT on the road west from Petrich.

It was certain that this movement would be covered by fighter patrols, and the fighters were sent off to carry out a sweep over the road and over the Greeks on Mt. Beles and in the Rupel Pass. Twelve Hurricanes met twenty Me109s and our fighters shot down five without loss to themselves. This disposed of any anxiety or over cautiousness which the squadron commander of the fighters had felt about the change over from Italians to Germans. Whereas, at the outset, the squadron commander expressed the view that his aircraft could not operate in formations of less than twelve, he now agreed that formations of six would be able to escort Blenheim formations across the line. This meant that the base area only had to be left completely unprotected when the Hurricanes went off in strength to patrol over our forward troops. In the circumstances, the wing commander considered it a reasonable division of fighter strength.

40. Communications between Force HQ and Wing HQ to Athens were now becoming extremely poor, and I was virtually out of touch not only with the wing commander but with the GOC, with whom it was essential for me to be in constant communication. Accordingly, I sent an officer of air rank to

take over operations in the forward area. The air officer took over at a time when, in view of the intention of the army to withdraw to the Olympus line, plans were being drawn up to withdraw the ground party of the squadron of Blenheims at Niamata and to use it only as an advanced landing ground.

During the next few days, until the complete evacuation of the Larissa plain on the 15th, enemy MT columns and concentrations and on the roads between Prilep and Bitolj and in the Amyntaion area were bombed successfully by our aircraft.

Our army had had little time to prepare strong positions in this area, which they had hoped would be protected for some time by the resistance of the Yugoslavs. A heavy burden was therefore thrown upon our air forces, which now virtually had to make up for the time lost by the caving-in of the Yugoslav forces. No stone was left unturned to delay the enemy and to shield our ground forces. Meanwhile, our army was engaged in fighting a rearguard action in the areas around Amyntaion and Kleisoura.

No sooner was the withdrawal to the Aliakmon line complete when, on account of the threat to its left flank, it became necessary for the army to make a further withdrawal to the Thermopylae line. Consequently, all RAF units on the Larissa plain had to be withdrawn at once with the utmost speed along roads which were already congested. At the same time the RAF continued to throw all in power into delaying tactics.

On 14th April, the weather improved and German air activity intensified. The Germans had brought their fighters forward to the Prilep and Monastir areas, where their engineers had prepared the necessary landing strips. The German air force was mainly directed in close support of their army, and heavy dive-bombing attacks were made against our troops. Our Hurricanes, escorting our bombers in attacking enemy MT on the roads near Ptolemais and disorganising his lines of communication, shot down many enemy aircraft.

41. On 15th April, the main effort of the German Air Force was directed against our air force, which had been delaying their military operations and had taken toll of their aircraft. Large numbers of short-range fighters made their appearance over the Larissa plain and ground strafed Niamata. In spite of AA, every aircraft of the Blenheim squadron located there was destroyed. Owing to the breakdown of the Greek observer system, our fighters were at a hopeless disadvantage. When, on one occasion, Me109s appeared over their aerodrome at Larissa without any warning, three Hurricanes were attacked whilst taking off and two were shot down. The third shot down one Me109. Although, when our fighters were able to get off, they played havoc with the enemy, the situation was obviously untenable. I was present on the Larissa aerodrome whilst this attack was in progress and I ordered the squadrons to withdraw to the Athens area forthwith.

42. The Greek army commander at Yannina capitulated to the Germans. As the situation in this area deteriorated, it became increasingly obvious that it was necessary to withdraw the RAF Western Wing, consisting of one Blenheim and one Gladiator squadron. This was successfully carried out in spite of difficulties which arose as the result of numbers of Yugoslav aircraft and personnel arriving at Paramythia aerodrome and requiring fuel and food right up to the last moment.

43. At this juncture, I decided to abolish the Eastern Wing and take over control of all operations from Athens. I left an RAF officer at Force HQ to act as liaison between the army commander in the field and me. Later, when Force handed over the direction of the withdrawal to Anzac Corps, this officer was attached there. The army commander desired only reconnaissance and fighter protection which we did all we could to provide.

45. The fighters were withdrawn to the Athens area, since no aerodrome north of this was free from ground strafing. The constant lack of intermediary aerodromes made it inevitable that, if our fighters were placed on an aerodrome from which they could give protection to our troops, they were in imminent danger of destruction by ground strafing as soon as they were on the ground. If, on the other hand, they were placed beyond the range of ground strafing, they were unable to protect our troops and the tightly packed columns of MT withdrawing along the roads. The utmost efforts were made to give the maximum protection to our continually harassed troops. All our machines were working to maximum capacity. Many of our pilots were working at extreme range, challenging untold odds and at times, after they had used up their ammunition, pursuing enemy aircraft engaged in ground strafing our troops.

On 20 April, approximately 100 dive-bombers and fighters attacked the Athens area; my whole force of fighters of 15 Hurricanes intercepted them, bringing down a total of 22 enemy aircraft confirmed and eight unconfirmed for a loss of five Hurricanes. Small as our losses were, they were crippling to our small force. Even after having been shot down, our fighter pilots would immediately take to the air in aircraft which had been riddled with bullets and by all normal standards were totally unserviceable. The courage of these men never failed nor looked like failing. Each day their fellows died, each day they stepped into their battered aircraft, not without a sensation of fear but quite undismayed. Each man was aware of his great responsibility in the face of great odds.

46. On 22nd April, I sent the remaining Hurricanes to Argos. From here, I intended that they should cover the evacuation of the British Army, but the German air attack became so concentrated, that after a number of Hurricanes

had been destroyed on the ground on 23rd April, the remainder were ordered to leave for Crete. In Crete, Blenheim fighter patrols were organised to cover the ships evacuating the troops from the beaches. These escorts were maintained throughout the evacuation without respite, and I consider it was due largely to their efforts that such a large proportion of the total British forces in Greece were evacuated.

Appendix VII

BILL'S WARS

CRETE, 1940–41: AN OFFICIAL OVERVIEW

Extracts from Official Reports of Air Chief Marshal Arthur Longmore, Air Marshal Sir Arthur Tedder and Grp Capt George Beamish

In the early months of 1940 the French had been developing plans for the occupation of Crete should Italy come into the war. With the French collapse these plans fell by the wayside. When Italy attacked Greece the Greek Government, afraid to offend the Germans, was not prepared to allow British troops to land on the Greek mainland, but it allowed troops to land in Crete in order to protect the naval refuelling base at Suda Bay, the use of which was required by the Royal Navy for its task of protecting the Aegean waters. The first British troops, therefore, landed in Crete early in November 1940.

There was, at the time, little prospect of a serious attack on Crete so long as the Greek Army was able to hold the Italians on the mainland, although between November and May there were a number of air raids on Suda Bay and Heraklion, but in these first weeks it was not known whether the Greeks would be able to hold the Italians. Preparing for the worst, the incumbent British troops were ordered to dig-in so as to enable the garrison to defend itself against airborne attacks on Heraklion, Retimo and Canea.

In the middle of November the Greek C-in-C insisted on the transfer of the greater part of the Cretan divisions to the mainland to take part in the campaign there. In consequence of this, it was decided to increase the British garrison in Crete to a division and to increase the anti-aircraft defences in proportion.

During these months no RAF operational units were permanently stationed on the island, although Suda Bay was used as an advanced base for Sunderlands of 230 Squadron. The FAA, however, maintained at Maleme a mixed fighter squadron (805) of reduced strength, consisting of Fulmars, Gladiators and a handful of Buffalos. In December, radar was installed at Maleme (252 AMES) as part of the defence system of Suda Bay. This unit fed information to the gun operations room at Canea. It had been intended

195

to detach a half squadron of fighters from Libya to provide fighter defence of Crete. The changed situation in Libya made it necessary to cancel that move and there is no immediate prospect of providing fighters in Crete.

With the German attack on Greece a new situation arose. It was, from the first, probable that it would be only a matter of time before the Greeks and their British allies were expelled from the mainland, and in a very few weeks it was clear that Crete's first task would be to receive the evacuated troops. At the beginning of April, Suda Bay was transformed from a refuelling base to a Fleet base. With the turn of events, it was now no longer merely a question of defending the Fleet base against a raid but rather of a total defence of the island against invasion. The enemy might attack at either or both ends of the island, or at Retimo in the centre.

In the middle of April reports began to come through of Italian concentrations in the Dodecanese for an attack on Crete. The GOC proposed to station an infantry brigade at the western end of the island and another infantry brigade in the centre. The defence of the eastern end of the island was to be entrusted to Greek troops. The GOC also advocated the construction of full-scale operational airfields for both bombers and fighters:

> Forces at my disposal are totally inadequate to meet attack envisaged . . . The forces here can, and will, fight but without full support from Navy and Air force cannot hope to repel invasion.

He was advised:

> Air support is difficult. We are going through very lean period as regards fighter aircraft but every effort is being made from home to reinforce as early as possible.

Towards the end of the month he was told to expect 25,000 evacuees from Greece and to arrange reception area for them.

On 17 April, Grp Capt George Beamish arrived to take over the duties of SASO in Crete. He established his HQ in Canea and set about establishing relations of co-operation and confidence with the Army commanders, but his HQ and operations staff were drawn from evacuees from Greece who had little or no experience of the work which they were now called on to do. The first task was that of protecting evacuating convoys from Greece and the forwarding of RAF personnel from Crete to Egypt. Sunderlands at Suda Bay and bomber/transport aircraft at Heraklion were used in these tasks.

Convoys were protected near the Greek coast by Blenheims, usually operating in flights of six at late evening and early morning, and by fighters during disembarkation at Suda Bay. 30 Squadron had 14 Blenheim Is, of which six to eight were serviceable at any one time, established at Maleme, and 203 Squadron was at Heraklion with its nine Blenheim IVs. Between 22 and 24 April, the remnants of 33, 80 and 112 Squadrons arrived from Greece, comprising six serviceable Hurricanes and about the same number of serviceable Gladiators out of the 14 that arrived. The evacuation of Greece was completed by 29 April, and personnel being taken on to Egypt by bomber transport and Sunderlands began on 23 April, while a large contingent left by sea on 29 April. Air Chief Marshal Longmore, AOC ME declared:

> There should be a reasonable chance of keeping Suda Bay usable by the Navy by one Hurricane squadron with 100 per cent reserve pilots and replacement rate of 100 per cent per month. Excellent scope for dispersal and concealment in vicinity of Canea, if Greek Government resign themselves to certain discomfort.
>
> Present location of King east of Heraklion not really safe and I have told GOC Crete. Question is whether possible to keep Hurricane squadron up to strength against heavy wastage, in addition to Libyan commitments. In meantime, Nos. 30 and 203 Blenheim fighter squadrons and 112 Gladiator squadron are doing their best from Maleme and Heraklion to provide more degree of air protection to ships coming from Greece and to Crete itself.

On 30 April and 1 May, since there was little further convoy work to be done and since the Blenheims would be useless against enemy fighters, 203 Squadron was returned to Egypt. This left in Crete the Blenheims of 30 Squadron, 33 and 80 Squadrons with six Hurricanes which had been combined to form a Hurricane Flight, 112 Squadron with a dozen Gladiators, but only a small maintenance party, and the FAA's 805 Squadron, with full squadron strength but only six aircraft. The combined strength of these squadrons was 36 aircraft, but only half were serviceable. There were also five Greek Avro 626s and one Avro 621 at Maleme, plus at least 800 Royal Hellenic Air Force personnel including 157 pilots, but these were of no use for the defence of the island and most found their way to Egypt over the next few days.

On 3 May, the Chiefs of Staff asked for an appreciation of the defence of Crete in relation to the situation in the Middle East as a whole, in the following alternative cases:

(a) Crete to be used as a fuelling base, etc.;
(b) Crete to be denied to the enemy.

The reply received from the C-in-C ME revealed:

> Main threat comes from air. Enemy has ample strength and operational facilities in the Med and Balkan areas to maintain very heavy-scale air

attacks on Crete, at the same time continuing operations in strength against Malta, Cyrenaica and Egypt.

In view of heavy recent fighter losses in Greece and Cyrenaica, new commitments Iraq, need to maintain strong air defence of main base area Egypt, and to watch the Syrian situation. Adequate degree of fighter protection for Crete impracticable until further reinforcements arrive and during this period use of Naval and air bases Crete liable to serious interruption.

Heavy casualty rate aircraft Crete inevitable. Landing of enemy airborne division supported by heavy air attack is possibility we are preparing to counter. Estimated minimum land garrison three infantry brigade groups. Present garrison one British infantry brigade and equivalent two New Zealand and one Australian infantry brigades ex-Greece – immobile and with low-scale LMGs. Propose eventually to relieve Anzacs by British formations. Equipment being dispatched to Crete includes four 3.7 howitzers and a number of 75mm guns, plus eighteen light and six infantry tanks. Hope eventually Greek troops, of whom 11,000 in island, may relieve position of British garrison, but minimum of three months required for re-equipment and training.

Anti-aircraft defences will require, eventually, three heavy and two light batteries in addition to present sixteen heavy, thirty-six light guns and MNBDO [Mobile Naval Base Defence Organisation]. Anti-aircraft cannot at present be diverted from other vital requirements. Consider reasonable chance of Suda Bay being sufficiently usable with one squadron of Hurricanes with 100 per cent reserve pilots and replacement rate of aircraft at 100 per cent per month, but if enemy really concentrated on the problem, there seems little doubt that harbour could be rendered untenable. Allocation of fighters for Crete from expected early reinforcements will, of course, depend on situation in Cyrenaica, Egypt, Iraq and Syria. In the meantime, present air garrison for defence purposes as one fighter squadron of Gladiators, a few Hurricanes and Fleet Air Arm fighters.

Worthwhile supplies of tanks and aircraft were on their way from the UK, with 'Tiger' Convoy heading for Alexandria. Comprising five heavily escorted large freighters carrying 295 tanks and 53 crated Hurricanes, on the safe arrival of the convoy depended any future plans for the area. Until this convoy arrived, Air Chief Marshal Longmore had available to him just 90 twin-engined aircraft (Wellingtons, Blenheims – both bombers and fighters – a few Beaufighters and Marylands) and 43 Hurricane fighters to cover all his responsibilities in Egypt, Libya, Iraq, Cyprus and Crete. Twenty-five Hurricanes and their pilots aboard the old training carrier *Argus*, intended for

Greece, had been diverted to Malta, where there was also a desperate need for fighters.

It soon became evident that the enemy's air attack was going to be far heavier than had been foreseen. The rapidity with which the Germans made operational the Greek airfields in a matter of three weeks after their occupation can only be described as remarkable, and contested most strongly with the length of time it took us to prepare airfields, whether in Greece or Crete. Of course it was now a dry summer, whereas we had fought in Greece in wet winter – and the Germans were ready at this date to operate from far less elaborate airfields than we were, as they were prepared [and able] to suffer a far higher rate of crashes than we could afford. Also, the Germans had abundant tools and materials (we had next to none) and ruthlessly conscripted local labour, which we were unwilling to do for political reasons, and to some extent were unable to do as all able-bodied men were at the front with the Army. There are grave disadvantages in fighting in an unfriendly country, but there are also advantages.

Throughout the whole of May, both before and after the attack, the enemy carried out continued photographic reconnaissance flights over Kythera Channel, but they met with losses which were too heavy to be borne. Grp Capt Beamish suggested that 30 Squadron be kept at Maleme for convoy protection only. He signalled Air Marshal Tedder on 11 May:

> I consider main requirement Air Force Crete; firstly fighter defence Suda Bay area and Heraklion, secondly sea reconnaissance of possible landing and approach of seaborne expedition, thirdly fighter protection for convoys. Suggested location: Four additional Hurricane aircraft [for] Maleme, making total of ten. Fleet Air Arm aircraft to be removed. Six Hurricanes [for] Heraklion, which I am now in a position to accept immediately for operations after maintenance personnel provided. Consider Hurricanes and pilots greater value here now than held as reinforcements in Egypt. 30 Squadron Blenheim I aircraft to be maintained Maleme for convoy protection only . . . would propose if possible return these aircraft to Egypt before enemy attack develops. Aircraft to be returned to Maleme after attack defeated.

Air Marshal Tedder compiled an appreciation of the overall situation, emphasising his prime responsibility to be that of security of Lower Egypt as an effective base. In the light of this and other considerations he wrote:

> The method of providing air support for the defence of Crete against impending attack must depend on the Army plan of defence. This is being discussed in Crete today [11 May]. There are at present in

Crete six Hurricanes and approximately 14 very old Blenheim Is and Gladiators. The former have been useful on convoy protection. We may be able to stage a low-flying Blenheim attack on Scarpanto, but apart from this there appears no useful role for either type in meeting attack.

In view of the need for minimising losses on the ground, my present intention is to maintain two Hurricane flights in Crete and hold reserve of aircraft and pilots in Egypt for immediate reinforcement. The most useful contribution towards the defence of Crete will be attack on [the German] departure aerodromes, and for this the maximum strength of Wellingtons will be needed. I am withdrawing Wellingtons from Iraq for this purpose and increasing Blenheims in Iraq instead.

Our fighter technique at this time was to maintain fighter aircraft at readiness. On the plotting of one enemy aircraft, one aircraft [fighter] came to standby. On the enemy's approach to the island the aircraft [fighter] took off and made contact with the Operations Room on R/T. Fifty per cent of the remaining aircraft [fighters] were then brought to standby and, if a raid of size developed, these took off, the remaining 50 per cent then again in their turn being brought to standby. Though the enemy's air attack was such as to compel our withdrawal from the airfields – only two fighters and one medium bomber were lost on the ground.

While ships were being unloaded at Suda Bay a constant patrol of one aircraft from Maleme was maintained every day. The warning system was admirable except for aircraft approaching from the south. A signalling system kept the aircraft informed if their airfields were still serviceable. Two boards were laid out in parallel lines if the airfield was serviceable and across at right angles if it was not. The fighters would also be kept informed of the state of their airfields by R/T from Canea and Operations Room Heraklion.

From 14 May onwards, the enemy switched his attack from shipping to airfields. As soon as it was understood how overwhelming was the air power which the enemy was able to bring to bear, both Grp Capt Beamish and General Freyberg [GOC] had been very dubious of the wisdom of keeping in Crete aircraft which must inevitably be overwhelmed by such an attack. Our fighters during their period of operations had given a good account of themselves, claiming to have destroyed 23 and probably destroyed 9 more enemy aircraft, and damaged 41, but there was no purpose in keeping aircraft in Crete merely to meet a certain destruction. It was proposed to keep two flights of Hurricanes to prevent the enemy from having everything his own way but to withdraw all other aircraft, with the hope, of course, of bringing them back again after the attack had been beaten off, and to confirm our effort to attacks on Dodecanese and Greek airfields by Wellingtons and Beaufighters operating from Egyptian, or in one case, Maltese, airfields.

The enemy began with spasmodic bombing and occasional low-flying attacks, but these grew in intensity. His attack on the Cretan airfields had become so devastating by 19 May, that in spite of a reinforcement of ten Hurricanes we had only three Hurricanes and three Gladiators left fit for operations at Heraklion. At Maleme there was only one Hurricane. Before the weight of the German attack the destruction of these aircraft was certain. No reinforcements were available from Egypt. Grp Capt Beamish therefore decided that there was no alternative but to fly even the Hurricanes back to Egypt and to abandon the air defence of the island.

Air Marshal Tedder reported the decision and his acceptance of it in a signal to the CAS on 20 May:

On 18 May, Beamish and Freyberg decided to send out remaining aircraft since they could do nothing against the scale of attack. I agreed this was sound and three Hurricanes and four Gladiators flew out at dawn on 19th. This morning Crete advised that our joint plan to send two flights of Hurricanes from Egypt to operate for limited period over Crete should be suspended. Force of 15 Wellingtons detailed to attack Greek aerodromes tonight in hopes they will be illuminated; making preparations for further operations tomorrow. Weather doubtful and moon waning, so big results unlikely but every little helps. The long-range Maryland sent to recce Athens–Crete pm today to assist Fleet against seaborne attack returned safe.

In truth, the only contribution apart from reconnaissance that the RAF could make to the defence of Crete in the circumstances was that of bombing the airfields from which the enemy was operating. This it did to the best of its ability. Photographic reconnaissance of Greek airfields on the 12th had shown 'large concentrations of all types of aircraft, maximum being about 150 at Menidi'.

Wellingtons attacked the aerodromes on the nights of 13/14th and 14/15th: 'Pilots' reports indicate considerable success.' The AOC also arranged for Beaufighters from Malta to attack the aerodromes at dawn on the 17th: 'Beaufighter dawn attack on Greek aerodromes from Malta appears to have been successful and emphasises value of long-range fighter.'

Forty-two sorties were made in 17 raids against aerodromes in Greece during this period. It is certain some enemy aircraft were destroyed. However great it may have been, there is no reason at all to think that it even deranged the enemy's plans.

Compiled by Air Historical Branch

Appendix VIII

BILL'S WARS

THE VICHY FRENCH IN SYRIA, JUNE 1941: AN OVERVIEW

In late 1940, Germany sent Werner Otto Von Hentig to Syria to execute Hitler's objectives to use the Levant as a staging area for the assault on Mosul's oil fields in Iraq and the Suez Canal in Egypt. Von Hentig met with several influential leaders of the Syrian nationalist factions, including future President of Syria Shukri Al-Quwatli. They discussed increasing German–Syrian economic co-operation and plans to undermine Allied influence in Syria.

In May 1941, Admiral François Darlan signed an agreement with the Germans known as the 'Paris Protocols'. Darlan signed on behalf of Vichy France and the agreement granted the Germans access to military facilities in Syria. Though the protocols were never ratified, Charles Huntziger, the Vichy Minister of War, sent orders to the High Commissioner for the Levant. In accordance with these orders, aircraft of the Luftwaffe and the Regia Aeronautica were allowed to refuel in Syria. These aircraft, disguised as Iraqi and painted as such, were en route to Iraq during the Anglo-Iraqi War. After a *coup d'état*, Iraq was controlled by pro-German rebel forces under Rashid Ali. The Germans also requested Vichy authorities to use the Syrian railways to send armaments to Iraqi rebels in Mosul. There was a threat of Axis support for anti-British parties in Iraq, thus endangering strategic oil supplies and communications. Gen Wavell, Commander-in-Chief of the Middle East Command, had to respond to the threat posed by Vichy collaboration with Germany and Italy.

The Allied offensive (Operation *Exporter*) was aimed at preventing the Germans from using the Vichy French Mandates of Syria and Lebanon as springboards for attacks on Egypt. Desperate times called for desperate measures. On 9 June, two French destroyers, the *Valmy* and the *Guepard,* exchanged fire with the British destroyer HMS *Janus*. The New Zealand light cruiser *Leander* and six RN destroyers came to the aid of *Janus* and the French destroyers retired. Close air support was provided by squadrons from the RAF and RAAF and the ground forces on the coast were supported by shelling from Royal Navy and Royal Australian Navy units.

On 15 June, with or without French approval, the Luftwaffe attempted to come to the aid of the hard-pressed French naval forces. Ju88s of II/LG1 attacked British warships off the Syrian coast. Hits were scored on two destroyers, *Illex* and *Isis*. That evening, French aircraft bombed British naval units off the Syrian coast. Next day (16 June) FAA Swordfish sank the French destroyer *Chevalier Paul*, which was on its way from Toulon to Syria carrying ammunition and supplies. On 25 June, HMS *Parthian* torpedoed and sank the French submarine *Souffleur* off the Syrian coast, and shortly afterwards the French tanker *Adour* was attacked and badly damaged by Swordfish. The tanker was carrying the entire fuel supply for the Vichy forces in the Levant. With total defeat facing the Vichy in the air, on land and at sea, a ceasefire came into effect on 12 July.

The Vichy French forces lost approximately 6,000 men, of whom about 1,000 had been killed. Almost 38,000 were taken prisoner. But when given the choice of being repatriated to France or joining the Free French, only 5,668 chose to join the forces of Gen de Gaulle.

Appendix IX

THE CRETE CAMPAIGN

B ill's involvement in the Crete campaign ended before the invasion began, the first German airborne forces arriving on 20 May, by which time he was safely back in Egypt. The hard-pressed RAF and FAA contingent left behind attempted to thwart the German onslaught.

Airmen in the Defence of Maleme, May 1941

For Operation *Merkur* the Luftwaffe air commander, Maj Gen Gerhard, had 10 air transport groups comprising some 500 Ju52s at his disposal, but most of these had, during the Balkan campaign, been engaged in ammunition and supply deliveries, and now urgently required overhaul. On 1 May, the whole fleet flew off to the north. Dozens of maintenance centres in Germany, Czechoslovakia and Austria dropped all other work to devote themselves to the task. Two weeks later some 493 of them, completely overhauled and many with new engines, had relanded at bases in the Athens area. It was a masterpiece of organisation and technical achievement.

A second problem facing the Luftwaffe was the airfields. Few had metalled runways and these were already occupied by the bomber units. There remained only small and neglected fields of sand. 'They are nothing but deserts!' the commander of KGzbV.4, Oberst Rüdiger von Heyking, bitterly reported. 'Heavy-laden aircraft will sink up to their axles.' Von Heyking had the misfortune to be based with his 150-odd Ju52s at Topolia, on an airfield, which an over-enthusiastic Army officer had ordered to be ploughed after its occupation 'to make it more level'. The consequence was that every take off and landing produced a cloud of dust, which rose to 3,000ft and blotted out the sun. In the course of a rehearsal, von Heyking worked out that after a squadron take-off it took 17 minutes before one could again see one's own hand and a second squadron could follow. Conditions were hardly better at the neighbouring airfield of Tanagra, where more Ju52s were based. The remaining four transport Gruppen lay at Dadion, Megara, and Corinth – their airfields likewise of sand. On the first morning of the invasion, a watching fighter pilot Ltn Josef Neuhaus recalled:

The clouds of dust whipped up by the first take-offs blinded the other pilots, with the result that by the time the transports reached their destination, our fighters and bombers providing the air cover had to dash back to refuel.

But the worst bottleneck was fuel. To transport the chief combatants to Crete would require three successive flights by the 493 aircraft, and that meant some 650,000 gallons of petrol. Brought by tanker to Piraeus, the port of Athens, it then had to be transferred to 45-gallon barrels, and finally transported by lorries to the remote airfields. With great efficiency, this was achieved.

At 0530 on the morning of 20 May the first of almost 500 heavily laden Ju52/3m transports began taking off, hampered by the billowing clouds of dust and requiring a 20-minute interval between the take-off of each Staffel to allow visibility to clear. As a result it took over an hour for the various Gruppen to assemble into formation over Kythera before heading south to approach Crete from the west, over the Antikythera Strait.

Disaster stuck immediately. First off had been the glider tugs of I/LLG1, with their DFS230 gliders trailing behind, each carrying ten fully equipped assault troops including the pilot, who was expected to participate in the fighting on landing. The glider carrying the commander of Luft Division 7 and six members of his staff was buffeted by the slipstream of a low-flying He111 of II/KG26 that passed close by, causing the towing cable to snap. The pilot was unable to retain control and the wings broke off under the stress, the fuselage spiralling down to crash on the little island of Aegina in Athens Bay; all aboard perished.

* * * * *

At Maleme the rear parties from 30 and 33 Squadrons numbered 229 officers and men, together with three officers and 50 ratings of 805 Squadron. A further 56 RAF personnel were attached to 252 AMES (radar). Everyone was on edge, anticipating an imminent dawn attack, as Sqn Ldr Howell noted:

> The minutes dragged by. We stamped our feet and moved restlessly to keep warm. It was getting light and the sky turned from black to purple, to blue. The landscape came to view. The matchless mountains to the south, dark against the sky. The blue Aegean stretching out to the horizon in the north. At seven o'clock the stand-by period was over. Just one more routine completed. We were free to go about the business of the day. I dismissed the men and they hurried off to breakfast. I strolled back to my tent wondering if I could snatch some more sleep. The sun was coming up and it was already getting warm.

I stripped to the waist and washed and shaved in the basin outside my tent. The cookhouse down the hill was as active as a beehive. Among the trees around me I could see Beale and the others also shaving.

For the heat of the day we wore only shirt and shorts. I was pulling on my shirt when the alarm bell went. The usual morning blitz, I thought. I strapped on my revolver and took my tin hat and started off for the ops room to find out what was on. Someone came running to meet me. 'A hundred plus,' he reported. The men were grousing at having their breakfast interrupted. But they were making for the slit trenches, which were dispersed throughout the olive grove. We had too much experience of air attacks to take them lightly. I headed for my usual vantage point, a trench out on the side of the hill overlooking the landing strip where I could watch the camp and the airfield simultaneously. I found Vernon Woodward and young Dunscombe already there. The trench could hold three at a pinch. It was a good one, deep and narrow.

The air reverberated with the noise of many engines. As yet we could not see them. But slowly it became apparent to me that this was bigger than the usual blitz. Nevertheless I could not believe that it would be more than a blitz. It seemed so suicidal for them to try dropping paratroops in broad daylight on to prepared positions. It was suicidal for many, but I underestimated the determination of our enemies.

The glider-towing He111s of II/KG26, joined by KG2 Do17s from Menidi, were first over Crete just after 0700, approaching the Maleme–Canea area and subjecting the defenders to intensive and concentrated bombing, many bombs falling around the airfield and on the slopes of Kavkazia Hill (known as Hill 107), which overlooked the airfield, and where 22nd New Zealand Battalion was entrenched. Due to the effective slit trenches that had been dug by the soldiers and airmen here in recent weeks, casualties were relatively light. Howell continued:

In any event our orders were clear. We were not to move till it was apparent that invasion was occurring. So we watched the skies as interested spectators watching the teams come out on the field for a rugger match. The first formations of bombers were in sight now and wheeling in to run up over us. We watched them closely, with a more personal and apprehensive interest now. They were clearly going to pass straight overhead. That meant we were the target. We waited till we heard the whistle and whine of several scores of heavy bombs on their way down, and then we went flat in the bottom of our trench. The bombs struck in twelves, earth spouted to the heavens, the crump and shock of impact crept closer up the hill. The noise was indescribable. The ground shuddered and shook under us as the bomb pattern passed over and beyond.

The whole area was shrouded in thick choking dust, and earth and stones were falling everywhere. We could not see more than a few yards. But we heard the whistle of more bombs on their way down and we kept below ground. The concussion of the bombs bursting close to us shook in the sides of the trench. We were covered in earth. Our eyes and mouths were full of grit. And still it went on. We were shaken by the earth shock till our teeth felt loose and we could hardly see. Debris continued to crash around us and the sides of the trench crumbled. We lost count of time.

There remained the continuous roar of aircraft overhead and the apparently continuous whine of bombs descending. Later these sounds were punctuated by long bursts of cannon and machine-gun fire as low-flying fighters came in to attack the anti-aircraft gunpits. These were already silent under the terrific weight of attack with the exception of one Bofors gun down by the beach. This went on firing for some time till a host of Stukas and Me109s fastened on it and shot and blasted it out of existence. I remember the sense of admiration for that determined British guncrew.

It seemed a long time later that I noticed there were no more bombs coming. It was eight o'clock precisely. We could still see nothing beyond a few yards due to the dust. But looking straight up you could see the blue sky. And there, only a few hundred feet above us, were passing packed formations of Junkers 52s. Gliders towed behind were casting off and circling down towards the west. They were to land in a dried riverbed about three hundred yards away, a very rough landing, but most of them survived it. Everywhere silhouetted against the blue were parachutes, strings and strings of them, all colours, floating rapidly down among us.

The tugs and gliders of I/LLG1 arrived at 0805, releasing the tows over the sea to allow a battalion of the Assault Regiment to land on target. Misty conditions and smoke caused a number of the glider pilots to misjudge their landing area, which was in the valley of the Tavronitis, just behind Hill 107. As a result several crashed on the rocky slopes nearby, killing or injuring the occupants. Others came down in isolated areas, where they were swiftly dealt with by the defenders. Airman Marcel Comeau of 33 Squadron was again in the thick of the action, two gliders crash-landing close to the trench in which he was sheltering. Approaching the nearest with some trepidation, armed only with a rifle, he was nonetheless sufficiently composed to shoot the first two dazed soldiers who came staggering out. As more men followed from both gliders, Comeau beat a hasty retreat to cover.

The Germans advanced on the camp areas of 22nd NZ Battalion at the base of Hill 107, where it had been hoped to catch the New Zealanders off guard and unprepared. The camp was nearly empty, however, so the Germans turned to their main objective, the capture of the hill. Since Hill 107 dominated the airfield, whoever controlled it, controlled Maleme – and the prompt seizure of one of the airfields was vital to the success of the whole operation. As the men advanced up the slopes they were suddenly met by a hail of fire from well dug-in defenders; among those who fell dead or seriously wounded was the German commander; the survivors were pinned down, unable to move.

Just a mile away to the west a dozen more gliders approached the dried-up riverbed, only to come under heavy fire from the fully alerted defenders. The vulnerable DFS230s, constructed as they were of tubular steel, canvas and wood, made easy targets during their slow descents, and many occupants were killed or wounded in flight. One glider went down in flames and another was hit by a heavy burst as it touched down. Others broke up on landing, but sufficient numbers of men survived to attack the New Zealanders on each bank of the river at its mouth, and to capture their positions, thereby silencing their AA guns. This extremely important if brief action was to ensure the ultimate success of the whole venture, for now at 0820 the first elements of the main paratroop force appeared overhead, the slow Ju52s flying a steady course at under 400ft to drop 1,800 men, very little anti-aircraft gunfire being experienced. Howell later wrote:

> I watched as if in a dream, as a formation of Ju52s disgorged their paratroops. My brain seemed numb and unable to appreciate the significance of the scene. The other two with me seemed to be in the same state. Suddenly a gaunt and grimy figure stood on the edge of our trench. It was Beale. Pointing up, he said, 'Hadn't you better get your men moving? I am off to the Battalion headquarters to see what I can do for the Colonel.' Memory sprang to life with his words. I realised that the long-awaited signal had been given. We jumped out of the trench and I sent Woodward and Dunscombe running to collect the men for whom they were responsible. I went also at the run to round up others. Soon I had a number with me, collected from the slit trenches in the middle of the camp. Aircraft were still roaring overhead only a few feet up and they were firing at every sign of movement round us. We kept close to the ground and crept in single file round to the gully.
>
> As we peered through the thick dust from the bombing and picked our way among the shattered olive trees where our camp had stood, there seemed to be a bomb crater at every step. We could see upwards

to the blue sky where parachutists still seemed to be coming down everywhere. Suddenly we almost stumbled over the crouched figure of a British soldier. He was bent over an empty oil drum. Inside it was a small stove with a billycan bubbling on it. His grimy face looked up at us. 'Like a nice cuppa tea, Sir?' he asked. At that moment the question could not have been more incongruous nor could it have been more welcome! We were parched with thirst, our mouths full of grit. I accepted gratefully and we shared sips of hot sweet tea as the battle continued to rage about us.

Within minutes hundreds of parachutists were disgorged over the Maleme area. Accompanying them were two heavy-weapons companies with 20mm anti-tank rifles and small pack-howitzers. One battalion was less fortunate. Because the 600 paratroops were due to land on or near the beach to approach Maleme village and the airfield from that direction, the 50 Ju52/3ms came in over Canea Bay and were forced to fly inland to prevent the parachutists being blown out to sea by the wind prevailing. This brought them over Bofors gun positions at Pirgos and near Modhion, several being shot down. One was seen to fall out of control into a batch of parachutists, while a second fell in flames as the men attempted to jump out, a third splashing into the sea. One more force-landed near Canea with one member of the crew dead, and a fifth aircraft was badly damaged, crash-landing on return to Topolia.

Most of the unfortunate battalion jumped over the slopes of surrounding hills, coming down on heavily defended New Zealand positions where they were greeted by intense small-arms fire. Many were killed or wounded as they floated down; others were caught in trees and shot before they were able to free themselves, while yet more were injured landing on the rocky terrain. Many of the survivors were never able to get to their weapons containers, while some came down among dwellings in the Modhion valley, where a number were cut down by machine-gunners attached to the New Zealand Engineers as they attempted to free themselves from their harnesses. Local villagers attacked others; men, women and children armed with knives, axes and even ancient flintlock rifles, killing several. Within an hour all the officers, including the commander were dead or seriously wounded; over two-thirds of this unit, nearly 400 men, would die in the fighting. Meanwhile, nine more gliders carrying a detachment with anti-tank guns, motorcycles, mortars and flame-throwers, came down in the Tavronitis valley with the objective of seizing the old iron bridge over the river. The objective was quickly achieved, demolition charges removed and the crossing secured. One German paratroop commander wrote:

Even from the air one already has the impression that the landing ground is alive. Small fountains of smoke and dust arise from the earth, and when they have cleared it looks as though an army of moles has been at work. Then comes the landing. The plane lurches across the ground, and to the roar of the engines is added the crackling explosion of bursting shells. Splinters rip through the cabin walls. A man cries out, grasping his shoulder. He is the first casualty. The plane comes to a halt with a sudden jerk. Everyone rushes for the door to get out as quickly as possible, but outside all hell is waiting. The fountains of dust which from the air looked so small and innocuous have suddenly grow to enormity, and from their midst there explode blinding red flashes of light. The crash of the explosions deafens you, yet in the whining of the shells you seem to hear a sound like the cry of a tortured animal. You throw yourself to the ground and flatten yourself, drawing up your legs, pressing your arms close to your body, and holding your breath. The distinctive smell of bursting shells burns your nose and gums. Then you jump up and dash forward – three or four paces, perhaps – until the howl of a fresh shell sends you sprawling again. And the edge of the first bit of cover is still so far, so very far away . . .

With many units of paratroops now down and armed, fierce fighting was developing at the eastern end of the RAF camp where groups of airmen were being cut off as the Germans infiltrated. One small party of six airmen from 33 Squadron held out in their trench until their ammunition ran out, and then attempted to retreat as paratroopers approached over the iron bridge. Only three made it, Airmen Cyril Banks, Ken Eaton and Tubby Dixon all being killed. An urgent call went out for medical aid on the airfield and 30 Squadron's ambulance, driven by LAC Henry Betts, with LAC Norman Darch as medical orderly, ventured out across the open area under fire. Although wounded in the back by two bullets, Darch helped rescue a number of wounded and got them to comparative safety. Betts was killed. The RAF and FAA men were congregating mainly on the lower slopes of Hill 107 in small parties, trying to reorganise and formulate some plans for defence and survival. It had been proposed that in the event of invasion, officers and NCOs of the two units would defend allocated sections, and would each be responsible for small groups of airmen. Howell continued:

We arrived first at the gully and lay in cover waiting for the others to arrive. Soon the imperturbable Woody appeared with a few men behind him. He had found difficulty in collecting them as some slit trench areas were cut off by pockets of enemy paratroops. Dunscombe was not long behind him and reported the same thing. We decided to move without waiting further. It was clear that the New Zealanders were fully occupied where they were. At their request, I sent Woody and Dunscombe with some men to prospect to the south. It was the last I saw of them. I led the rest up the hill to the east and found some New Zealanders behind a stone wall. They did not know what was happening elsewhere, so I decided that we should hold this ground against possible attacks from the west. Others now arrived with P/O Myhill in charge and I appointed him to command one sector, while Sergeant-Pilot Butterick took over the other sector. Both men were cool and capable and ready for anything. I walked from one end of our line to the other, gratified to find my brain working clearly again and the sense of fear gone. Aircraft still roared overhead and bullets kicked up the dirt, but I was too busy to worry about them.

To the north, a huge formation of Ju52s was dropping more paratroops. Everywhere, the sky was busy with aircraft. I decided it was time to contact the colonel and report my action to him. I left Myhill in charge and walked round the hillside to the headquarters. More paratroops were being dropped to the east round Galatos. Bullets from various sources still whined past and there was still the occasional crump of a bomb. But the blitz had lifted and the land battle was on.

I found Beale wondering about the safety of our respective orderly rooms. Colonel Andrew had decided to come with Beale and me to see how his own forward elements were faring. We walked up over the crest of the hill together. On the far side, we found a little group round a badly wounded soldier. He had been hit in the lungs and was coughing blood. He was pretty far gone. Three of his pals were round him holding his hand as he prepared to make his last journey. We left them and went on down the hill into the olive grove. At the end of the gulf there should have been an advanced post of New Zealand infantry. Their trenches were empty. The Colonel decided to go back to his headquarters and await runners from his companies.

Beale and I walked on, keeping in cover as far as we could. There was intermittent fire coming from down on our left where the glider troops were forming up after landing in the riverbed. We kept out of sight of them as we moved across the face of the hill. We came to a coloured parachute. There was nothing tied to it and there was no one in sight. But I had a hunch the place was unhealthy and we went back a few yards. Here we found a slit trench with two airmen in it. They had rifles. We took them with us and went forward again. Beale was in the lead. I followed with my revolver ready. Then came the two airmen. We crept quietly forward.

All of a sudden Beale pitched forward about five paces with a cough and grunt. He had been hit in the stomach. Fortunately the bullet came out between his ribs without damaging his vitals. But he and we were not to know that. I leant over him, speechless in stupid concern. There was nothing I could say, so I said, 'Are you all right?' A ridiculous question under the circumstances. The idea was in my mind that he had been hit by a stray bullet from an aircraft, so I was not taking any special precautions myself.

As I uttered the words, however, I felt a tremendous blow on my left shoulder. It picked me up off my feet and spun me in the air. My right arm flung out and was also struck violently. I found myself on the ground. My left shoulder was quite numb and blood was spouting from my right forearm where the artery had been cut. I had been hit by two Tommy-gun slugs from a nearby paratroop. He had also hit one of the airmen a glancing blow on the ribs with another slug. We were all flat on the ground now and in cover from further fire for the moment. My arm was a nasty sight. Part of my forearm had been carried away as the slug spread on the bone and tore it out. I found it difficult to move myself as neither arm could be of any help. Beale struggled over to me. One airman came with him. Together they took out a field dressing and tied it on my arm by the elbow. They started to tighten it up with the help of a stick to make the tourniquet effective. As they tightened it, however, the stick broke.

In the meantime, bullets were whining past us again. We were in an unhealthy position. There was not time to do more. So my tourniquet was left as it was. An extraordinary thing was that it was just tight enough to slow up the flow of blood from my artery enough to let it clot and so stop, without being so tight as to stop the blood supply to the rest of my arm. As the tourniquet remained on for three days that fact saved me from losing either my life or my arm. The others decided to crawl back to the gully, where they would be under cover again to walk back to our lines. I was unable to crawl, as both my arms were broken. So they helped me to my feet and I started to run back across an open stretch to where there would be cover to walk. It was about a hundred yards. I set my teeth and ran. The bones ground together with a sickening noise as my helpless arms flapped about. The pain was excruciating. When I had only about five paces to go, I relaxed the attention, which had been focused completely on my objective. The result was a blackout. I fainted and fell, just short of cover, in the open, exposed to fire from two enemy positions.

I was oblivious to the passage of time. The next thing I knew was that Beale and the airmen were beside me. They lifted me up. I made a supreme effort of concentration and tried to walk. I was half carried to a place a few yards away where a tent had stood before the blitz.

It was dug into the hillside and afforded good cover. I watched a stick grenade or explosive shell pitch five yards ahead of us. The dirt flew and the explosion cracked on us, but miraculously no one was touched by splinters.

They laid me down on my back in the pit and sat close in to review the position. Beale's face was white and haggard. His wound kept him bent almost double with pain. Only his amazing spirit kept him going. He was determined to reach our lines. He promised to send a rescue party to bring me in and set off on his own. He got back all right only to be taken prisoner later when the aid post where he was being attended to was overrun.

Two airmen, who had been accompanying the small group, returned to see what comfort they could provide:

The airman had my revolver. I told him to give it to me. He put it into my left hand, which was lying helpless on my chest. I made a terrific effort of concentration and got the muzzle under my chin. But the strength to pull back the hammer had left my fingers. The airman was shocked and took the gun from me. I asked him to shoot me but he was clearly horrified at the idea. So I gave up and sent him off to try to get back to our lines. He and the other man were captured on their way.

A rescue party, led by one of his own officers and made up of airmen, counter-attacked and reached Howell. But they found him unconscious in a pool of blood. His right arm lay across his stomach from which the blood appeared to have come. He was covered in flies and without sign of life.

Meanwhile, the battle raged. Following on the heels of the bombers, StG2s Ju87s arrived, accompanied by Staffel upon Staffel of Bf109s and Bf110s, strafing from low level. The Luftwaffe's attack seemed well co-ordinated for whenever the marauding fighters came under fire from any well-concealed AA guns the Stukas appeared to be called in to deal with them; the intensity and accuracy of the resultant attacks invariably silenced the particular target. On the airfield the empty pens, remaining gun positions, and the wrecks of the Hurricanes and Buffalos were repeatedly strafed by fighters that appeared suddenly from behind surrounding hills, or along the beach at very low level.

Intermittently the defenders scored successes against the low-flying strafers, as when six Bf109s were seen circling over Theodhoroi Island, just east of Maleme, prior to sweeping across the beach towards the airfield – every gun that could fire put up such a terrific barrage that almost at once the leading aircraft, Black 3 of 5./JG77, flown by Oblt Berthold Jung, was hit and he broke away back out to sea, trailing black smoke. The following pair both took hits in the engine, Oblt Gerhard Rahm and Obfw Werner Petermann crash-landing White and Black 1 on the beach. Meanwhile, Jung, obviously fearing that his damaged fighter would not get back to Greece, turned back again and crash-landed near Maleme, while the three remaining fighters gave up their attempt to attack and fled out to sea. The defenders believed these had been hit also, for all were observed trailing black smoke, but this was obviously caused by the engine exhaust. All three pilots who had been shot down survived, but one of the wingmen was assaulted by local peasants, who pulled him out of his cockpit, a Cretan woman hacking off his ring finger, complete with engagement ring, with a carving knife before troops could get to them and take them into custody.

Ill-armed and in a hopeless position the various groups of airmen were now led away from the vicinity of the airfield by their officers or NCOs, some aided by New Zealand officers; most headed inland for safety. Fighting side by side with them had been the FAA personnel, remnants of 805 and 815 Squadrons. Lt Alfie Sutton RN, who had been acting as Cdr Beale's principal assistant, had dug a hole near a Royal Marine gun position with his bayonet, taking pot-shots at paratroops from here until Ju87s attacked the Marines and put the guns out of action. Under constant sniper fire they managed to get one gun working again. At the bottom of the hill LAC Denton, an RAF mechanic attached to 815 Squadron, manned a Lewis gun until the barrel burned out, then retreated up the hill. Lt(A) Alec Ramsay, now in charge of 805 Squadron, mustered his party on high ground overlooking the camp, and although inadequately armed and under constant attack both by aircraft and paratroops, they held onto their position, inflicting many casualties. A second group from this unit were led to high ground by Sub-Lt(A) Roy Hinton, arming themselves from a German weapons container. Concealed in olive groves, without food or water, they consoled themselves from a gallon container of rum, liberated from the mess.

When the attack on Maleme commenced, a number of airmen were in sick quarters suffering from dysentery, including Lt(A) Lloyd Keith, a Canadian pilot of 805 Squadron, and 30 Squadron Medical Officer, Flt Lt Tom Cullen. Although feeling very groggy, Keith vacated his sick bed and spent most of the day stalking German snipers, armed only with his revolver; reputedly, he accounted for more than one. Although too weak to walk properly, Cullen attended to wounded throughout the fighting, continuing to do so until his post was overrun and he was taken prisoner. Even then he carried on alone in a nearby village, without sleep for three days, until captured New Zealand medical officers were sent to assist him. Over 1,000 wounded would pass through his hands before further aid was made available. Meanwhile, other airmen had joined New Zealand troops in hunting the paratroops, among them a party from 33 Squadron led by Woody Woodward, including the indomitable Marcel Comeau.

Over Maleme strafing fighters continued to mill around, Bf109s seeking to winkle out the defending guns. Members of 30 Squadron not occupied in holding the lower slopes of Hill 107 gave support to the New Zealanders. Plt Off Crowther, in charge of the detachment, led a handful of men to mop up a band of paratroops on the far side of the hill, where some 30 or so RAF and FAA personnel had been captured. So desperate was one German officer to seize the hill that he employed these prisoners as a human shield in an attempt to gain a footing. Some of the prisoners were shot by New Zealanders who mistook them for Germans as they approached, but PO Wheaton of 805 Squadron and a 30 Squadron airman, LAC Holland, were then ordered to approach the New Zealand lines and tell them to surrender.

As they reached shouting distance, the pair called out that they were going to make a dash for cover, but at that moment Crowther's 30 Squadron party, and men of 33 Squadron led by Cpl Harrison, suddenly attacked the Germans from both flanks. The remaining prisoners attempted to reach safety during the confused fighting, but about half of them were killed before the Germans were shot down or dispersed. LAC Holland was one of the casualties, badly wounded in the back, but was rescued by the New Zealanders. Crowther then led his band in a counter-attack on some Germans who had gained control of the eastern side of the RAF camp.

Despite constant strafing by Messerschmitts and fierce close combat with the paratroops, the RAF camp area was regained, and with the failure to capture the hill, the paratroops called in Ju87s and Bf110s to attack the defenders again. Late in the afternoon a pair of Junkers transports again tried to land on the airfield, but were driven off by a hail of small-arms fire from the troops on the beach. Finally, during the evening two detachments from the Assault Regiment managed to take Hill 107 despite fierce New Zealand resistance. Their victory found the Germans almost out of ammunition, but no counter-attack came. They had secured ultimate control of the airfield by this coup, and from this point the battle was lost for the defenders.

As the first wave of Ju52/3ms returned to Greece, they had lost no more than seven of their number over Maleme, Canea and Suda Bay, but as they reached their airfields most were forced to circle to allow the clouds of dust thrown up by the first down to subside. Several aircraft collided on the ground after landing, or were damaged in other accidents. Anxiously awaiting news from the invading forces, Headquarters of XI Fliegerkorps in Athens were ignorant of the catastrophes that had befallen much of both Groups, many of the radio transmitters carried in the DFS230s having been damaged or destroyed in the landings.

Meanwhile, at the same time as the initial glider landings had taken place around Maleme, Group Centre had commenced its assault on Canea and Suda Bay. The DFS230s came under heavy fire from their proposed objectives, three or four being hard hit and caused to crash, while the survivors were widely dispersed. More than half the force became casualties, while most others were swiftly rounded up and captured. Eight more gliders came down near the gun battery they were to put out of action south of Canea, but one landed near a Royal Marine section whose fire raked the glider, killing three of the occupants. As the remaining troops clambered out, all were shot down.

To support the valiant assault units, some 1,800 men were to be dropped west of Canea, to land in Prison Valley on either side of the Canea–Alikianou road, near Karatsos and along the coast road. These areas were heavily strafed by Bf109s just before the landings commenced, the first wave of over 150 Ju52/3ms then approaching. Although several gun sites had been put out of action by the glider troops, others put up a sustained fire, causing the transports to veer away and break formation. The result was that the parachutists fell over a wide area in scattered groups. Leading his men of the 3/Battalion was Hptm Baron von de Heydte:

> Then suddenly, from the mountains behind me, there came a screech of engines – not the ponderous roar of a transport plane, but a sound more like a siren followed by a fierce crackle of machine-gun fire. Automatically I hurled myself into the ditch – a deep, concrete ditch bordering a large field of corn – and at that moment a German fighter, with all guns blazing swept over within a few feet of where I lay. A stream of bullets threw up fountains of dust on the road and ricochets sang away into the distance. Then, as suddenly as it had appeared, the apparition passed. The fighter pulled up high and disappeared over the olive groves in the direction of what I took to be Canea. So the first shots to be aimed at me during this attack had been made by one of my own countrymen! No one could have thought of laying out identification signals so soon after landing, and the fighter pilot, whose task it was to support our attack, had obviously never imagined that this lackadaisical figure wandering in such unmilitary fashion down the centre of the road could possibly have been the commanding officer of a German battalion!

At Canea both sides had sought to consolidate their positions while Messerschmitt fighters cruised above, obviously uncertain of the locations of their own troops. During one sortie Hptm Paul Kleiner's Bf110 of 4./ZG26 (3D+HM) was shot down near Canea with the loss of the crew, while JG77's low-flying Bf109s continued to take regular losses. Fw Niemeyer of 4 Staffel was shot down and killed in Yellow 9, while Oblt Otto Grobe, from the same Staffel survived being shot down in Black 5 and managed to evade capture, later returning to his unit. A third Bf109, this from 7 Staffel, was lost when Fw Dietrich Saake was similarly brought down in White 6, becoming a prisoner.

With the end of the day the surviving para/glider troops found themselves in an almost hopeless situation. Surrounded by greatly superior enemy forces, they struggled for survival. Their signal equipment had been smashed during the airdrop and they were therefore unable to establish contact with the nearest friendly forces. Although they were completely on their own and faced by an uncertain fate, they were determined to hold out to the end in the vicinity of the two airfields so that they would tie down the defending forces and thus assist their comrades in the western part of the island.

Morning on 21 May found the Germans most favourably placed at Maleme, where daybreak attacks by Bf109s and Ju87s prevented the New Zealanders launching any organised counter-attack against the critical Hill 107. Apart from the constant strafing, however, it was relatively quiet here and around Canea with only skirmish activity occurring. The various RAF and FAA parties, mainly without arms, were gradually being led away from the forward areas. The two largest groups had congregated to the east of Hill 107, the 30 Squadron party with 23rd Battalion near the village of Dhaskaliana, while the main 33 Squadron party was along Vineyard Ridge with 21st Battalion. Everyone was keeping their heads well down, as Hs126 spotter aircraft were meandering overhead, looking for targets for the Stukas and Messerschmitts. To the south of the hill was the radar station, and this came under air attack by Bf109s and Bf110s during the morning, 17 of the 56 RAF personnel becoming casualties, or subsequently being captured.

Many of the FAA personnel had gathered in the same area, including Sub-Lt(A) Hinton's small party, as he recalled:

> Dawn found myself and about four of my troops in a trench covered in bracken. We had a field of observation downhill and due east. After some time I got out to have a pee and behold, some Germans were coming over the top of the hill. This was an occasion when I was thankful I was the open champion sprinter at school. We made it to the hollow of the valley, scrambled up the opposite side and fortunately came across a motley crowd of our own troops. We lay along the ridge taking pot shots at the Germans on the other side of the valley. To my horror I found I was receiving some 20 shots in return to every one fired by me and realised I was firing tracer bullets!

As the majority of the RAF and FAA were unarmed, Lt Sutton RN requested permission for them to be withdrawn. It was agreed that they could make for

Canea, but would have to defend their present positions first until the return of the New Zealanders from their attempted counter-attack. Lt(A) Ramsay and the armed FAA party took the right flank, while Sutton and the RAF group covered the left; the unarmed men were ordered to remain under cover; the group was now about 160 strong. At 1600, the first Ju52/3ms began landing at Maleme, one behind the other. As soon as each aircraft touched down the alpine troops poured out and rushed for cover. Then the aircraft, unloaded as rapidly as possible, would try to take to the air again.

At last, at 0330 on the night of 21st/22nd, the 20th New Zealand and 28th Maori Battalions launched a counter-attack on the airfield at Maleme, supported by three light tanks of 3rd Hussars. Despite fierce opposition, the New Zealanders were nearing their objective at dawn, threatening both the airfield and the important high ground to the south, but one tank had been knocked out by an anti-tank gun, the other two suffering gun stoppages. While being withdrawn, they came under air attack, and one more tank was destroyed. By mid-morning the whole of 5th Brigade had been committed to the battle, but the ground gained could not be held, and all units began withdrawing. With the airfield still in their hands, the Germans continued flying in men and supplies at an increasing tempo, Ju52/3ms landing at the rate of one every five minutes.

Aircraft continued to pile up on the airfield, at least 20 more crashing, crash-landing, or suffering less severe damage, while aircraft were shot down. A further dozen were in a damaged condition, or crash-landed on arrival due to the state of the runways there. Around midday, the Luftwaffe again made heavy attacks on the Suda Bay area, but in doing so lost a Ju87 of Stab/StG77 and a Bf110 of II/ZG76 (MB+FN: Ltn Werner Hoffmann); a further Bf110 from II/ZG26 crash-landed at Maleme. By now 5th New Zealand Brigade, together with the surviving RAF and FAA troops, had begun pulling out of the Maleme area, taking up reserve positions behind 10th Brigade in the Canea area.

With Maleme firmly in their hands, the Germans began gathering in the wounded – both their own and British – from the various medical posts and from the field. 33 Squadron's badly wounded Sqn Ldr Howell had been found by passing paratroops after lying unattended in the open for three days. Realising that he was still alive, they gave him some water, and a little later a German rescue party carried him to a nearby village where he received some rudimentary treatment from Flt Lt Cullen, the 30 Squadron doctor. Howell vaguely remembered:

> The sun beat down from the blazing sky. My thirst was extreme. I was
> so weak that I could not twitch a finger. The flies crawled over my face
> undisturbed. Clouds of them gathered around me, attracted by the

pool of blood in which I lay. Big shiny black flies. They saved my life. They laid eggs in my wounds. Later I was crawling with maggots. The maggots ate the decaying flesh and prevented gangrene. But at the time the flies were the last torment. Tortured with pain and thirst I lay in the sun with a deep desire for death.

Time passed slowly. I was intermittently conscious. Sometimes conscious of noise as machine guns rattled nearby. Always acutely conscious of thirst. I craved for water as I had never before craved for anything. Some say that, faced with death, the past comes before the fading gaze in shifting scenes. I had no such experience. I was alone and dying from loss of blood and thirst. It was a race to see which won. I only desired the race to end.

Somehow, he hung on to life:

The sun blazed down again. I had lost all sense of time. I must have been unconscious for most of that day and the following night. On the third day I had a spell of consciousness again. There were men passing just by me. I tried to croak at them. They saw that I was alive and came round me. Six young German paratroops. My tongue was dry and swollen. They saw my need and produced their water bottles. The first drops to pass my throat were more precious to me than life. I drank and drank. I seem to remember draining many water bottles. Someone had cold tea with brandy in his. Another gave me some dried fruit from a cellophane packet. I was sick. And drank again. 'Water' was the only word I could whisper through my cracked lips. Someone pulled a blanket over me and I was alone again. Only the craving for water remained. I remember being carried in on a stretcher. Every lurch of the stretcher was agony. I passed out again into merciful oblivion. Then I was lying among a crowd of other wounded and dying men in the village street.

Other 33 Squadron groups had also fared badly: Plt Off Ray Dunscombe had been killed in the fighting, while Sgt Alec Butterick had been seriously wounded. His group had engaged in hand-to-hand fighting with the paratroops during which he was shot through the left knee by a burst of machine-gunfire. Taken prisoner, he would be held in a barn for several days without care and food, with a group of other prisoners, including some civilians; the civilians were then taken outside and shot. Two other pilots from the unit were captured, Sgts Glawil Reynish and Fred Leveridge. Those seriously wounded were soon to be flown to Athens in Ju52/3ms, including Cdr Beale RN. Here, Sgt Butterick would have his shattered leg amputated, while Sqn Ldr Howell would make a remarkable recovery from his wounds.

Airman Comeau and his party were also making for safety, but not without a few close encounters:

> We joined the Canea road. On the beach a Messerschmitt 109 lay new and artificial-looking with its nose in a clump of feathery reeds. With the airman's in-bred curiosity my companions forgot the war for a while and left the road to clamber all over it. Not until their 'technical' examination had been completed did they move on again. A few minutes later they were all lying full length in a shallow ditch, holding their breath while three hedge-hopping Me109s flew down the road towards them. We soon discovered that fighters were maintaining a standing patrol between Canea and Maleme, passing low overhead at intervals of fifteen minutes. It was a nerve-racking business. Sometimes there was no opportunity to find cover and the men could only sprawl by the road edge and keep very still.
>
> There was a 30 Squadron Palestinian beginning to crack up under the strain. Then he lost his head completely, darting across the path of the fighters he scurried towards a small stone cottage on the other side of the road. A Messerschmitt flicked a wing – taking a good look. It was time to move quickly. Before the Germans could come back again the party had all bolted into the cottage behind the Palestinian. A few moments later cannon shells were exploding outside, scattering tiles from the roof like playing cards, their bullets thudded into the walls like hailstones. In one darkened corner sat an old woman, softly sobbing and crooning to herself. We suddenly felt ashamed for having invaded her house and left her our last few blankets.

But it was not all bad news for the airmen troops, since survivors of Lt(A) Keith's party and the group commanded by Sub-Lt(A) Hinton reached Suda Bay on the evening of 23 May, being evacuated by the destroyers *Jaguar* and *Defender* together with some 200 other naval personnel. Flt Lt Woodward's party was close on their heels, arriving at Suda Bay with many tales of frightening experiences, as Woody recalled:

> We crawled, at one point, through part of a New Zealand anti-personnel minefield in a vineyard, much to the consternation of the New Zealand troops who were watching our progress through binoculars.

He was now informed that he would be flown out in a Sunderland that evening, and was told to stand by. At the last moment, however, he was directed to take charge of a party of walking wounded and to lead them to a rendezvous with the Australian destroyer *Nizam* in Suda Bay. This warship, with *Abdiel* and *Hero*, took aboard some 930 wounded and surplus personnel, including merchant seamen from the many sunken vessels, and naval personnel including Lt(A) Alec Ramsay's 805 Squadron contingent. Among those missing were the two TAGs, L/Airmen Tom Jary and Bill Jarvis, both of whom had been killed in the fighting.

With the departure of Woodward, command of the 33 Squadron party was assumed by Flt Lt Mitchell. His group now numbered just 41 out of an original 102 airmen, and they were ordered to make for Sphakia on the south coast, two trucks being provided for their transport. Just before they departed, a Do17 flew over the area dropping leaflets, printed in English and Greek, threatening reprisals against anyone, man or woman, found guilty of ill-treatment of German prisoners. In the Sphakia area to which this group was now heading, was the 50-strong 30 Squadron party, who had also lost more than half their original number. Meanwhile, Lt Sutton's mixed RAF/ FAA party was also making for Sphakia.

Even as the retreating troops were making their way south, the Luftwaffe began flying in to Maleme, as Fw Johann Pichler of 7./JG77 recalled:

> About 100 crashed aircraft were lying around the airfield and landing was a risky operation. All day long we sat in the slit trenches with nothing to eat or drink. It was extremely hot and we were under constant attack by Blenheims and Hurricanes. However, Maleme had the advantage that we no longer had to make the frightening flights over the sea and we could fly sorties in record time against the fiercely resisting British anti-aircraft and artillery positions. Each pilot took off singly, attacked the target, fired all his ammunition and returned to be re-armed and refuelled for another sortie, all while Ju52 transports were landing or unloading troops and supplies and with the damaged or burnt-out Ju52s still lying around. It was a real graveyard for the Transportflieger and a hectic scene of confusion and disorder.

Between 5,000 and 6,000 troops were now crossing the mountains of central Crete, many on foot and many wounded. Some of the latter had received only very rudimentary treatment, but still staggered on the 30 miles to the embarkation area, many of them in considerable pain. There were men with amputated arms, severe leg wounds, and even one with a bullet-punctured chest, who nonetheless completed the trek with the aid of his comrades. All came under frequent air attack, which continued at night, amber flares being dropped to illuminate the packed single road to the south. On this occasion the Luftwaffe behaved impeccably, however, and parties of wounded who displayed large Red Cross flags were not attacked. Indeed, one instance was reported when a Bf109 pilot, having aborted his attack when he obviously spotted the flag, flew round above the group until they reached the coast, apparently protecting them from assault by other aircraft. He was even seen to lean out of the side of his cockpit and wave before departing.

The first departure from Sphakia was made at 0300 on 29 May, the destroyers having first offloaded urgently needed stores and rations. They took away with them 744 persons, including the 33 Squadron party under Flt Lt Mitchell, and Lt Sutton's party; also aboard were two children and their pet dog! With daylight came the threat of air attack, and just after 0900 four Ju88s appeared, their bombs near-missing *Nizam* and causing slight damage. Apart from this single attack, the passage to Alexandria remained unhindered.

Airmen in the Defence of Heraklion Area, 20–31 May

The defenders at Retimo and Heraklion – that included 140 RAF personnel plus a further 37 attached to 220 AMES radar – had been spared the 20 May morning assaults by the air landing forces, although a reconnaissance Do17P of 2.(F)/11 had appeared over the latter airfield at 0800, a high-level bombing attack then following; from then until midday aircraft were constantly overhead, bombing and strafing, but causing few casualties. At Retimo defence was provided by two Australian battalions and by two Greek battalions, with two tanks in support. There were no heavy AA guns, the Australians relying on tripod-mounted Brens and a few Vickers machine guns.

At 1600, several Staffeln of Bf110s commenced strafing the area while Ju87s went after specific targets and Do17s bombed and strafed from low level. The Australian gunners put up an intense barrage which shot down two of I/KG2's Dorniers and severely damaged a third. Both Oblt Heinz Schmidt's U5+EH and Ltn Max Graf von Durkheim's U5+BH fell in flames; two more of these bombers from III/KG2 also suffered damage.

Fifteen minutes later two dozen Ju52/3ms were counted approaching from out to sea, these crossing the coast to the east of the Australian positions, but then turning to fly parallel with the coast, where advanced units began dropping. More and more transports followed until an estimated 160 were over the target zone. Despite the lack of any opposition in the air, the drop was highly disorganised, troops coming down in the wrong sequence, and as a result being scattered over a wide area. Partly this was due to the confusion by then reigning on the dispatch landing grounds in Greece where Staffeln were being ordered off as soon as they were refuelled. It was also to an extent occasioned by the intense fire put up by the Australian gunners. Groups of aircraft were broken up as bullets and shell fragments riddled the fuselages of the slow-moving Junkers, killing and wounding many of the men inside. At least seven aircraft were seen to fall in flames, two or three crashing near Perivolia, while others headed out to sea trailing tails of fire; two more collided.

At much the same time Heraklion had also come under renewed fire. Following a lull in the air bombardment, a continuous stream of attackers appeared from 1600 onwards, striking the airfield and gun sites here. At one point an estimated 50 Stukas were overhead, these being aircraft of III/StG2 from Scarpanto, but courageously the defenders continued to hit back. When He111s of II/KG26 came in at low level two were hit, 1H+ZP (Oblt Kurt von Stetten) and 1H+MP both crash-landing on the airfield where von Stetten's crew was taken prisoner, the other crew evading capture. Strafing Bf109s were joined by Rhodes-based CR42s, and these were followed by Bf110s of II/ZG26. The latter were hunting for surviving gun sites, but accurate fire shot two 4 Staffel aircraft down into the sea. The Staffelkapitän, Oblt Reinhold Heubel (3U+AM) and his gunner were killed, but Uffz Otto Stein and Gfr Dietrich Hermann managed to ditch 3U+CN and reached the shore where they were captured; they would be released later.

Shortly after 1800 the first of some 240 Ju52/3ms came in, flying at about 100ft over the sea, but climbing up to 250ft to drop their charges. The results were close to disaster for the Germans. Gunfire enveloped the formation, hitting many aircraft and killing numbers of paratroops before they could even jump. Several transports fell away trailing flame and parachutes as men aboard tried desperately to get clear. One unfortunate was seen to catch his parachute on the tail of one aircraft as it headed out to sea. The big transports crashed, or glided down to force-land all round the area, 15 burned-out wrecks subsequently being found in the immediate Heraklion sector alone, while others fell in the sea.

Owing to the lack of information coming from the Retimo area, but believing the landing ground to have been captured, Air Headquarters in Athens ordered a Fi156 communications aircraft (believed from 2.(H)/31) to be dispatched to this sector to obtain an up-to-the-minute situation report. Arriving during the early evening the pilot landed at Retimo, only for he and his observer to be taken prisoner by the Australians, thus leaving Air HQ none the wiser.

At Heraklion, early morning air reconnaissance on 22 May was followed by supply-dropping Ju52/3ms while Bf110s strafed and dropped bombs on the airfield and its defences. Some bombing of Heraklion town and areas to the west also took place, intensified at 1800 when Do17s and Bf110s carried out a heavy attack as a preliminary to a further paratroop drop. At least two of the troop-carriers were shot down, but some 500 men landed to the east of the airfield and 300 more to the west of the town. Some of the latter got into the built-up area under cover of darkness, but were soon mopped up next day, even civilians and priests taking part in the action. The remainder dug themselves in 2 miles west of the town, cutting road communications with Retimo and Canea.

During the night the Royal Navy had thwarted an attempted seaborne invasion and, next morning, German seaplanes were active in rescuing survivors. One of these apparently came too close to the shoreline and was shot down into the sea, as related by Cretan soldier Andreas Manouras:

> While we were deliberating about what to do next, my brother Manolis appeared. He was carrying a gun, which he'd got his hands on I don't know how. I always thought he was unarmed. It must have been about 7.30 when a hydroplane flew very low over us, heading for the city and firing. I turned my machine gun towards it and emptied a cartridge band. It circled the city and headed back towards us. I emptied a second cartridge and the plane lost its balance and plunged into the shallow waters near the beach at Perivolia. It was the second one I had hit successfully with the machine gun.

Heraklion continued to be assaulted from the air and ground, day after day. Even so, a flight of six Hurricanes from Egypt managed to land on 23 May, in a belated effort to help the garrison. But there was hardly any fuel or ammunition available, and the aircraft departed the following morning having accomplished very little. Plans were being made to evacuate the survivors by sea. By the morning of 28 May, destroyers were on their way to pick up troops in the Heraklion area from the small harbour, while those at Retimo were to be taken from Plaka Bay. Others were to be evacuated from Tymbaki, but there was no question of being able to get out the main forces around Maleme–Suda Bay area other than from the south coast, and these units were to make their way over the mountains to Sphakia.

Over 4,000 men were plucked from under the noses of the Germans at Heraklion, but the RAF contingent at the airfield failed to get away. Among those captured were the OC Heraklion, Sqn Ldr Tony Trumble, and Flt Lt Charlie Fry of 112 Squadron, plus attached pilots Flg Offs Garside and Hutton, although two others, Flg Off Dick Bennett and Plt Off Len Bartley did reach the south coast. Mixed fortunes were experienced by Flg Off Stan Reeves and Plt Off Neville Bowker. The former was captured making for the south coast but Bowker, who had been captured early in the fighting, simply walked out of a German field hospital and succeeded in joining up with a party of British troops, who were then evacuated from Heraklion harbour.

While the troops who had reached Sphakia waited for the warships to arrive, the ridges above the harbour, the village itself and the areas to the east and west of the beaches were repeatedly bombed and strafed. But when the ships did arrive, the Luftwaffe failed to target them, thus allowing many hundreds to escape capture, or worse. Among those sheltering in the Sphakia area were Gen Freyberg and Grp Capt Beamish, both of whom were ordered to depart with their staffs aboard two Sunderlands sent to collect them. When the evacuation finally ended, some 16,500 men had been withdrawn (including 312 RAF personnel), but 12,500 had been left behind, including

226 RAF personnel. A further 71 had been killed. Many of those left behind had already been captured but to those still free, Gen Wavell gave discretion to surrender, fight on or escape if they might. By the end of 1941 over 1,000 escapees from Crete, the Greek mainland and the Aegean islands, had arrived back in Egypt by various means and routes.

Bennett and Bartley of 112 Squadron, having reached Tymbaki on the south coast, joined forces with 4 other officers and 66 men in an attempt to reach Egypt in an abandoned and damaged landing craft they had found. Three days out to sea they were intercepted by an Italian submarine and ordered to stop. The officers were told to swim to the submarine, but one drowned while attempting to do so. Those remaining were instructed to return to Crete but, once the submarine was out of sight, they propelled the landing craft towards the North African coast and four days later reached Mersa Matruh.

RAF Sacrifice in Vain

While the fighting on Crete was at its height, RAFME decided to send Marylands and Blenheims to attack Maleme, and to dispatch a flight of Hurricanes to operate from Heraklion, which remained in British hands.

On 23 May, five SAAF Marylands bombed and strafed Maleme, followed by four Blenheims, one of which was shot down. Later, two Beaufighters strafed Maleme. A total of ten Ju52s were claimed destroyed on the airfield by returning crews, whereas six were admitted destroyed. 73 Squadron at Sidi Haneish was ordered to dispatch six Hurricanes to Heraklion, from where it was hoped they would be able to operate in support of the ground forces. En route they overflew British warships, which put up such a tremendous barrage that the formation was scattered; five returned to Sidi Haneish but the sixth, flown by Sgt Bob Laing RNZAF, continued towards Heraklion:

> Having passed over the bleak looking slopes of the mountain range I soon sighted the crossed runways of Heraklion, close by the township of Canea. Having circled the landing strip I noticed some good-sized bomb craters in the runway but as the place seemed deserted I decided to land. I made a good landing, running down to the south-east towards the beach. The propeller clanked to a standstill and there was not a sound, which to say the least was most eerie! I stepped out of the aircraft and decided to walk to the nearest building, a stone hut some 300 yards away. Having gone a few yards a machine gun opened up on the aircraft and myself, with some degree of accuracy, and I realised I was not alone.
>
> To return to the Hurricane would have been of little use as it was merely a sitting duck and I decided to run for it. Bullets began to

whistle round and I dived for a small depression in the ground, which gave me a little cover. I remained there lying with my head towards the direction of the machine-gunfire to make a smaller target; also my dark blue tunic against the runway was quite fair camouflage. They gave the Hurricane and myself the works for quite a time and I tried to pluck up courage to make a bolt for it – luckily my mind was made up for me by the approach of a British Matilda tank, which rumbled up and shielded me from the fire of the machine gun. The tank commander, an Army major, lifted up the trap door of the tank, greeted me with a smile and apologised for the reception I got. Having exchanged views on the situation and the Bosch in particular, he suggested I taxi the aircraft down to the revetment area, about half a mile down the runway, where I would find some shelter. Apparently he wanted to save the aircraft, as in those days pilots were more easily replaced than aircraft. Fortunately the engine was not damaged and I was able to taxi down at high speed, helped along with bursts of fire from the Bosch machine guns, who were very active at this time.

Within half an hour six Bf110s arrived and commenced strafing the gun positions. The Hurricane was soon sighted and was reduced to a blazing wreck. Bob Laing sheltered with others as the airfield was constantly bombed and strafed, and added:

We could do nothing about it, except the Aussie-manned guns accounted for several aircraft but at a very heavy cost to themselves. Without my plane I was a mere spectator of the operation in progress, and one experienced a terrible feeling of frustration to witness Heraklion being reduced to a shambles.

Back at Sidi Haneish, 73 Squadron was ordered to repeat the operation, a replacement pilot joining the other five, who set out at 1520. Just about dusk in the midst of yet another raid by about a dozen Ju88s, the six Hurricanes arrived. Despite being low on fuel, the fighters attempted to intercept, both Flg Off Benny Goodman and Plt Off John Ward claiming bombers damaged during a brief skirmish as they pursued them over Canea and out to sea, before they were obliged to break away and head back to Heraklion. The airfield had been heavily pitted with craters, two Hurricanes breaking their tailwheels on landing as a result. The airfield was still under small-arms fire from the paratroops positioned on the ridge and behind rocks on the perimeter, and as the pilots headed for shelter, they had constantly to throw themselves flat for cover. Two Hurricanes were rapidly refuelled and were sent up to patrol until dusk, but nothing more was seen. After a hurried consultation with the OC Land Forces, Goodman learned that there was no stock of .303 ammunition for the Hurricanes and only limited fuel available. It was decided that as the Hurricanes could offer little assistance they should return to Egypt in the morning.

Following a night's desultory sleep, the six Hurricanes prepared to depart, Laing and Goodman squeezing into the cockpit of one, Goodman using his companion's knees as a seat, the parachute pack having been discarded and stowed into the fuselage. Before heading for Egypt all pilots were to use up their remaining ammunition by strafing enemy positions around the airfield, which they did. Bob Laing continued:

> Our journey back across the Mediterranean was uneventful from enemy point of view but we struck a head wind during the last hundred miles and with petrol low, we were feeling anything but comfortable. We finally landed at Sidi Haneish in a sandstorm with our petrol gauge registering zero. Surely Allah had been with us and my only complaint was that I was so stiff and numbed after sitting for three hours in a cramped cockpit and used as a cushion for the pilot. However, I gave the flight commander a big hand and said: 'Thanks Benny – a lot.'

They were the first to arrive, landing at 0830, but were followed shortly by Plt Off Ward; no others returned to base. It was later learned that two had run out of fuel and force-landed at Fuka and the other had come down just inside Ras el Kanazis. Of the other two, flown by Plt Offs Bob Goord (from Kenya) and Bob Likeman, nothing was ever heard. It was believed that both had been shot down by gunfire from British warships.

On 25 May, meanwhile, 204 Group's involvement in the battle over Crete was much increased. Already during the night Wellingtons had set out to raid Maleme, although only two actually reached and bombed the target. At dawn, four SAAF Marylands appeared overhead, bombing and machine-gunning the airfield and surrounding troop positions. They were followed by six Blenheims, the crews of which saw a number of Ju52/3ms already on fire as a result of the South African's attack, and added their light bombs to the carnage. An estimated two dozen aircraft were considered to have been destroyed or badly damaged, although many of those hit were almost certainly already wrecked.

At Gerawla, 274 Squadron had received four Hurricanes fitted with long-range tanks. The pilots were not happy, however, for not only did the tanks slow the Hurricanes down and make them less manoeuvrable, but also the armour plating behind the seats had to be removed and ammunition reduced to compensate for the weight of the extra fuel. One stated:

> The additional tanks gave the Hurricane a range of 900 miles compared with the normal range of 600 miles. There were two additional tanks –

228

one port, one starboard. The port tank emptied first, then the starboard tank. Air locks were liable to develop owing to bad refuelling or severe bumps in the air and throw the system out of commission. You never knew when the port tank emptied if the starboard tank was going to feed through. If your starboard tank refused to work over the sea, that was the end.

Nonetheless, the four Hurricanes prepared to leave for Maleme at 0530 accompanying two Blenheims of 45 Squadron. One fighter burst its tailwheel on take-off and aborted, but the other three rendezvoused with one of the Blenheims, the other having crashed on take-off from Sidi Barrani. Near Crete the little formation entered dense, low-lying cloud and became separated, all but one Hurricane abandoning the strike and returning separately to Egypt. Only Plt Off Archie Hamilton continued alone towards Maleme. Over Suda Bay he encountered an aircraft identified as a Ju88, claiming this shot down in the sea. The only Luftwaffe loss recorded was Bf110 3D+CP of II/ZG26, which reportedly ditched 30km west of Melos due to engine trouble, Gfr Heinz Nagel and his gunner being posted as missing. However, Hamilton's aircraft now developed the feared fuel problems, and he landed at Heraklion where the undercarriage suffered severe damage on the cratered runway. He would later be taken prisoner. Three Blenheims that attempted a later strike were all shot down by defending Bf109s.

The final strike of the day against Maleme was to be made by three South African Marylands and two Hurricanes from 274 Squadron. Off at 1530, one Maryland soon developed a fault, turned back, and force-landed at Sidi Barrani. The two remaining bombers went in first, bombing and strafing the area. One failed to return. Meanwhile, the two Hurricanes flown by Flt Lts Dudley Honor and Hughie Down, had followed the Marylands in, as Honor later recalled:

> As we crossed over the mountains there were so many enemy aircraft in the sky that I was undecided whether to have a crack at the ones in the air or carry out my original orders and attack the aerodrome. I decided that I had better carry out my original orders. Down and I dived along the river valley. As we approached, we saw two transport aircraft circling to land. There were so many aircraft on Maleme that it was just a congested mess. Some were on their noses, some obviously burnt out. It was difficult to decide in that mass which of the aircraft on the ground to attack. I decided to have a crack at the two which were landing. I thought they were probably full of troops and equipment. They came in too fast for us. We were still about 2,000 yards away as the second one started to touch down. I opened fire at this range and continued firing as I approached the aerodrome. I

passed over at about 50 feet, spraying everything I could see. Down's aircraft was about 300 yards astern of me.

I saw three 109s taking-off from the aerodrome, going in an easterly direction. I thought they were going after the Marylands. I got to the north boundary, still at about 50 feet and noticed some troop-carriers, German and Italian (there is no evidence to suggest that Italian [sic] transport aircraft were involved), coming into the aerodrome along the line of the Cape Spada peninsula; they were at about 1,000 feet. As I passed over the northern boundary the AA guns opened up; the sky was black around me with ack-ack bursts. I pulled up to the line of troop carriers, head on. They stretched right along the peninsula, with about half a mile between each. There was an endless line of them, away to sea. I managed to get up to the same height as the leading aircraft – it was an Italian S.79 [sic] – and gave it a very short burst at dead range. It made no attempt at evasion and burst into flames and went straight down into the sea. I carried straight on and had a crack at a second, a Ju52 loaded with troops. He half turned away from me and went down. I saw him as he turned over on his back and hit the water.

Meantime, Flt Lt Down was being pursued by Bf109s of II/JG77 – possibly those seen taking off by Honor; he did not return. He may have shot down a Ju52 before his own demise, a German paratrooper recalling:

At the height of the landing operation RAF Hurricanes suddenly appeared – one of them following a Ju52 as it steadied for a landing, and destroying it before it could get down. But it was the Hurricane's final victory, a vigilant Me109 from the fighter umbrella over Maleme swooped down to rake the British fighter with its guns, and the Hurricane blew up in a rosette of flame.

The other German pilots gave chase to Honor, apparently joined by at least one Bf110, as he recalled:

Suddenly there was a series of explosions and my control was gone. A 110 had attacked me from underneath and behind. I did not observe it before the attack. I started to take what evasive action I could. My controls were very badly damaged. I could only try to dodge him. The chase lasted about 15 minutes and I got closer and closer to the sea. I worked in as close to the cliffs as possible, watching him in the mirror. Each time I saw a white puff coming from the front of him I did a skidding turn.

I saw the cannon shells bursting in the sea alongside. He must have used up all his ammunition without hitting me again because he sheered off. A 109 then took up the fight. He employed the usual tactics on me, diving and then climbing. I was unable to turn with him but managed to get him round the north of the peninsula, out of sight of the aerodrome. There was cloud at 2,500 feet but I could not climb to get up there. After about five minutes a burst of fire hit my engine; there was a horrible bang and an awful smell of cordite in the cockpit. I was about 20 feet from the sea when I was hit. I could not pull out so I steered straight ahead to make a landing on the water at high speed, at about 220 mph. I reduced speed in order not to hit the water too hard and touched down at about 120 mph. After about 15 seconds the aircraft began to sink. I still had the cockpit hood closed and my safety harness was still fastened. I went down 40 feet before I realised what was happening. I noticed the sea turning from blue to dark green . . . I opened the hood, which luckily had not jammed . . . and turned the knob of my Mae West. I was wearing a German Mae West, which inflates automatically, whereas the RAF type had to be blown up by mouth. I drifted to the surface slowly, noticing the water grow lighter and lighter. It seemed a long time. I broke surface to find the 109 still circling overhead at about 50 feet. Fortunately the pilot did not appear to see me and after a couple of circuits made off round the peninsula towards Maleme.

In this engagement the II/JG77 pilots claimed a total of three Hurricanes shot down, one by Uffz Schmidt, who had earlier shot down two Blenheims, one by Fw Otto Köhler of 4 Staffel, and one by FjGfr Günther Marschhausen of 5 Staffel. Dudley Honor, meanwhile, continued to float in the water:

The sea was very rough; I was about half a mile from the cliff and after swimming for about a couple of minutes, I realised I was floating stern upwards. I still had my parachute on . . . I jettisoned it and my trousers, which were hampering me. I carried on swimming for about three hours until I was just about 20 yards from the cliffs, which were about 100 feet high, not only sheer but overhanging. Each time I tried to get a handhold I was dragged away again by the suction of the retreating wave. My nails and flesh were torn by the rocks . . . I found it impossible to get to the shore so I relaxed and allowed myself to drift round into a small cave. By this time it was nearly nightfall. I saw a German seaplane fly along the cliffs very near me . . . I thought he might be searching for me. Eventually I was washed into another cave and although smashed up against the end by the drive of the sea, managed to hang on by grabbing a rock stalagmite and crawled up onto a little ledge.

The ledge was about two feet wide and just long enough to hold me. It was covered over by the waves, but above the level of the sea when the waves receded. After I had recovered my breath and got my strength back, I found I was ice-cold and trembling. My hands had shrunk in the water. I had a signet ring on the small finger of my left hand, which I had not been able to get off for years, and it had slipped off in the water. After a time, I managed to climb on to a higher ledge in the cave and sit on the stalagmite, in a kind of saddle worn by the action of the sea. I took off my clothes and wrung out the water and sat there shivering. I draped my shirt round my legs to keep warm. All this time the waves that hit the end of the cave were spraying over me.

I had done eleven-and-a-quarter-hours' flying in a single-seater plane in two sorties that day, and I was pretty tired. I kept myself awake for a long time by singing songs. I dozed off several times but woke up when I started to fall off the stalagmite. The sea was highly phosphorescent. I could see trails all about made by fish.

Dawn broke. I looked round for a means of getting out of the cave. I managed to walk along the cliff from ledge to ledge until I got into the open. I then thought it would be an easy task to climb to the top of the cliff. I made three attempts and got up halfway. I could get no farther. And each time I was scared to go down again. In the end, I managed to peer round a corner of the cliff and saw what appeared to be the mouth of a dry riverbed about 200 yards away. I put on my Mae West again. As the waves receded from the point to which I had worked my way along the ledges, I took a flying leap into the sea. I sank like a stone. I rose and started swimming towards the dry riverbed. I was swimming for about an hour. It was only about 200 yards, but I was swimming against the waves. I eventually reached the riverbed and crawled ashore.

Here, I found that my Mae West had been punctured on the rocks. I knew now why I had sunk when I jumped into the sea. I groped in my pocket for a tin of 50 cigarettes, which I had husbanded throughout my trials. I opened them and then remembered what I had forgotten before, that I had broken the tin sealing them to get two or three out earlier. The cigarettes were just a soggy mass. That was a bad moment. The flesh under my arms was very painful. My Mae West had worn away the skin and cut deeply into the flesh as I swam. The wounds were raw and looked very angry. They certainly felt angry. I put my Mae West, together with my revolver bullets, in a little cave and covered them over with rocks. Then I laid out all my clothing on the rocks to dry in the sun. After about two hours my boots and clothes had dried, and I set off walking in my shirttails.

I climbed up the riverbed to the top of the peninsula. There was absolutely no sign of life. There was no vegetation, just rocks. I started walking down the peninsula, over the hills and rocks southwards towards Maleme. Then suddenly I heard a bell. I looked round me and saw a flock of mountain goats with bells round their necks.

Some of the hills were still hidden in cloud. I looked round for some sort of human habitation but did not find any. I carried on walking south. All the time I could see Ju52s coming in on each side of the peninsula and occasionally I could hear 109s take off and fly overhead from Maleme. I also saw formations of bombers, Ju87s and 88s, and of some Ju52s and S.79s coming in carrying troops and equipment. Suddenly, I heard the rattle of machine-gunfire and saw a long-range Hurricane shoot a Ju52 down in flames into the sea. Then 109s took off from Maleme and came overhead. I heard cannon-fire and the 109s went back again to Maleme. I did not know if they had got the Hurricane, but I was to learn later that they did.

Back at Gerawla, 274 Squadron received a further six long-range Hurricanes, while at Sidi Haneish six replacement Hurricanes and pilots had arrived for 73 Squadron. The six long-range Hurricanes were to go after the transports flying into Maleme, three setting out at 15-minute intervals commencing 1310, followed by the other three at 1415. New Zealander Flg Off Owen Tracey was first to arrive over Maleme. Here he promptly claimed a Ju52 shot down, but a Bf109 then fastened onto his tail, and he dived towards the steep cliffs, his Hurricane taking several hits in the fuselage, in the fuel tanks and in the propeller. Reaching sea level, Tracey pulled clear at the last moment, believing that the pursuing Bf109 had plunged straight into the sea behind him. Having nursed his damaged aircraft back across the sea to Sidi Barrani, he force-landed; he claimed both the Ju52 and the Bf109 as destroyed.

While Tracey was fighting for his life, a second Hurricane flown by Sgt George Kerr, had arrived off Maleme, and he too at once claimed a Ju52 shot down in flames into the sea. Like Tracey, he was also pounced upon by a Messerschmitt, and soon followed his victim into the sea. Kerr survived the crash and managed to get ashore. It seems probable that the German pilots involved in these engagements were Hptm Herbert Ihlefeld and his wingman, Ltn Fritz Geisshardt of Stab I(J)/LG2, both of whom claimed Hurricanes on this day over Crete. A Maryland also failed to return.

Meanwhile, Dudley Honor was still trying to find help:

I reached the highest point on the peninsula. I had no food or water. I was sucking a pebble to keep my thirst down, but I did not feel weak for lack of food. I felt nothing at all. I sat down for a rest and heard a whirring noise overhead. Looking up, I saw two great eagles circling above me. I picked up a handful of pebbles, but they did not attack me. I carried on walking and saw in a valley two or three stone buildings.

I approached them circumspectly. I thought they might have been occupied by Germans. When I arrived, I found two stagnant wells. The water was covered over with green slime. The wells were too deep to enable me to get at the water. One of the buildings was a small chapel, tumbling in ruins. I went inside. The building was about 15 feet square and built of old stone. There was an altar, but it did not look as if the chapel had been used as a place of worship for a long time.

I found a small glass tumbler hanging by a length of wire from the ceiling. It had evidently been used as an incense burner. In the church I also found a box of German matches. I took the glass, which was oily inside from the incense, and the wire it was hanging by, and used them to dip some water from the wells. It was dark by now, and I made a bed of twigs in the church and went to sleep. My slumber was very disturbed.

The next lone Hurricane, flown by Frenchman Flt Sgt Marcel Lebois, evaded the now-alerted Messerschmitts but did encounter the Junkers transports, one of which he also claimed shot down. He arrived safely back at Gerawla at 1800, where he awaited news of two of his fellow countrymen flying in the final section to Maleme. On nearing the island these three Hurricanes separated and hunted for the transports individually, Flt Lt Paul Jacquier soon encountering one making for Maleme. He recalled:

I was flying at approximately 3,000 metres about 20 kilometres north of Maleme when I noticed a single Ju52 flying very low (100–200 metres) heading for Crete. I attacked from the rear, made a single pass, disengaged above and banked upwards to the right. I saw it disappear into the sea. Some minutes later I saw a second lone Ju52, at the same altitude. Again I attacked from the rear and broke away upwards and this also went into the sea. In both attacks the Ju52s only returned fire at the last moment. I regained altitude and continued to Maleme to strafe. While I was attacking, five Bf109s and two Bf110s on aerial defence were circling at about 500–1,000 metres, at slow speeds – with undercarriages down – no doubt for identification by German airfield defence. I dived at great speed from 3,000 metres, going west to east (sun behind me). I shot a Ju52, which blew up, and levelled out some metres above the ground. On the eastern edge of the airfield I received a shock – the engine was hit – it cut and petrol flooded the cockpit. Using my speed I glided along the beach between Maleme and La Canee (Canea) and landed wheels up amongst the German forward positions. I was captured immediately. Apart from rough handling by Austrian mountain troops on capture, I was treated well in accordance with the Geneva Convention. I was wearing the badges of my rank in the RAF and at my first interrogation by the Germans at Maleme, I indicated that I was French-Canadian. Some time later I met, in the PoW camp, Lt Courcot and two others (the crew of a shot-down Maryland) in French uniform – and I decided that I would share the same fate as my compatriots. Thus, at my second interrogation, in Athens, I stated that I was French.

From this second trio of Hurricanes, only Flg Off Antoine Peronne (the other Frenchman) was to return, landing back at Gerawla at 1915. During his five-hour sortie he too had met a Ju52/3m and claimed this shot down. The third pilot, Sgt Colin Glover, had been killed when his Hurricane was intercepted by Oblt Walter Hockner of 6./JG77 and shot down into the sea; whether he encountered any transports before his demise is not known. At least six of the Junkers had been claimed by the Hurricane pilots; records indicate that at least three aircraft were shot down and three more obliged to crash-land at Maleme.

Six Blenheims were then briefed to make a dusk attack on Maleme, but just prior to their take-off at 1700, two more 274 Squadron Hurricanes flown by Sgt Peter Nicolson and Wt Off Charles Coudray, another of the French pilots, were sent off to strafe, both carrying out their missions and returning safely. The Blenheims arrived to find the defences alerted, and while the three 55 Squadron aircraft again escaped interception, those of 45 Squadron were caught by patrolling JG77 Bf109s of 6 Staffel, led by Oblt Hockner and two were shot down; the third escaped but crashed on return.

Flt Lt Honor's third day at large brought better luck:

> I pushed on again at first light next morning. The transport aircraft were still coming in. I had to bob down behind rocks as German fighter aircraft came overhead. I was on the Maleme side of the peninsula, and I decided to walk over to the west side to see if I could find any human habitation. After walking most of the day, climbing over cliffs and up dry riverbeds, I found a goatherd's hut, with the door padlocked on the outside. There were two wells near by. I broke open the door and after searching round the place found a rusty knife and some dry lentils and beans, also some very dirty cooking-pots.
>
> I dipped some slimy green water from one of the wells. I was scared by snakes of various colours, chiefly green and brown, which went slithering about on the brink of the well. I lit a fire with my German matches, and with the aid of paraffin I found in the hut boiled some lentils, which I ate, and parked down for the night on a bed of twigs. I was still early afternoon, but I was very weary.

In the air the confrontations – and losses – continued. The final operation of the day was launched at 1530 when two Hurricanes of 274 Squadron rendezvoused with a Blenheim directed to attempt further interception of the Ju52 air convoy, still streaming into Maleme. As the trio headed towards the south coast of Crete, however, they encountered six Ju88s of II/LG1 and attacked at once. The Blenheim pilot made a port beam attack on one low-flying bomber, the crew claiming that considerable damage had been inflicted and that the Junkers had probably been destroyed, although they did not see it crash. Both Hurricane pilots, Flg Off Sam Weller and Sgt Peter Nicolson, also engaged, each believing that they had shot one down, and indeed the Blenheim crew reported seeing one Ju88 falling in flames and two others hit the sea. In fact only one was lost, Ltn George Freysoldt and his crew perishing in L1+EW; presumably all three fighters had attacked the same aircraft, each unaware of the others' involvement. Following the fight the Hurricanes became separated from the Blenheim, and after an uneventful patrol hunting for transport aircraft, both landed at Heraklion, from where they returned next day, at daybreak. Meanwhile, the Blenheim returned direct to its base. Of the rapidly dwindling Blenheim strike force, no fewer than six were lost during the day, two having collided and four crashing or force-landing in the desert on return, their fuel tanks dry. Three more were lost next day, only one of which fell to enemy action.

Honor's saga continued:

> Next morning I rose and carried on towards the west side of the peninsula. Ju52s and S.79s were still coming in. About midday I came to a valley. It was a lovely sight, green and gold fields in the midst of that wilderness of rock. There were little houses along each side of it. It took me about four hours to reach the village. I found lots of little children and cows. After I explained my plight in French to one of the villagers, who spoke a little French, and established my identity as an Englishman, the villagers told me there was another pilot there who had been shot down the previous day.
>
> They gave me some goat's milk, brown bread and cheese, and while I was eating this the Englishman they had been talking about came out of a house. He was dressed in borrowed clothing, including holed shoes too large for him, but I recognised him under his fancy dress as Sergeant-Pilot Kerr of my own squadron. 'Jesus Christ!' I said. 'How the hell did you get here?' 'I was shot down by a 109 yesterday,' he said. 'But I got a 52 first.' After questioning him I realised that this was the Hurricane I had seen shoot down a Ju52 the day before.
>
> I wanted to get to Heraklion to join the British forces there. I believed the British at Heraklion were still holding out, and there was

an aerodrome there where I thought I might get an aircraft. I spent two days and nights with Kerr in the village. I slept at night on a twig bed covered with a counterpane and plentifully supplied with fleas. But the rest and regular food restored my strength. The villagers had outposts stationed, watching for the approach of enemy patrols, and there was little chance of our being surprised.

On the morning of the third day, Kerr and I decided we would have to be moving on. We started out with four guides and climbed up mountains and over the other side, drinking at a well halfway and eating food we had brought from the village. I had been unable to get another pair of trousers and was still walking in my shirttails. We arrived at another village after about four or five hours. The people seemed very frightened of reprisals. They had had people shot by the Germans already for having helped British troops. They advised us to give ourselves up. We did not want to do this but thought it might be advisable to conceal our feelings and push off when we got the chance.

There were some Greeks in a house nearby who had been captured previously when the German paratroops dropped around Maleme. Some of them were wounded. We went round to see them. They were very friendly and dressed my sores with some first-aid kit they had and boiled some eggs and gave us a bottle of water each. They also gave me a pair of Greek sailor's trousers. A Greek sailor wanted to go with us, and two of the other Greeks felt our position so strongly that they burst into tears at the thought of us being taken prisoner. One, an Evzone, who couldn't speak a syllable of English, nevertheless by gestures and outcries made it plain that he was avowing allegiance to England. He explained to us through an English-speaking Greek officer that he had already helped a British senior officer to escape and had shot four Germans and been wounded himself in the chest. He offered to guide us to Heraklion, which he said should take about four days.

We were summoned to a council of village elders, which was sitting, and found they had decided to send for a German guard, which was only 15 minutes' away, to escort us to German headquarters. We decided this would give us just enough time to get out of the place and to accept the offer of the Evzone to guide us to Heraklion. The Evzone was delighted. He was a most evil-looking fellow, thick-set, with hair cropped right down on to his skull. You wouldn't have trusted him ten feet on his looks, but he was a good friend to us. We christened him George, because we could not pronounce his name.

Rather than continue the suicidal attacks against transport aircraft operating in and out of Maleme, the dwindling Hurricane force was required to provide protection for the many ships evacuating troops from Crete. During the daylight hours of 29 May, 21 protective sorties were undertaken over various returning warships during the morning and early afternoon by Hurricanes of 274 Squadron. These patrols consisted of two or three aircraft at a time, usually accompanied by a single South African Maryland or a Blenheim. At 1200, a Maryland was circling over the ships when the crew spotted a lone aircraft at 13,000ft. The Maryland turned to investigate and the crew saw that it was a Ju88 – a reconnaissance aircraft of 2.(F)/123, which at once dived away. The Maryland followed and opened fire with its front guns before being hit by return fire. As the Junkers attempted to escape, pouring black smoke from its damaged starboard engine, it was attacked by one of the escorting Hurricanes flown by Flg Off Tracey, who applied his *coup de grâce*; 4U+EK came down into the sea with the loss of Fw Ernst Chlebowitz and his crew. Meanwhile, another of the Hurricane pilots, Plt Off Arthur Sumner, reported engaging an aircraft he believed to be a Do17, which he claimed to have damaged before it evaded his attack and disappeared.

During one of the earlier escort sorties, Sgt Peter Nicolson was detailed to break away and make a dash over central Crete to the Retimo area, where he was to drop a message bag to the besieged garrison. As Nicolson attempted to carry out this duty, his Hurricane was intercepted by Oblt Erich Friedrich of Stab/JG77, and was shot down into the sea with the loss of the pilot. Whether or not he ever got to drop the message bag is not known.

Throughout 30 May, 274 Squadron's Hurricanes flew 30 sorties over the two naval forces, sometimes accompanied by a single Blenheim IVF or Beaufighter. Their first contact with the opposition was made just after 0800 when a section of three Hurricanes encountered three bombers that were identified as He111s. Despite the identification these would seem to have been Do17s of I/KG2. Flg Off Peronne, one of the French pilots, gave the nearest bomber a quick burst and saw it fall into the sea; Uffz Heinz Hövel's U5+GL was lost.

Late in the afternoon Plt Off George Tovey was accompanying a Beaufighter when they came across Ltn Walter Fischer's He111 (1H+KN) of II/KG26, which was on a ferry flight to Cyrenaica. The Beaufighter attacked first, but closed so rapidly that it collided with the bomber, although both aircraft seemed to escape serious damage. This allowed Tovey the opportunity to nip in and shoot the Heinkel down into the sea. As dusk approached the final sorties were being flown by three Hurricanes and a Beaufighter. In the fading light a reconnaissance Ju88 (7A+HM) of 4/(F)121 was seen, and was apparently attacked by both the Beaufighter and Hurricane pilot Plt Off Arthur Sumner, although each was unaware of the other's presence. The Beaufighter pilot claimed a probable, Sumner a definite victory. The Junkers crashed into the sea with the loss of Oblt Franz Schwarz-Tramper and his crew.

The two RAF fugitives Dudley Honor and George Kerr, together with their Greek guide, were still at large and making progress:

> We heard sounds of gunfire and shooting in the distance, but did not see any Germans. We had to pass twice over roads that German motorcyclists were using. Each time George [their guide] went out to spy out the land before signalling to us to dash for it. Riverbeds gave us cover on each side of the roads. Three times he reported German sentries, and each time we crawled along and managed to pass without attracting attention.
>
> We stopped at a house where a woman gave us bread and cheese and a drink of water. She was sympathetic but very frightened and anxious to get rid of us. It was evening, and we passed on over some hills to another village where German troops were living. We had to skirt this village and passed within 300 yards of the German officers' mess. We kept out of sight in the trees and grass. After a few hours wandering among the trees we came to a house with lights showing. The Evzone knew the people. They hid us away in a back room and gave us a bed for a few hours.
>
> We rose in the dark and started walking again. While we were walking we heard the sound of bombing coming from the direction of Maleme. We hoped it was the RAF getting back at the Germans. At daybreak we came to another village, where we met a man who spoke English with an American accent. He warned us that German patrols were searching round all the villages. We stopped at lunchtime, very tired, and ate some brown bread and cheese and a boiled egg. After walking in the blazing sun, we crossed over the highest mountain, about 8,000 feet, trying to find the Plain of Omalos, which is in the heart of the mountains.
>
> We eventually arrived. It was now dark. We saw fires burning and lights from little houses round the side of the plain. We made our way down to the houses, passing through herds of goats and cows. A man came along who spoke quite good French and a little English. He asked us to dine with him, although the hour was late. He produced fried eggs on chips, exquisitely cooked in oil, with hot goat's milk to drink. That completed 17 hours walking again that day. Our host advised us not to go to Heraklion, which had been our primary objective. He said he understood the Germans were almost there. He told us the British troops were being evacuated from Sphakia.

Among those sheltering in the Sphakia area awaiting embarkation were Gen Freyberg and Grp Capt Beamish, both of whom were now ordered to depart with their staffs. A Sunderland was due to take them and their key personnel to safety, and just before 1800 two of these big flying boats arrived. One aircraft took on board the GOC's party, totalling about 45 Army and RAF, while the other flying boat was due to pick up his passengers from Sphakia Bay. Some difficulty was experienced in finding the actual spot, so two members of the crew rowed ashore in a dinghy, but found no trace of anyone. On returning to the aircraft, they spotted a light flickering on Gavdhos Island and realised that their position was six miles to the south-west of their destination. The Sunderland was taxied to the correct position where a boat with the passengers aboard was located.

274 Squadron at Gerawla had received a further influx of pilots to aid in the long patrol sorties. Three South Africans from 1 SAAF Squadron included the highly experienced pair of Capt Ken Driver DFC and Lt Bob Talbot DFC. 73 Squadron also sent over three pilots, all Frenchmen, and these included another highly skilled pilot, Sous-Lt Albert Littolff.

The SAAF section was soon in action on the morning of 31 May, when they encountered two Ju88s. Lt Talbot fired two bursts at one bomber, but it evaded him, then Capt Driver and Lt Bester made beam and stern attacks on the other, which then dived for the sea. Talbot and the accompanying Maryland pilot gave chase for some 70 miles before Talbot succeeded in getting in a burst, which hit an engine. At this stage the Maryland overhauled the Hurricane, closed in on the damaged Junkers and poured all his remaining ammunition into it. The same engine appeared to have been hit again, for it now stopped and the bomber was last seen flying just 10ft above the sea. It was assumed to have crashed, but in fact the pilot managed to nurse it back to Heraklion, where he crash-landed the badly damaged bomber. It was subsequently written-off, reportedly due to severe AA damage. Capt Driver reported meeting three or four other Ju88s and claimed to have shot one of these down into the sea; no other Ju88s were reported lost.

It would seem that the relieving section of Hurricanes from 274 Squadron that arrived to take over from the South Africans also met the Ju88s reported by Driver. Flown by three of the attached French pilots, these engaged the bombers, Sous-Lt Littolff claiming one shot down. He then reported meeting a lone Cant Z.1007bis, apparently a reconnaissance machine out from Libya, claiming this damaged before it escaped. However, one of the Hurricanes flown by Sgt Auguste Guillou failed to return; it may either have been hit by return fire from the Ju88s, or shot down by an escorting Bf110, for during the day the Germans were to claim four Hurricanes shot down south of Crete. Early in the afternoon the three South Africans were up again on patrol when an intruder was seen. While Capt Driver and Lt Bester stayed with the ships, Lt Talbot set off in pursuit, identifying another Z.1007bis, presumably also a Libyan-based reconnaissance aircraft. After chasing his quarry for 100 miles westward he finally got into a position for an attack, reporting that he shot it down into the sea 50 miles off Tobruk.

After dark, two Sunderlands again flew to Sphakia at dusk to pick up more key personnel, including Maj Gen Weston and his staff. Flt Lt Frame, back again in 228 Squadron's T9046, flew low and slowly along the coastline, flashing prearranged signals at places likely to conceal parties of evacuees. No response was seen, so after ten minutes he alighted. An SOS was then seen flashing from the shore. Dudley Honor's account of the final day of the great trek revealed:

> Kerr and I were both feeling very weary, and we did not want to get up. But in spite of our being thoroughly footsore and reluctant, George [their guide] dragged us out of the twig beds we had slept on in our host's house. We started off at dawn. About midday, we insisted on stopping for a bath – the first either Kerr or I had since reaching Crete. It was very refreshing. We washed our clothes and dried them in the sun and pushed on once more. We could hear shots all the time we were going down the gorge. In the evening, after many hours marching, we came to the coast about 10 miles west of Sphakia.
>
> We started to walk along the coast. We travelled along a narrow belt of sand, overhung by heavy cliffs. Halfway along the coast we suddenly heard a noise of aircraft engines. We looked up and saw three 109s passing along the coast about 300 feet up. We dropped behind some rocks. I think they saw us, but they did not come back. We saw them climb and start ground-strafing in the half-light. Several formations of 109s passed across and ground-strafed within a few minutes of each other. We thanked our lucky stars they did not pick us up.
>
> We kept on walking and eventually night fell. We sat down and ate some more bread and cheese. The beach had petered out. About 11 o'clock we heard the sound of an aircraft approaching. We crouched down behind some rocks and waited, thinking it might be German. We saw a silhouette against the faint moon as the aircraft passed above. 'That's a Sunderland,' Kerr said. I agreed with him. We heard it landing on the water. Unfortunately, Kerr's feet had given out by this time. He was wearing shoes too large for him, and his feet were rubbed raw. I decided to go on ahead with George to get help to carry Kerr.
>
> We had to scramble over the cliffs for about a mile in the darkness, and had been going for about a quarter of an hour, barking our shins, when we heard the sound of an aircraft. We thought it was taking off from the water and gave up hope, but continued to walk forward to see if there were any people about. We came to a party of about

30 Greeks. They told us that the flying boat had landed on the water. They were signalling with a pocket torch from the cliff edge, and it was their signals that had caused the Sunderland to land. They had signalled SOS. This raised my hopes again. What I had thought was an aircraft taking off was, in fact, a second Sunderland landing. I took over the flash lamp from the Greeks and signalled, in Morse: 'RAF here.'

'Swim for it,' a voice shouted. 'I can't,' I shouted back. 'I'm done.' I could not swim because my arms were raw. We tried to interchange messages in Morse, but not being an expert, I was not very successful. But eventually a one-man rubber dinghy arrived at the foot of the cliff. It was manned by one of the pilots of the Sunderland. He took me on board, two of us crowded into a tiny rubber dinghy. I had promised to take George [the guide] to Alexandria, but we were unable to go back even for Kerr, because the sea was rough and growing rougher. We had to leave him [them] behind.

On boarding the Sunderland I was told that it was only by the merest chance that it had landed at that very spot. It had come from Egypt to take off General Weston and his staff from Sphakia. The crew were watching the coast for signals and had landed at the wrong place, misled by the SOS from the Greeks. I directed them down the coast to Sphakia. We taxied on the water the whole way. There we took on General Weston and his staff. They were absolutely exhausted. The wireless operator gave me a packet of Woodbines. They tasted sweeter than any cigarette I had ever smoked. I gave one to the General and sat smoking the others while I had six cups of tea.

The evacuation was practically over – some were lucky and escaped, others were about to start at least four years' internment as prisoners of war.

Extracts from Christopher Shores, Brian Cull and Nicola Malizia, Air War for Yugoslavia, Greece and Crete *(Grub Street, 1987, edited and updated); Wg Cdr Edward Howell,* Escape to Live *(Grosvenor, 1981); Baron von der Heydte,* Return to Crete *(WDL, 1959); Costas Hadjipateras and Maria Fafalios,* Crete 1941 Eyewitnessed *(Efstathiadis, 1989); and John Hetherington,* Airborne Invasion *(Harborough, 1957).*

* * *

The occupation of Greece and Crete brought about terrible hardships for the civilian population. Over 300,000 civilians died from starvation, thousands more through reprisals, and the country's economy was ruined. At the same time Greek Resistance, one of the most effective resistance movements in

Occupied Europe, was formed. These resistance groups launched guerrilla attacks against the occupying powers and set up large espionage networks, but by late 1943 began to fight among themselves. When liberation came in October 1944, Greece was in a state of crisis, which soon led to the outbreak of civil war.

Appendix X

FOUND – A MISSING BROTHER

By Alan Sykes (since deceased)

In November 1940, my eldest brother Harold [Bill] was flying in a formation of six Gloster Gladiators of 80 Squadron on an offensive patrol over the border between Greece and Albania, when they were intercepted by nine Italian Fiat CR42 fighters. In the ensuing combat, his aircraft collided with one of the enemy's causing both to crash. According to the records of the Commonwealth War Graves Commission, Harold has no known grave and is commemorated on the El Alamein Memorial, his squadron being on detachment from Middle East Command.

According to a newspaper article written in January 1941 by the *Daily Mail* Special Correspondent, Yannina, his grave lies beside that of a Greek Evzone, in the churchyard of the Greek church of the Twelve Apostles in the remote mountain village of Drovian. In the article, the correspondent described how he and three RAF men reached the village after a two-hour ride on horseback over mountain paths and, by finding his grave, solved the mystery of the fate of Flying Officer H. Sykes, who had been missing for six weeks. Some 55 years later, I came across this article amongst family papers during a visit to Australia and decided to follow it up with the aim of getting Harold's name taken off the unknown grave list and obtaining official recognition of the site in Drovian.

The most comprehensive official confirmation of the accuracy of the *Daily Mail* article, which I was able to trace, came from the Air Historical Branch of the RAF. Their more detailed records agreed completely with the search and findings as outlined in the newspaper. So similar were the two accounts that it is safe to assume that the Special Correspondent tagged along with the search party sent out by the squadron as soon the area in which the aircraft fell was surrendered to Greek troops. It is also safe to assume that although the gravesite had been located, nothing could be done about it and commemoration on the Alamein Memorial was the obvious and only answer at that time.

Now that the reliability of the newspaper article was confirmed, the next step should be for me to travel to Drovian and find the gravesite for myself –

but there was a problem; someone had moved the frontier and Drovian was no longer in Greece, but was now in Albania.

After the war, Albania had become one of the most isolated countries in the world under its paranoid leader, Enver Hoxha. All links with both the USSR and the West were severed and even the ties with China, which were maintained for some time, were eventually cut. One of Enver Hoxha's more bizarre decrees called for the removal of all evidence of Allied assistance in driving the Italians from Albania. Such evidence included the British War Cemetery in the capital, Tirana, so this was totally obliterated, as were a number of isolated graves. This action was not supported universally and, especially in those villages which formed Greek enclaves within the borders of Albania, the people protected the war graves from desecration by removing the markers.

I did not know about this, just as I did not know about the border changes, when I started my search. If I had known, I think I would have found the prospect of looking for an unmarked grave in the remote mountain village, in an officially declared atheist state which had become isolated from the rest of the world for half a century, far too daunting, especially if a major language barrier were thrown in for good measure.

As it so happened, my ignorance worked to my advantage. It led me to the Greek desk in the Foreign and Commonwealth Office, where a most helpful person not only put me right about the boundary changes, but also put me into contact with two people without whose help I would have got nowhere: the Deputy Head of Mission and the Vice-Consul in the British Embassy in Tirana.

As soon as the snow melted and the mountain roads became passable, they started a ground search in their own time at weekends and public holidays – such an activity was not included in their official duties. Their search involved round trips in excess of 600km on atrocious roads and mountain tracks better suited to travel by mule.

They used the small ferry port of Saranda, about 300km south of Tirana, as their base and from the outset the gods smiled on them. They chose to stay in a small guesthouse where the co-owner was an English-speaking Albanian, with a military school background, who, *inter alia*, organised mountain treks and knew the surrounding area well. This was a godsend as road maps showing mountain tracks to isolated villages were non-existent, as were such features as signposts. Without this chance contact the embassy pair would have had major problems. With his help they reached Drovian, visited the Church of the Twelve Apostles and found Harold's grave. In his account to me, the Deputy Head of Mission said that the exact location of the grave was known to many of the villagers and that, unprompted, some of the older ones told him about the dogfight and the collision which had taken place between an Italian and a British aircraft. The caretaker of the churchyard, Christopher Pappa, was a teenager in 1940 and was a member of a group of villagers who collected the body from the crash site and carried it for burial in Drovian.

You would need to stand in the centre of the village, as I did in the summer of 1997, and view the distant mountain ridge behind which the Gladiator fell, to appreciate fully the physical effort involved. During my visit to Drovian, two of the villagers insisted on giving me parts of what they said came from my brother's plane. As I thought that it was more than likely that they were telling me what they thought I would like to hear, I was reluctant to accept, but could not possibly decline.

I had the parts examined at the Fleet Air Arm Museum (the FAA also flew Gladiators during the war) and sent photographs to the Imperial War Museum and the Shuttleworth collection. The consensus of opinion on the part which I now use as a paperweight was that it is a counterbalance weight from a variable pitch propeller of, perhaps, a Fiat CR42. There was no consensus on the part which I use as a wastepaper bin, but the FAA Museum suggested that it's a side-mounted ammunition canister, possibly from a Gladiator. As throughout I have been favoured by chance, I would like to think that I have a part of each of the two planes that collided over Drovian in 1940.

After all, it was chance that put me into contact with two surviving pilots of 80 Squadron who were in the same dogfight as Harold when he was killed and witnessed the collision, and unbelievable chance that placed me next to a man in the Yeovil Library who volunteered the information that he had served in 80 Squadron, operating from Yannina in 1940/41. He had been prompted to recall those days by seeing the cover of the *Blue Guide to Albania*, which I was browsing through prior to travelling there.

The Commonwealth War Graves Commission have agreed to commemorate Harold by marking his grave in the churchyard of the Twelve Apostles, and a standard war pattern headstone is currently being prepared in Italy. Christopher Pappa, who helped to bury Harold in 1940, will now be the official keeper of his grave.

NOTES AND REFERENCES

Introduction

1. The third of four sons of Lt Col Dr Albert Jones DSO, MC, Edward Gordon Jones was born on 31 August 1914 at Widnes and educated at the local grammar school. His early childhood had been spent in India, where his energy caused his three brothers to christen him 'Doolally Tap', a vernacular expression meaning 'slightly mad'; the nickname 'Tap' remained with him for the rest of his life.

Preamble

1. Framlingham College website: www.framlingham.suffolk.sch.uk/college

Chapter 1

1. RAF Halton website: www.raf.mod.uk/rafhalton
2. Richard Townshend Bickers, *Home Run* (Pen & Sword, 1992).
3. Gordon Kinsey, *Martlesham Heath* (Dalton, 1983).
4. Extracted from Air Vice-Marshal Tony Dudgeon, *The Luck of the Devil* (Airlife, 1985).
5. Wikipedia: http://en.wikipedia.org
6. Flt Lt John Oliver later commanded 85 Squadron during the Battle of France, and was awarded the DSO and DFC.
7. See E.C.R. Baker, *Ace of Aces* (Crécy, 1992).

Chapter 2

1. See Baker, *Ace of Aces*.
2. Wikipedia website: http://en.wikipedia.org
3. In June 1939 two Royal Iraqi Air Force pilots, Lts Ghani and Abdulla, were attached to 80 Squadron to gain experience on modern fighters. They did not remain long, having crashed two Gladiators on landing.

Chapter 3

1. Dean was nicknamed Dixie after the famous English footballer of the time.
2. Håkan Gustavsson's website: surfcity.kund.dalnet.se
3. It should be noted that many entries in Bill's logbook, particularly for his operational flights in the Desert and Greece, were not entered in his own hand. It was not unusual for a pilot to get a clerk to complete the summary of flights from the Flight's Authorisation Book, although this procedure would have been frowned upon by his seniors had they known. It therefore seems likely that the dates of some of Bill's combats do not comply with 'official' records. His first, on 1 July 1940, may have been a case in particular.

247

4. Flg Off Gray-Worcester was killed in a flying accident on 18 July, two weeks after his successes.
5. This was the blackest day of the whole war for the 8ºGruppo CT. Six CR42s had been shot down and four more damaged, three pilots were killed, two taken prisoner and three wounded.
6. Plt Off Michael Sheckleton of 113 Squadron.

Chapter 4
1. Roald Dahl was later to become the internationally famous author of children's books.

Chapter 5
1. Count Ciano was Mussolini's son-in-law and Minister of Foreign Affairs.
2. Harold 'Bill' Sykes was born on 6 August 1918 in Alexandria, Egypt. His parents were John Sykes, a British Citizen, and Inez Barbier, an Italian subject born in Egypt to an Italian mother (Astori) and father (Barbier) who was of French descent. They were residing in Atbara, Sudan, while working for the Sudanese Government Railways. Harold's two younger brothers, Percy and Alan, were born in Atbara. He joined the RAF on 23 August 1937. (See also Appendix X.)
3. See Baker, *Ace of Aces*.
4. See Richard Dimbleby, *The Frontiers Are Green* (Hodder & Stoughton, 1943).
5. See Baker, *Ace of Aces*.
6. Son of Sir Henry and Lady Ripley.

Chapter 6
1. As an example of the confused situation and bad record keeping, Bill's official account of this action is dated 26 January (Air 27/674), whereas the battle actually occurred on 27 January. To make matters even worse, Bill did not record the flight nor his claim in his logbook, which goes to prove that his logbook was written up at a later date (and not even in his own hand), hence the many dating errors.
2. Bill later annotated his logbook 'Did not return. POW', but against the date 31 January; the author believes this to have been an error and that it should have been 13 February.
3. Bill must have been mistaken. The person he had seen was unlikely to have been Richard Dimbleby, although he had been in Greece a few weeks earlier. According to his autobiography, *The Frontiers Are Green* (1943), Dimbleby had returned to Libya by this date, and in response to the author's enquiry to his son, the distinguished journalist and television personality Jonathan Dimbleby wrote: 'It is a very interesting story, but I cannot think that the incident involving my father bears any relation to reality as I knew it. He was in Greece but, having scoured through the history of his career for my biography of him, I do not think that it can possibly either fit the facts or his character.' It seems probable that Bill had observed one of the American war correspondents rather than Richard Dimbleby. The Americans, not in the war, were able to converse with the Italians.
4. Account extracted from a letter to the author from Bill's friend Sqn Ldr John Hopper.

5. See Baker, *Ace of Aces*.
6. With the onset of the Greek civil war in mid-1944, Paramythia suffered one of the first tragedies when Greek fascists commenced ethnic cleansing to oust Albanian Muslims from the region. In the town of Paramythia, on 27 June 1944, a total of 673 men, women and children were killed. By March 1945, some 2,877 Albanian men, women and children had been massacred and 68 small villages razed to the ground. After March 1945, the remaining Albanian Muslims (around 30,000) were expelled from their ancestral lands and forced to flee to Albania or Turkey.
7. Bill claimed that he later came into possession of an Italian reward poster, offering 'thousands of lire' for his capture, dead or alive. This he showed to his friend Sqn Ldr Hopper. The author has seen this item and considers it to have been one of Bill's practical jokes.

Chapter 8
1. Affectionately named after the Army Liaison Officer who 'discovered' the flat piece of land for the squadron.
2. See M.G. Comeau, *Operation Mercury* (Tandem, 1961). Marcel Comeau, a fourth-generation Englishman of Nova Scotian descent, had joined the RAF in 1938. In October 1941 he was awarded a MM for his performance at Crete: 'In the course of a heavy bombing and machine-gun attack on an aerodrome, a bomb exploded on a trench causing 2 soldiers, both Greeks, to be buried in the debris. AC Comeau, displaying great bravery, left the shelter of his trench and although the station was under continuous fire, managed to dig them out with his hands. One of them subsequently died. Later on in the face of enemy fire AC Comeau secured from another position a gun which greatly improved the defence of his own position.'
3. JG77 history (Jochen Prien) via *Kieler Zeitung*.
4. Christopher Buckley in the official history *Greece and Crete* (HMSO). The quoted 22 victories seem to have been made up either of an addition of the 14 'confirmed' and 8 probables, or alternatively of the total claimed by the defences for the whole day, including the two claimed by the gunners; both these equations add up to 22.
5. Luftwaffe losses would appear to have been greater than previously believed, as noted by eminent historian Erik Mombeek (*Strike in the Balkans*): 'The available Luftwaffe records for this period show some discrepancies and even the Quartermaster General's loss lists, considered reliable by many researchers, contain some anomalies. According to the personnel loss lists, the Stab, II. and III/JG77 lost five pilots killed and one wounded in action during [Operation] Marita, figures which appear correct as the names of the pilots can be confirmed by other sources. Material losses for the seven fighter Staffeln suggest a total of 14 aircraft completely destroyed and 12 more than 50% damaged [aircraft 60% damaged were considered written off]. However, if these figures are reliable, then at the end of the Balkan campaign the Geschwaderstab and two Gruppen of JG77 should still have possessed about 50 serviceable aircraft, but the recollections of the pilots indicate that this cannot be correct. 8 and 9./JG77 had to fly together over Greece in order to carry out their assigned patrols and escort missions and some personnel from JG77 have confirmed that the strength of each Gruppe had

been reduced to just six or nine machines. To increase their strength, the fighter units were forced to recover as many as possible of the Bf109E fighter-bombers which II(Schlacht)/LG2 had left behind.'

6. Maj Gen Sir Howard Kippenberger, *Infantry Brigadier* (OUP, 1961).

Chapter 9

1. See Comeau, *Operation Mercury.*
2. See Costas Hadjipateras and Maria Fafalios, *Crete 1941 Eyewitnessed* (Efstathiadis, 1989).
3. Adolf Dickfeld went on to become one the Luftwaffe's top aces; he died in 2009.
4. See Hadjipateras and Fafalios, *Crete 1941 Eyewitnessed.*
5. See Martin Pöppel, *Heaven & Hell* (Spellmount, 1996).

Chapter 10

1. Sqn Ldr John Hopper.
2. Christopher Shores, *Dust Clouds in the Middle East* (Grub Street, 1996).
3. French historian/author Chris Ehrengardt states: 'I can say that S/Lt Brondel, Jacobi's wingman, is adamant about the fact that his leader was shot down by AA fire. His report was published in my own book, *L'Aviation de Vichy au combat, vol. II – La Campagne de Syrie.* No air-to-air combat was recorded by GCIII/6. As to N°80 Squadron, you'd better question most of their claims, including Dahl's, which are pure fantasy.'
4. A large number of civilians were killed in the crossfire or died fighting as partisans. Many Cretans were shot by the Germans in reprisals, both during the battle and in the occupation that followed. The Germans claimed widespread mutilation of corpses by Cretan partisans, but much of this was down to the breakdown of dead bodies in the very high temperatures as well as carrion birds. One Cretan source puts the number of Cretans killed by German action during the war at 6,593 men, 1,113 women and 869 children. German records put the number of Cretans executed by firing squad as 3,474, and at least a further 1,000 civilians were killed in massacres late in 1944.

Chapter 11

1. H.E.T., probably meaning Higher Education Test.

Appendix III

1. See Hadjipateras and Fafalios, *Crete 1941 Eyewitnessed.*
2. See Betty Wason, *Miracle in Hellas – The Greeks Fight On* (Museum Press, 1943).
3. *The War Illustrated*, 4 July 1941 (London).

BIBLIOGRAPHY

Primary sources

RAF Museum, Hendon, Sqn Ldr Bill Vale's logbooks
The National Archives, Air 27/366-372, 33 Squadron ORB
The National Archives, Air 27/673-676, 80 Squadron ORB

Secondary published sources

Baker, E.C.R., *Ace of Aces* (Crécy, 1992)
Bowyer, Chaz, *RAF Operations 1918–1938* (Kimber, 1988)
Buckley, Christopher, *Greece & Crete* (HMSO, 1942)
Comeau, M.G., *Operation Mercury* (Tandem, 1961)
Dahl, Roald, *Going Solo* (Cape, 1986)
Dimbleby, Richard, *The Frontiers Are Green* (Hodder & Stoughton, 1943)
Dudgeon, Air Vice-Marshal Tony, *The Luck of the Devil* (Airlife, 1985)
Hadjipateras, Costas, and Fafalios, Maria, *Crete 1941 Eyewitnessed* (Efstathiadis, 1989)
Hetherington, John, *Airborne Invasion* (Harborough, 1957)
Howell, Wg Cdr Edward, *Escape to Live* (Grosvenor, 1981)
Kinsey, Gordon, *Martlesham Heath* (Dalton, 1983)
Kippenberger, Maj Gen Sir Howard, *Infantry Brigadier* (OUP, 1961)
Mackenzie, Compton, *Wind of Freedom* (Chatto & Windus, 1943)
Mombeek, Erik, Roba, Jean-Louis, and Pegg, Martin, *Strike in the Balkans* (Classic, 2002)
Pöppel, Martin, *Heaven & Hell* (Spellmount, 1996)
Prien, Jochen, and Stemmer, Gerhard, *Jagdgeschwader 77 Volume II* (Schiffer, 1992)
Shores, Christopher, Cull, Brian, and Malizia, Nicola, *Air War for Yugoslavia, Greece and Crete* (Grub Street, 1987)
Shores, Christopher, *Dust Clouds in the Middle East* (Grub Street, 1996)
——, *Fighters Over the Desert* (Neville Spearman, 1969)
Stowe, Leland, *A Lesson from the Greeks* (Glasgow, 1942)
Townshend Bickers, Richard, *Home Run* (Pen & Sword, 1992)
Von der Heydte, Baron, *Return to Crete* (WDL, 1959)
Wason, Betty, *Miracle in Hellas – The Greeks Fight On* (Museum Press, 1943)
Wisdom, T.H., *Wings Over Olympus* (Allen & Unwin, 1942)

Periodicals

The War Illustrated, 4 July 1941, London.
Der Adler, various issues, 1941

INDEX

252